Fever Trees of Borneo

Mark Eveleigh

Edited by Gordon Medcalf

Published by TravellersEye

Fever Trees of Borneo

1st Edition

Published by TravellersEye Ltd, October 1999

Head Office:

    30 St Mary's Street

    Bridgnorth

    Shropshire

    WV16 4DW

    tel: (0044) 1746 766447

    fax: (0044) 1746 766665

    website: www.travellerseye.com

    email: books@travellerseye.com

Set in Times

ISBN: 0953057569

Copyright 1999 Mark Eveleigh

Cover photograph Paul Bailey

Photographs, Paul Bailey

Printed and bound in Great Britain by Creative Print & Design Ltd

For Blanca, who showed me the way when I couldn't see the wood for the trees.

Contents

Introduction

I don't think that I ever consciously thought that I wanted to be an 'Explorer.' It's such a dated word, tainted with colonial conceit. Anyway, born less than two years before man first set foot on the moon, surely there was nowhere left for someone like me to explore.

I spent the first eight years of my life in West Africa. It was home to me and certainly didn't feel like the unexplored continent of Livingstone and Stanley. Raised on the adventure stories of Willard Price, and later the travels of Gerald Durrell, I dreamed (although even then I knew it could only be a dream) of being a 'bring-'em-back-alive man' - capturing rare and dangerous animals for the world's zoos.

In my late teens I showed what was perhaps my first sign of promising behaviour by dropping a job that I could see was leading nowhere and, almost on a whim, leaving home to see the world . . . or at least Cornwall.

My first 'big trip' took me to Venezuela where, within two weeks, I found myself swinging by a frayed cable in the world's highest cable-car. Two people died in that accident and the six hours that we swung there was a time for deep contemplation for all the survivors.

I spent the next decade travelling and intermittently working at whatever I could do to raise the next airfare. I began to notice that as I travelled I was seeing less and less of the places that the guidebooks recommended and I developed a nagging urge to seek out areas that were little known and often uncharted. I hesitate to say 'unexplored' areas because, in truth, there are very few countries that have never been crossed even by locals. Nevertheless, I soon realised that if you push far enough into the world's undeveloped countries there are still a great many places into which the western world has never penetrated. There are less of those challenging blank spots on the world's maps but when you understand that most of them have been covered by 'educated guesswork' from aerial photos – and when you finally see at first hand how misleading they can be – you realise that the challenges are as forthcoming as ever.

The world is still an immensely wide and wild place. I yearned for that obscure thrill that comes suddenly – whether in the middle of a rice padi or a rainforest – when you look around and think: 'how did *I* ever get here. This is not for someone like me. This is 'Explorer Country."

I was never a globetrotter, preferring to concentrate instead on getting to know a relatively small region and its people as well as possible. For the latter there is no shortcut to learning the local language and, although you could never say that I'm 'gifted at languages,' I always set out for a new country with at least the basis for market-place conversation.

As is so often the case, money was the greatest factor limiting how far 'off the beaten track' my travels could lead me. It was not until after many thousands of miles – clocked-up wherever possible in a combination of walking and hitching – that Heineken Export offered me a chance to reach the parts that 'real explorers' had not yet reached.

I read about their 'Wildest Dreams' travel bursary and immediately started on the path that would lead me deeper into the jungle than I had ever been. I was yearning for what I vaguely termed 'a real jungle trip.'

A return to the Amazon was quickly over-ruled in favour of the equally mysterious but less documented island of Borneo. The amount of equipment that would be needed for a 'real jungle trip' meant that I needed a travelling companion and my first choice was Paul Bailey. We had travelled together before in South East Asia and I knew that we would have no problems spending up to four months in each other's company. It was an added bonus that he was a talented photographer.

Borneo and Paul fitted well into the jigsaw. What we had to do next was to decide on our mission. I started reading everything that I could find about Borneo - looking for the final elusive piece that would win us the confidence of Heineken Export's panel of judges.

At last I was able to report: 'I have researched extensively and believe that I have located the last large nomadic territory of the mysterious Punan tribe. This is the last resort of these elusive jungle-dwelling nomads – 'the Wild Men of Borneo' - believed by other Dayak tribes to be so primitive that they have tails!'

In 1882, Carl Bock spent a single afternoon in the company of a band of Punan. His was the first reliable report on the tribe:

I believe these savages to be the true aborigines of Borneo. They live in utter wildness in the central forests, almost entirely isolated from all communication with the rest of the world.

Mr Bock's account of his explorations showed him to be an observant and accurate reporter and it seems unlikely that he would have left it unmentioned if these Punan had been equipped with tails. Still the myth persists even today amongst the other Dayak tribes in the central jungles that these 'wild people' do indeed have tails with which they move through the treetops and, no less imaginative, that they wean their babies on panther's milk.

This is not to say that all members of the Punan tribe are the epitome of the legendary wild men of Borneo. To a certain extent, members of all the interior tribes (all tail-less) have integrated into mainstream life throughout all the territories of the island. Others live in semi-nomadic groups which emerge from the rainforest periodically only to trade natural latex, aloeswood or bird's nests, as they have done since the Chinese first arrived in the sixth century.

The Punan that we hoped to meet were those about who occasional rumours (but nothing more) are still transmitted to remote villages by hunters who have ventured far enough into the apparently uninhabited wilderness. It seems that even today there are bands of nomadic Punan who live entirely self-sufficient lives: sleeping, it is said, under lean-tos of leaves, running when they smell approaching men and leaving no trail of their passage. Most reports suggest that they are shy and peaceful and I had no reason to worry that we were setting off on the trail of a murderous tribe of headhunters.

Charles C Miller, who travelled in Borneo in 1942, would not have shared my optimism:

There are three tribes in Borneo seldom visited by white men, partly because they have no home in which to be visited, and partly because they are so tough, so cold-blooded and so utterly fearless that they would regard a social visit as an invitation to commit murder. These nomadic gangsters of the jungle are called the Hebans, the Punans and the Bukats.

Mr Miller was a Hollywood cameraman.

I plotted the locations of as many of these reports as I could find and the result was a rough circle around the Müller Mountains – and a thoroughly unrealistic picture of the Punan. Inside my circle there were no reports - but that was only natural, since nobody had ever been there.

The logic was inescapable. The Iban headhunters, the scourge of Borneo, raiding steadily inland had been the first forces to drive the peaceful nomads deeper into the sanctuary of the rainforest. Then, increasing pressure from the outside world had combined to push them further into what I came to believe must be one of the largest undocumented regions in the world. Borneo is navigable in most places only by river and I planned to travel into the interior up the mighty Kapuas River, the longest in Indonesia. I imagined it as the main artery through which we would be injected into Borneo's secretive and treacherous heart.

To Heineken Export this all seemed reasonable enough. Apparently they mistook the lunacy in my eyes (the natural effect of a dismal Bethnal Green winter) for burning commitment and unshakeable determination, because they generously agreed to finance the expedition.

The jigsaw was complete and plans were finalised. I'd already spent several months teaching myself Bahasa Indonesia. This is the *lingua franca* of Kalimantan, the southern two-thirds of Borneo, at the heart of which lay our destination. Paul was as enthusiastic about our mission as I was and as our departure date rushed forward to meet us I was grateful to be able to pass some of the organisation on to him. My plans necessarily ended at the headwaters of the Kapuas. Once there I decided (with blind faith) we would find a guide, speaking both Bahasa and Punan, who would lead us into the Müllers – across the blank bits on my maps and into the territory of the 'wild men of Borneo.'

It all looked so simple on paper.

Chapter One

Shipwrecked

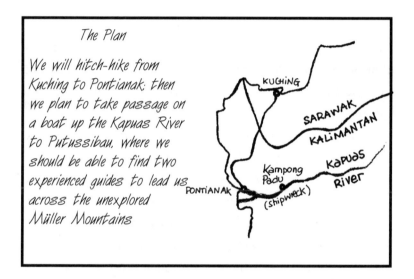

The Plan

We will hitch-hike from
Kuching to Pontianak; then
we plan to take passage on
a boat up the Kapuas River
to Putussibau, where we
should be able to find two
experienced guides to lead us
across the unexplored
Müller Mountains

KUCHING

SARAWAK

KALIMANTAN

Kapuas

River

Kampong
Padu

PONTIANAK

(shipwreck)

The old truck rattled through the tangled jungle, heading away from the border hills of Sarawak. We gripped the rusty bars behind the cab and leaned into the bends, allowing our knees to take the shock of the potholed road.

Paul and I had been in Borneo for just over a week and, barely two hours into Kalimantan, I imagined that we were now seriously going 'up-country.'

'Up-country.' I kept flipping the phrase over in my mind. For almost two years I had been planning for a trip into the interior of the world's third largest island. This was just the beginning and we were still only trying to get to first base - merely cutting a corner.

The countryside here was still hilly but occasionally we would swoop down, kamikaze style, and out onto sunlit padi fields. The view was almost a cliché; farmers, knee-deep in lush green stalks, would take off their conical hats and wave when they saw two foreigners grinning at them from the flying truck.

Paul waved back and whooped as the truck's tyres skittered through a shaded gully. His foot was jammed tightly against his precious camera bag. We were still travelling light. By the time we started for 'second base' we would be loaded down with the supplies and gifts that would be needed upriver. My mind wandered into an old B-movie western: a gnarled chief, puffing a long pipe, gasped when I folded out a blanket to reveal a miraculous pile of beads and mirrors. My imagination was running away with me. After two years dreaming of this in London, I was high on being out on the road.

Our battered packs were stuffed with everything I thought

we would need for survival in the jungle: mosquito nets, hammocks, our trusty British army jungle-boots and the medical kit that was our pride and joy. We had creams, powders, balms, tablets and lotions for everything from acute angina to zits.

Our ignorance of what truly lay ahead of us in the jungle was amply balanced, we imagined, by our blind enthusiasm.

Paul and I have hitchhiked together and individually for years, and we are both convinced that it is absolutely the best way to travel. A ten-hour bus journey could have replaced the uncertainty of a journey that had so far seen us riding in five different types of vehicle. But uncertainty and freedom was what we had travelled all this way for.

In the tropics the added incentive for hitchhiking is that, more often than not, you find yourself in the back of a truck stoking up your suntan in a cooling breeze, with ample leg room, and a three hundred and sixty degree field of vision. There is also the chance to meet travelling traders and the opportunity to rap on the roof and get down and walk whenever you see a place that you like.

Neither of us would ever consider more formal transport while there is any possibility of hitching. For appearances sake we had taken a bus only the necessary distance to get us past the watchful eyes of the Indonesian border guards. Hitching is not always accepted by the authorities as the pastime of a respectable person: yet another good reason for doing it.

The three lads in the truck's cab made a living by tearing along this strip selling plastic buckets, bags and beakers and buying up empty bottles for recycling. In a bustling riverside village we bought the boys a meal of cold curry with rice and hard-boiled eggs. Afterwards, whilst Paul wandered around taking more photographs of squealing kids, I tested my Bahasa.

The younger men appeared to be following the outline of my plans but it was not until the driver took up what was obviously a more familiar subject that the glazed expressions cleared from their eyes.

"The Dayak is not happy," he was saying, "The police are all from Java. All power is in Malay hands."

His harangue seemed to be aimed at the world at large and, as his speech got louder and more passionate, I began to feel less and less comfortable. Some passers by stopped in the doorway to listen.

"The Dayak is very angry!" The driver slammed his hand onto the table.

I had little experience of free-speech Indonesian style but, nevertheless, this conversation was making me very uneasy. I paid for the curries and eased the boys out onto the dusty street.

"Wah!" he emphasised his final volley as he wrenched open the truck's door, "Will be big problems all over Indonesia by year 2000."

We climbed back onto the flatbed.

"Citizen Smith was really goin' into one, wasn't he?" said Paul with typical crispness.

Soon the hilly forests gave way entirely to the lush padi-field plains of West Kalimantan. The hamlets of stilted riverside huts became more frequent. Children dropped their wooden spinning tops to wave and old men brought their bicycles to a squealing halt to turn and stare after us as we sped past.

Orang barat gila - crazy westerners.

The sky darkened and suddenly it was raining in thick, driving sheets. Paul and I crouched behind the cab and hunched up our shoulders out of the now icy wind. A row of red lights on the truck's roof made the water sloshing around our feet glitter. We were already soaked when, a couple of minutes later, the truck skidded to a halt and the two younger men jumped onto the back. With practised speed they slid a bamboo pole across two uprights and threw a tarpaulin over the whole flatbed.

We towelled ourselves dry with sarongs and sat under the dripping canvas staring out at the slanting rain as it turned to silver in the headlights of the city-bound traffic.

First base was Pontianak, a dirty, bustling city close to the South China Sea coast. From here we planned to find a boat that would take us all the way up the Kapuas, the longest river in Indonesia. Second base would be the jungle trading-centre of Putussibau where we would try to find guides who could lead us into the Müller Mountains.

Checking into Pontianak's grimy Hotel Kalbar, we hoped that it would not take us long to arrange our departure.

The hotel was situated right next to the wharf and on its balconies and along the corridors furtive, pouting gays and slovenly prostitutes lounged in their dishevelled boredom. When I went apprehensively down to the shower cubicles one of them, a grubby tee shirt strained across her breasts, barged her way into the room. I bowed politely to the side and as I strode down the corridor I heard Paul explaining to her: "No, no, but I don't need a flend!"

We hid most of our cash and our travellers' cheques under the insoles of our jungle-boots; we reasoned that as they were about four sizes too big for anyone in Kalimantan it would take a particularly thorough thief to steal them. Then we dashed through the rain into the shelter of a food stall and ordered *mee rebus*, boiled noodles with some lumps of gristly and unidentifiable meat. Paul was disgusted.

A 'lady-boy,' a transvestite with darkly made-up eyes and shiny leggings squeezed onto the bench between us. "Hello mister. What your name? *Orang Belanda?*" - Dutch?

I tried to force down my *mee rebus* with the thought that before we left Borneo we would probably have eaten much worse.

I was right, we would – but only just.

Pontianak was just too depressing. We wandered to the town centre, fearing all the while that our hotel room had already been looted, and under an awning by a stinking black canal we drank several bottles of warm Guinness. We sat in silence, reluctant to voice our worries and unable to predict our triumphs.

Independent travel is a daisy chain spiked with thistles: times of great happiness are separated by sudden unexpected downers.

I tried not to think about the previous evening. Back in Kuching (already a world away) on a moonlit tower, overlooking the city lights and the rushing Sarawak River, I had been achingly happy in the company of a pretty English nurse. I knew that it was, at least partially, the romantic surroundings that affected us but we had felt so contented that we were unwilling to leave the solitude of our tower until the first tinge of dawn was already showing above the tree-line.

I wondered how she was feeling now - was she thinking of me? The pangs at being so suddenly separated were made even more bitter by the shivering prostitutes at the next table and the greasy rain rushing in the gutters of Pontianak.

With the coming of daylight the poison goes, and when I woke the next morning the equatorial sun was already steaming the pavements dry.

I wandered along the wharf and watched the cargo being heaped onto the roof of an old timber hulk. Six tattooed deckhands were stacking a mountain of chunky truck tyres onto the already groaning roof. If they were all being taken up into the interior then there must be more logging going on than I had been led to believe, even by the pessimistic anthropologist with whom I had lunched back in London several weeks ago. He had warned me that I would be lucky to find any virgin forest at all.

I walked over to inspect the cargo that was waiting to be loaded into the shuttered hold: five new motorbikes, several television sets, towers of egg trays, sacks of sugar and rice and a bundle of twisted pink plastic labelled in English, 'Large Vinyl Fancy Cases.'

On the trader's peeling bows a scrawled inscription in darker blue read *Sinar Bulan* - Moonbeam. I liked that.

I called up to the boys on the roof in my clumsy Bahasa, "*Pergi ke mana?*"

They were leaving for Putussibau in a few hours.

The captain was a stocky, barrel-chested Malay and, after only a cursory haggling session, we were bound for Putussibau for a fee of just over nine pounds each (for a five-day voyage with meals included).

Within twenty minutes we were on board the *Sinar Bulan* staking out our sleeping area on a roll of oil-stained linoleum.

We took a cycle trishaw to the modern section of town and,

in an air-conditioned bank lobby on a wide boulevard, we finally managed to find somebody who knew how to change travellers' cheques. This would be the last place that we could change cheques until we arrived back on the coast in two months.

"I didn't think it was going to be so easy to get away," said Paul, stuffing rolls of bank notes into his boots, "I thought you were going to have to work your passage to get us out of here."

'A few hours' turned into twenty-seven. The captain let us sleep on board and we were grateful for the company of the crew and the deckhands who isolated us from the more blatant low-life of the wharf.

In the riverside market we bought fruit and drinks for the journey, and gifts for the people we hoped to stay with up-country. We bought packs of Balinese sarongs, plastic sewing kits, spools of strong thread, waterproof pocket torches, batteries, fishing line and hooks, plastic combs, sachets of 'Loveli dan Glossi Sampoo' and a huge bag of balloons.

Our last purchase was three bottles of *arak* (rice spirit) - as an icebreaker for the crew.

Only after our little party got rolling did we realise that the crew of the *Sinar Bulan* did not drink (being devout Muslims) and we ruined all our good intentions by drinking on the boat's roof with the crews of the other traders.

Coolie, a gnarled Iban with a walleye, a Charlie Chan moustache and an eagle tattoo on his muscle-knotted chest, became more and more affectionate as he quickly became drunker. He had obviously decided that he would set himself up as our devoted protector.

In my western homophobia I invented what I considered to be a harmless lie. To my shame it was to haunt us all the way up the Kapuas. The *arak* was disarmingly drinkable and before it was finished Paul and I had convinced the crew not only that we were both happily married but that we had a total of five children between us.

I gave a pony-tailed Iban some money to buy five more bottles of *arak* and it was not too long before he came running back - with three and a half. Free enterprise, I shrugged. Someone dragged a beaten old guitar up onto the roof and the party started roaring.

"*Ngiropai! Ngiropai!*" someone yelled in Iban - drink up boys!

At the pony-tailed lad's insistence we traded tee shirts and he howled his way through 'Sweet Child o' Mine' before we all murdered 'Imagine.'

We made the sounds that drunken men make all over the world in the moonlight when there are no women - only guitars. When Coolie started breaking his old alley-cat wharfy's heart, groaning an Indonesian love-song ("Aaah man, that's beautiful," sighed Paul), I had to stagger below to get my recording equipment.

"*Ngiropai! Ngiropai!*" I could hear through the timbers.

With tears rolling down his cheeks Coolie crooned into the microphone and, weeks later, when we played the tape back to some Malay girls, they were disgusted by his drunkenness and we felt sorry for him.

After a while we ran out of songs and the silver river soothed us as it rushed skeletal pieces of the jungle towards the South China Sea.

Some of the boys were already asleep on the roof and Paul

had crawled to his sleeping bag when a spindly canoe came bumping along the hull of the *Sinar Bulan.*

A thin figure stood up and waved his torch from side to side. "*Selamat pagi,*" he hissed, although it didn't feel like morning yet. The two men in the canoe were shrimp fishing and, not wanting the night to end, I asked if they had room for me.

We drifted downriver in silence whilst the man at the stern guided the canoe under the piers and into the canals flanking the wide rush of the Kapuas. Using his torchlight as a lure the thin man would pluck shrimps out of the water with a wide net. Then I would flip the top off the polystyrene box between my knees and his catch would join the primordial soup writhing inside.

It was peaceful with the moon cutting dimly through the clouds and across the wide stretch of shining river the opposite bank appeared as a dark band. I must have dozed off and after about an hour we eased up to a rickety jetty and the thin man told me to jump out. 'Just stretching our legs,' I thought, as I clambered onto the greasy boardwalk.

Waving goodbye cheerfully they started to pull away from the jetty and I realised with a shock that they were going to leave me here.

I had no idea where I was except that I was some indeterminable distance downriver. In my impotent fury I started to shout abuse at them. I stamped my bare feet on the rough wooden boards but as the boat dissolved into the darkness I heard only their laughter.

As I turned to try to get my bearings the rain started to hammer down as it can only in the tropics.

I figured that it would take me at least an hour to find my

way back to the *Sinar Bulan* and muggers would be only one of my troubles in this rough, dirty stretch of town. Perhaps I should find a doorway in which to try to sleep until daylight or at least until the rain stopped. But I was already soaked and it was probably safer to stay alert and keep moving.

If the police found me barefoot on the streets with no identification at this time of the morning how could I explain? I knew nothing of Indonesian policemen but I did know about those of Latin America and I was painfully aware that I was not in an ideal position to start a discussion with a bored and bitter *guardia*.

These and other questions occupied me as I hurried off the jetty and past a shivering bundle of rags curled in a doorway. I turned the corner of a warehouse, splashing my feet through oily puddles. I stepped onto the edge of a wide marketplace, intent only on staying close to the river, and was halfway across before I recognised the stall where we had eaten the *mee rebus* the previous evening. There, just to my right, was the *Sinar Bulan*.

I thought of the two men who had invited me on their fishing trip and whom I had just been abusing. Even in my solitude and under the cool rain I felt my face grow hot with the shame of it. They wouldn't be picking up any hitchhikers for a while.

It was still a few hours until sunrise and my troubles were not yet over. All the shutters on the *Sinar Bulan* were firmly battened down and I was not keen to start hammering at three am and wake everyone - with the notable exception of Paul, who could sleep through a gale in a foghorn factory.

I clambered disconsolately onto the roof to look for shelter and found it in a wire-mesh cage under a tarpaulin. Later I discovered that this pen was used for transporting chickens. Thus

I was committing yet another social *faux pas*: a decent Indonesian looks upon the cleanliness of chickens as we do of pigs (of course they feel even worse about pigs).

I slept only sporadically, shivering in my Indonesian chicken-sty under the dripping tarpaulin.

The next morning I found that somehow, somewhere I had bashed my right big toe. The nail had turned almost completely black overnight and I went happily to wake Paul with what I considered to be my badge of honorary Dayakhood.

Our experiences with guide-hunting were to lead us to hypothesise that a Dayak's proficiency in the jungle was in direct relation to the disfigurement of his toenails. I was proud that my 'Dayak toe' was already ugly enough to compete with some of its less seriously mangled Pontianak contemporaries.

About mid-morning, whilst most of the wharfies were smoking their clove-scented Gudang Garam cigarettes in the shade, a small rowing-boat drifted silently under the trader's bows. The chubby Malay at the oars waited until he was about ten feet from the dock before his loud, clear shout turned the wharf into a hive of frantic activity. Word swept up quickly to the covered market across the road and people came running out to see whatever it was that was bundled in the boat's belly.

With the air of a showman, his fame now assured, the Malay peeled back a plastic sheet to display the body of a drowned teenage boy.

Already slightly bloated the corpse was trying belatedly to exhale the river water and snowy foam covered its nose and mouth.

The crowd jostled for a better look.

Some unspoken code forbade either of us from acknowledging this ill omen even by mentioning the event.

The *Sinar Bulan* finally stuttered her engines to life a bare half-hour before sunset whilst Paul and I were in the market. The captain had to send Eddi, the youngest crewmember, to find us.

Coolie was among those laughing loudest as we scrambled up the greasy gangplank onto the boat. Eddi led us up onto the roof of the wheelhouse. From this position we shouted *"selamat tinggal"* to the wharfies and the crews of the other boats as the *Kapuas Eagle* and the *Teladan Star* manoeuvred to let the *Moonbeam* out into the current.

As we passed under the conspicuously modern Kapuas Bridge the sky, already tinged pink by the dying sun, was peppered with bobbing kites. Many were sent aloft from the canoes and rowing boats which were now scurrying away from the old trader's bullying bulk.

The floating platforms bordering the river were swarming with townsfolk performing their evening ablutions and the tin dome of a small mosque blushed sensitively in the last glow of the sun. Although the fact was as yet unknown, the *Sinar Bulan* had embarked on her last voyage.

Darkness fell quickly and we moved out of the city into what seemed to our intoxicated and expectant eyes to be The Interior.

The *Sinar Bulan* had been trading up and down the Kapuas for fourteen years and her arrival had become an important event in the lives of the people who live along the river.

She was a great square hulk of a boat: a floating warehouse with a storage area about equal to half a tennis court. Along both sides she was equipped with removable shutters; the upper sections were swung up and tied to the roof beams and the lower halves were lifted out and stowed inside. When the rain slanted in across the river one side could be battened down and the muggy smell of Caterpillar tyres and rice dust became stifling and drove all the passengers to the open side of the boat.

There were about fifteen passengers in all, sleeping wherever they could lay out their pieces of linoleum or threadbare carpet. This was their idea of a pleasure cruise. A relaxing four-day voyage was far more enjoyable than sitting on a dusty, uncomfortable bus – even if the bus could cover the same distance in a quarter of the time.

There was a large Malay woman who never stopped laughing. She was travelling with her six-year-old son who was strangely and obviously effeminate beyond his years. His pale skin was never subjected to direct sunlight without a liberal coating of the white powder that middle-class Malay women use to maintain their complexion.

Transvestism is not only tolerated but enjoyed throughout much of South East Asia and from the way his mother pampered him it seemed that the boy was being deliberately groomed for the persuasion.

Ahmed was a middle-aged Indian man returning home to Sintang (two days upriver) with his wife and four children. A small oil burner kept them supplied with sweet black *kopi* and their baby gurgled, bouncing contentedly in a knotted sarong on a spring secured to the beams. Ahmed's obvious delight in his young family was as touching as his pride in the gleaming red Vespa scooter that had been the reason for his visit to Pontianak.

To get up front to the *Sinar Bulan's* wheelhouse it was necessary either to climb out of the shutters and down over the front of the roof or to risk life and limb in almost complete darkness on a shifting dune of plastic hairbrushes, flip-flops and 'Large Vinyl Fancy Cases.'

Eddi sat up on the roof with us and kept up an incessant stream of chatter. At fourteen he was small for his age and, in common with most of the crew, he had taken the job to earn money for his family during the school holidays. He hoped that if we were to be travelling together for the next five days I would teach him some English. I, in turn, hoped that he would let me practise my Bahasa.

The captain stepped out onto the rope-strewn bow below us and told Eddi to come down and prepare dinner. Climbing back down off the roof was nerve-wracking - especially for Paul, burdened as always with photographic equipment. Getting a firm grip on the ropes that were lashed across the tyres we had to swing out over the churning water and find a tentative foothold on the edge of one of the shutters before easing ourselves back into the security of the hold.

Within twenty minutes we were eating fried rice, onions, peppers and fish fried in a wok on a gas burner at the back of the boat. Washed down with *kopi,* it was wonderful.

We sat with our legs swinging over the muddy water, watching the dark trees slipping back towards the South China Sea and looked forward to the next few days: a relaxing period of slow acclimatisation and mental preparation for whatever lay ahead.

A question with which we would be dogged throughout our stay in Kalimantan interrupted my thoughts: *"Sudah mandi, pak?"* - already showered?

"Belum," I answered, - not yet - and turned back towards the river.

A moment later another voice instinctively asked, *"Sudah mandi?"*

"Belum."

After a while, shamed into moving, I made my way to the shower in the stern with my sarong over my shoulder (quicker drying than a towel). Other people enquired, *"Mau mandi, pak?"* - going to shower?

"Mau mandi." There are no equivalents for 'yes' and 'no' in Bahasa. You can only repeat the phrase or, in the case of a negative response, the phrase is preceded by *'tidak'* (not).

Every morning and evening all over Kalimantan the same question would be bandied around so that soon even Paul and I were greeting each other with *"Sudah mandi, pak?"*

Mandi-ing was not as easy on the *Sinar Bulan* (nor indeed elsewhere in Kalimantan) as I had imagined - which may explain the preoccupation with it.

The two wooden shower cubicles had oval holes cut into the floorboards and were equipped with cracked plastic buckets. The former being markedly smaller than the latter, I looked around for some other way of drawing water out of the river which I could see rushing two feet below the floorboards. I was further disturbed by the fact that the river seemed to be running so swiftly that it would probably tear a bucket straight out of my hand the moment it dipped into the water.

There must be some obvious system that I was overlooking here. I looked around and scratched my head. The only clue was a plastic pipe sticking out of the wall - a disappointingly dry plastic pipe.

I was aware that the crew, lounging outside by the 'galley,' had seen me enter the cubicle. The longer I stayed inside the more embarrassing it would be when finally I had to admit that I could not figure it out. So I went back out and, pointing at the door, I asked "*Bagaimana?*" - how?

"*Tunggu*," came answer - wait.

So I waited and, when there was a convenient pause in the conversation, I asked again.

"*Tunggu*."

As short a time as I had been in Kalimantan this seemed to me uncharacteristically rude and, suppressing my impatience, I wandered back to our little encampment. "Never wanted a bloody *mandi* anyway," I muttered to myself.

I had totally given up on my shower by the time we pulled away from a riverside hamlet, which had been all but devoured by vegetation, and chugged out again into midstream. Then Eddi was at my shoulder, "*Mandi. Mandi, pak.*"

Back in the cubicle water was gurgling merrily out of the pipe and it didn't stop until the *Sinar Bulan* did.

Early the next morning Paul was sitting reading on top of the heaped rice sacks and I was dozing, cocooned in my sheet sleeping bag. Suddenly there was a grinding crunch and the boat shuddered violently and lurched over onto one side.

Paul was thrown from his perch onto an upright post by the unexpected jolt and only narrowly avoided being catapulted into the river. I shot upright, quickly dragging my legs away from Ahmed's Vespa, which was rocking violently against the cargo straps.

It took a moment for my sleep-befuddled mind to register that the cargo had slipped over and its uneven weight was dragging the boat down. The crew came rushing back from the wheelhouse. The captain followed them, barking orders. The hold was in uproar with women screaming and children crying. I saw Ahmed trying to cluster his family on the upper edge of the hold which was suddenly three feet above the water level.

I kicked my legs out of the tangled sheet and Paul and I leapt forward to help the crew heave the rice sacks back over the pile. They were heavy and we had to work in pairs, climbing carefully over the avalanche, hauling one sack at a time back to the port side. The rice had taken several hours to load and we were going to be allowed only a fraction of that time to re-stack it before the *Sinar Bulan* went down.

Water was jetting into the hold from the engine room below and I realised that something had smashed a hole in the boat's hull. The old diesel engine spewed great clouds of blinding steam up to where we struggled.

The boat was tilted at a crazy angle now, with the port side five feet higher than the starboard. It was obvious that merely redistributing the cargo was not going to save the *Sinar Bulan*. The wind chop on the river was already lapping the gunwales and it was clear that once the water started pouring over the side she would sink very quickly.

Ahmed and his wife were undressing the children in

preparation for the swim. The Malay woman was wailing and smothering her son in her ample breasts. We were a hundred metres from the bank and the current was running fast. Above the noise of screaming passengers and the roars of the captain I shouted to Paul that we should grab the cash from our boots and be ready to swim with the kids.

The riverbank here was sparsely inhabited. It was extremely lucky there was a small hamlet further upstream. Hearing the passengers' shrieks the villagers were already ploughing three canoes towards us. Lacking anything more useful to do we redoubled our efforts to balance the cargo whilst one family at a time was shuttled to the riverbank. The timbers were creaking with the strain and we began to throw some of the sacks over the side to try to ease it quicker. Finally the captain told us to grab our packs and get in a canoe.

Twenty minutes later everyone was regrouped safely on the shore. With a crack like a rifle shot and a billow of rice dust the *Sinar Bulan's* roof caved in.

Kampong Padu translates as Unity Village - a grand name for a hamlet of two shacks and a schoolroom. Luckily for us the headman had visitors that day who more than doubled the population of his *kampong* and had supplied the canoes and manpower to effect our rescue.

The crew began hurriedly to ferry back whatever could be salvaged, throwing a bizarre assortment of goods up to helpers on the bank. It was a dangerous job. The *Sinar Bulan* was in a highly unstable condition; the strain that her twisted timbers were under seemed to be almost visible from the village.

All along the riverbank were soaking sarongs, piles of plastic shoes, stacks of leaking egg-trays and huge nylon sacks of instant noodles. Three soggy police hats for the Putussibau constabulary were officially handed into the keeping of the headman. Truck tyres were cut loose from the roof to be collected later downriver. I never saw the 'Large Vinyl Fancy Cases' again - doubtless they would be sorely missed by some trader in Putussibau.

Spotting Ahmed watching the salvage operation I went over to give my condolences on the loss of his scooter. I knew that it was a powerful loss.

"*Nasib*," he shrugged - destiny.

Soon a huge pot of rice was bubbling on a fire next to the schoolhouse. The headman's wife and the jolly Malay woman were throwing in chopped vegetables, pieces of fish and numerous packets of instant noodles. Suddenly we realised how hungry we were.

As we ate, unknown vegetable matter forming a sort of hessian mat in our mouths, we watched the salvage operation from the shade of the trees. A breeze blew up the valley and was refreshingly cool. Instantly everyone was screaming and running . . from us.

Paul and I looked at each other, dumbfounded, and then towards the headman's veranda, from where Ahmed beckoned us. Feeling foolish we tried to effect a sort of semi-nonchalant dogtrot.

"Durian!" laughed Ahmed, pointing into the treetops.

There, high in the foliage swung the huge green cannonballs of the durian fruit. Looking like some medieval weapon, this legendary fruit is most famous for its penetrating odour.

Durian means thorny in Indonesian and the fruit's jagged leathery hide protects it as it plummets to the jungle floor with such force that it literally half-buries itself. It is more than capable of manslaughter and I made a mental note never to sling my hammock under a durian tree.

When most of the other passengers were asleep in the schoolroom, we sat on the headman's veranda looking through the gloom of the river towards the triangle of roof that was all that was left of the *Sinar Bulan*. Two of the crew strummed their guitars quietly and the headman's three daughters hummed a melancholy accompaniment.

All attention turned to a spotlight cutting out of the shadows of the river and moving purposefully towards us. Soon three policemen were climbing up the bank, nodding greetings all around and shaking hands with the headman.

This was obviously an official call and the Sergeant explained that they had heard that there were *orang barat* on the *Sinar Bulan*. He was anxious to ensure that we were unhurt. I felt uncomfortably conscious that it was only westerners who warranted this official notice.

The Sergeant asked me to write a *surat keterangan* - a 'clearance statement' to the effect that we were in good health, had lost nothing and were content to stay in Kampong Padu until the next boat came by. After these formalities were over one of the officers produced a camera and with stern, fugitive expressions we were mug-shot either side of the chief.

The police relaxed, took off their hats and sat down. The guitars restarted their quiet melody. Like most of the police force in Kalimantan these men were from Java. They would work here for a year before they could take a two-week leave to visit their families. One of them had extremely long thumbnails. This is a sign of upper-class pretensions all over South East Asia; it is impossible to do manual labour without breaking nails that are over an inch and a half long.

It is also very difficult to play a guitar and when it was offered to him he quickly and casually bit off this impediment to his art and spat it out into the darkness. All who witnessed this sacrifice held their breath. Here perhaps was Indonesia's answer to Eric Clapton.

We were sorely disappointed and within two minutes he had lost possession of the instrument and spent the next hour sulkily contemplating his deficient thumbnail and resulting loss of status.

The captain of the *Sinar Bulan* was very quiet, perhaps considering the disgrace that was destined to fall squarely on his shoulders when the boat's owner arrived from Pontianak.

Eddi explained that *kaptin* had trapped a finger when a shutter slammed down during the salvage operation and he was '*pusing kepala.*'

I flipped through my dictionary: '*pusing*, dizzy; *itu memusingkan kepalanya*, this gave him a headache, he had to cudgel his brains.'

Obviously we had to do whatever we could to help before the captain cudgelled his brains. But it took all my powers of persuasion even to get him to let me see the damaged finger. He held it protectively against his chest, wrapped in an oily rag. I gave him a couple of painkillers and we left him for half an hour until the pain had lessened sufficiently for us to soak the rag away from the wound in sterilised water.

His middle finger was sliced through to the bone and certainly needed stitches. When we began to clean the ragged gash, to cover it with antiseptic cream and bandage it he turned a deathly white and was struggling not to faint. Every time we looked away he tried to grip the throbbing finger in his oily rag.

With luck he would be in Sintang the next evening and I stressed the importance of going to the hospital there to get it stitched. I gave him enough painkillers to last and strict instructions on when to take them.

At least the captain now appeared less ambitious to cudgel his brains. He was even able to force a grin when we positioned him in the centre of the hut with his rampant digit held aloft. We slipped a condom over the whole wound, explaining that it would be excellent waterproofing - and, more importantly, it would make a cracking photograph.

Chapter Two

Gateway to the Jungle

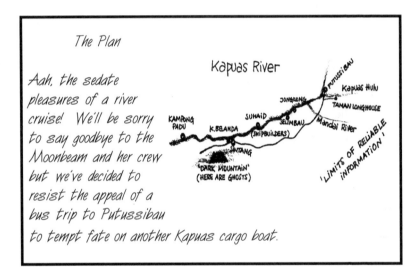

The Plan

Aah, the sedate pleasures of a river cruise! We'll be sorry to say goodbye to the Moonbeam and her crew but we've decided to resist the appeal of a bus trip to Putussibau to tempt fate on another Kapuas cargo boat.

Kapuas River

PUTUSSIBAU

Kapuas Hulu

JONGKONG

TAMAN LONGHOUSE

SUHAID

SELIMBAU

Mandai River

KAMPONG PADU

K.BBANDA

(SHIPBUILDERS)

NTANG

'DARK MOUNTAIN'
(HERE ARE GHOSTS)

'LIMITS OF RELIABLE INFORMATION'

Eddi shook us awake before dawn the next morning and we dashed around scrambling our baggage together. We dug out some gifts for the headman and within five minutes we were standing - trailing bootlaces, shirtsleeves and camera straps – on the riverbank.

The *Teladan Star* crawled towards us through the dawn mist. We stood waiting as she passed the last buckled corner of the *Sinar Bulan's* roof - standing out in mid-stream like a memorial. As the trader drew level with us we could just make out the crew watching from the bow.

We were still standing patiently when, with a playful hoot of her horn, the *Teladan Star* disappeared around the next bend. We turned and went back to bed.

At that moment, the only people in Kampong Padu who had a boat were the policemen. Even the headman was not keen to take upon himself the responsibility of waking them. So we were stuck until such time as a cargo boat should happen to pass at a more civilised hour. The *Raja Wali Kapuas* was expected about mid-morning but, since the *Sinar Bulan* herself had departed exactly twenty-seven hours late, we decided not to place much confidence in timetables.

We breakfasted on instant noodles. The population of Kampong Padu and much of the surrounding jungle would be dining on shipwrecked instant noodles, three times daily, for the next few weeks. Ahmed and the other passengers had already left to walk four miles to catch a bus to Sintang. They'd had their fill of the cargo boats. In the early afternoon only Paul and I remained to be ferried, in the skipping police boat, out to the *Raja Wali*. Word of the disaster had travelled swiftly down the river and, knowing some of the crew already from the *Sinar Bulan's* last party, we were greeted aboard as celebrities.

With a clumsiness that was fast becoming legendary I heralded our arrival by cracking my head violently on a roof beam as I leapt into the hold.

The *Raja Wali Kapuas (Kapuas Eagle)* was interesting in that, on this voyage at least, it was more concerned with carrying passengers than cargo. Each captain touts for his business at the beginning of a voyage and a question of timing had meant that the *Sinar Bulan* had collected the majority of the week's goods from Pontianak, leaving the *Raja Wali* and the *Teladan Star* to carry passengers.

We were disappointed to find that Coolie, our wall-eyed Iban protector, was not aboard. Apparently he had been hired only as a dockhand in Pontianak. Instead an obliging fellow with a cherubic face and the unlikely name of Norman became our constant companion. He was dedicated and informative, always ready to answer questions and quick to correct my Bahasa. The time was coming when I would have to negotiate with the guides who would lead us into the jungle and I was worried that my command of the language would barely be equal to that test.

There were sixty-seven passengers on the *Raja Wali* and a well-organised community had developed within a short time of leaving Pontianak. Rigid (though unwritten) rules had been devised governing sleeping positions: families and girls slept with their feet inward from the starboard side and single men (there were only eight of us) formed one row, feet inwards, from the port side.

In the mornings, when I first stepped onto the bow, I would stare at the dark walls of vegetation between which we cruised, trying to judge whether the banks had crept any closer during the night. In the proportions of this massive river we were moving so slowly that for a long time the difference was barely perceptible.

We spent most of our days on the boat's roof, reading and sunbathing blissfully, cooled by the breeze of the river. From this vantage point we stared in awe at the seemingly endless expanse of trees, stretching out flat across the Kapuas basin. For an entire day we moved nearer to Gunung Kelam, the Dark Mountain. Its bleak, cloud-draped tabletop dominated the surrounding jungle.

"No good," said Norman, shaking his head grimly, "*ada hantu*" - there are ghosts.

It was impossible not to think of Joseph Conrad creeping slowly up the Congo:

Going up that river was like travelling back to the earliest beginnings of the world. When vegetation rioted on the earth and the big trees were kings.

Occasionally we would pass a *kampong* of stilted huts and I would ask Norman which tribe of Dayaks lived there. Usually he described the inhabitants as *orang melayu*. These are not Malays, but Islamised Dayaks.

When an individual or a community adopts the official religion of Indonesia and becomes Muslim they cease forever to be, even nominally, Dayaks. I had the feeling that it was almost an indelicate question, but . . "What kind of Dayaks did they *used* to be, Norman?"

"*Orang dayak*," said Norman, nodding authoritatively.

"*Tetapi orang dayak suku apa?*" – yes, but which tribe - I asked, rephrasing the question. It was no use; it was as if their entire history had been erased at the moment they entered Islam.

I was never able to discover Norman's lineage. To an Islamised Dayak there are only two denominations - *orang dayak* and *orang melayu*. Norman was definitely the latter - before that there was nothing.   Our 'search for the wild men of Borneo' or 'the mystery of the lost tribe of the Punan' (in the words of the newspapers that had reported on the expedition) meant that I had already become involved in trying to define the tribal territories of this part of Kalimantan. In interrogating Norman I had stumbled deeper into the obsession that has created conflicts in the reports of most of the explorers and anthropologists who have tried to classify the Dayaks. Within the tribal groups there are countless subgroups and, historically, the problem of identifying who is related culturally to whom has been a sort of anthropological Chinese puzzle. But is this really a problem? As Carl Hoffman wrote in *The Punan - Hunters and Gatherers of Borneo*:

It became evident rather early on in my fieldwork that trying to ascertain the "real names" of Punan groups was a matter far more important to me than it was to the Punan themselves.

I was intrigued when Norman pointed out a *kampong belanda* (a Dutch village) near the town of Sintang. He said that the community there speak Dutch, are faithful to the Dutch Reformed Church and, apart from necessary trade, keep themselves aloof from the surrounding peoples. I wondered how they had survived the Japanese occupation when almost all the westerners on the island were either imprisoned or executed. Some Dutch settlers made desperate escape attempts into the eastern Müller Mountains, where they lost their heads to Dayak swords.

I imagined these *orang belanda* living here in a sort of

expatriate limbo: some of them had perhaps returned to Holland after Indonesian independence in 1949 and found that it fell short of their hopes and ideals. In some ways they seemed very much like the nomadic Punan. They had chosen this isolated settlement as their last bastion - how long could *they* hold out against infiltration?

By the end of the last century Sintang was one of Holland's two principal administrative centres in Borneo, and they had stationed a large garrison here to 'tame the interior.' This city of twenty thousand is still the key to the heart of the island and when the Dutch left it was predictably the Chinese quarter that became the hub of the city. It is through here that most of the trade between the *hulu* (literally 'upriver') and the coast passes.

Much of the *Raja Wali's* cargo of plastic and cotton goods were destined for Sintang's markets and whilst the crew were unloading we ate greasy doughnuts at a dockside canteen. We washed them down with three cups of white coffee. *Kopi susu* in Kalimantan is always served at least one part condensed milk to two parts strong *kopi*.

We were discussing the impropriety of ordering another *kopi susu* when an old man sidled up to us. He had a long package under his arm. Without a word he laid the package on our table, untied the string and reverently folded back the grubby cloth.

Inside was a *mandau* (a headhunting sword) with a beautifully carved scabbard and an antler handle representing a dog's head. A tuft of deer hair sprouted from the dog's mouth - in the good old days this would have been human hair. There was a dirty red rag bound around the sheath. If, like many of its peers, this *mandau* had been used in anger even as recently as the Malaysian border skirmishes in the early seventies then this rag could very likely be a shred of a captured Communist flag.

We were unhappy to leave this fine sword behind but neither of us was willing to take on the responsibility of looking after it from so early on in our travels. I believed that we would see better and cheaper examples later.

In the back yard of the government building on the dock an exciting competition was going on. A court, like that used for badminton, was scratched out in the dust and six boys were showing full commitment to a game of *sepak takraw*.

This sport is played over much of South East Asia. Its rules are similar to those of volleyball, but the hard plastic ball (traditionally made of wicker) must be kept off the ground using only the feet, the head or occasionally - a very flashy manoeuvre - the back part of the upper arm.

Having played *sepak takraw* often in Thailand and Malaysia, Paul and I were itching for a game. Every now and then a lad would fly up in front of the net, feet uppermost, and in a wide sweeping kick he would try to slam the ball downwards into the opposition's court before thudding onto the ground on the back of his neck. These boys were too serious for us.

The lack of privacy in the hold of the *Raja Wali* was sometimes hard to bear; invasion of personal space and gratuitous body contact are something that we English in particular find difficult to come to terms with. I had to make a determined effort not to draw away when, nose-deep in Herman Hesse's *Siddhartha*, one of the crew would lie down next to me with their head up against mine to ask what this word meant, or that.

We learnt to *mandi* when the showers were at their quietest and washed our clothes cautiously on the narrow stern platform, letting the surge from the propellers perform the rinse-cycle (instant death if you get dragged in).

The sleep that was so slow to come on the vibrating timber boards was fitful when it did arrive. We were amazed by what we considered a total lack of respect for people who were sleeping. It was perfectly normal for someone to wake during the night and yell across the hold to a friend to check if he also was awake. Nobody else ever seemed annoyed by this and we did our best to restrain ourselves to a mild "Shhh!"

Two girls, travelling home from college in Pontianak, showed an inordinate interest in the subject of our fictional wives and children. Kustinah (she listed her hobbies with her address in my diary: 'swimming and drinking milk') and Endang were obsessed by the lie that was spawned in my misguided homophobia directed at Coolie. Because many of the crew had been at our party, the lie had followed us here and the girls had made it their mission to uncover the truth.

Once, several hours before dawn, I was shaken out of my slumber by Kustinah. My optimism was short-lived – it was one in the morning and she wanted to borrow my dictionary. There was nothing that I could do but get up with as much grace as possible and dig the book out of my pack for her.

The crew slept in relative luxury in a tiny room above the wheelhouse. There they had installed a karaoke machine and – far more alluring – cushions.

One afternoon, whilst I dozed in a truck tyre on the bow, the captain woke me to ask if I wanted to take my siesta upstairs. I didn't need to be asked twice and with infinite gratitude I climbed the ladder behind the driver's seat.

One of the crew was already asleep and barely suppressing my groans of contentment I lay down with my head in the shadows behind the speakers. My hips and knees were bruised and the soft, grimy carpet eased me into sleep within moments. Suddenly there was a crash and the prolonged shriek of a tomcat being castrated behind my neck. I leapt up, crashing my temple against the corner of the amplifier. There, sat on the top step of the ladder, was a pimply teenager - two hands on the microphone - wailing some heart-rending Indonesian classic of unrequited love.

Like the rock-star that at that moment he believed he was, he gave me a saucy wink and picked up tempo and volume as he lurched into his chorus. Feeling like rending his heart with my own bare hands I climbed - bleeding from the ears - back down the ladder to find the captain lolling in my truck tyre.

Personal property was another concept upon which our opinions differed. The frequency with which my guidebooks circled the hold was dizzying. I would eventually stumble across a crowd staring at the pictures, giggling at the distended earlobes of the Kenyah Dayaks or the tattooed Iban women.

There was no malice in the way our fellow passengers would remove things from our bed spaces, and there was never a fear that anything had been stolen. In fact, there was an element of charm in the way my penknife (which I had not yet realised was missing) was casually returned by an old lady who had borrowed it from my backpack to slice a papaya.

Norman was one of the worst culprits and he exasperated Paul with his insatiable curiosity. He found Paul's precious camera equipment irresistible and, returning from a brief photographic operation, Paul would find Norman engrossed in emptying his bag *yet again* - gazing intently through lenses and opening film canisters.

Whilst we unloaded at a rickety jetty one morning Paul decided to take the opportunity to shave on terra firma. The operation always proved entertaining for our almost hairless travelling companions and Norman placed himself to get the closest possible view. They were sat side-by-side with their legs dangling into the coffee-coloured murk of the river when, from my position on the boat's roof, I heard Paul's gasp: "Aah Jeez! I don't believe it!" I looked over the side to see a hilariously shame-faced Norman who, while systematically examining the contents of the toilet bag, had just dropped Paul's toothbrush through the slats of the jetty.

There was a pleasant, unhurried routine to our days: *kopi* on the bow with the captain, people to visit with, *sudah mandi?,* lunch time, more *kopi, sudah mandi, pak?*, siesta in the sun, *sudah* . . .

At sunset we would cover up against the voracious mosquitoes and climb onto the roof to watch the sun drop through the bleeding sky onto the shadowy forest at the end of the boat's wake. It was sad when our little community began to dissolve into the chain of *kampongs* along the Kapuas.

All the way up the river we sparred with the *Teladan Star*. One boat would overtake the other every few hours and the crews would square off on broadsides to fire over a volley of abuse: "*Hati, hati!* – Careful with those *orang barat*. Did you hear what they did to the *Sinar Bulan*?"

The cargo boats caused great excitement wherever they

docked. At one *kampong*, in an inlet that swirled with oil rainbows, the school was dismissed to come out and watch the boat unload. Paul made the children scream with laughter with a wild tap-dance on the roof.

Most of the *Raja Wali's* customers were Chinese traders (West Kalimantan holds the highest concentration of Chinese in Indonesia) and a large number of these operated from floating warehouses called *bandungs*. These 'mobile stores,' some half the size of the *Raja Wali*, are throwbacks to the old days when the traders often had to cut loose from the riverbank to escape raiders.

At the village of Suhaid Norman took me to meet the carpenter who had built the *Raja Wali Kapuas*. He was now hard at work on another big trader that would take four months to complete. The smoothly tapering bow was already built and he was fitting the deck-boards - they were numbered (1a, 1b, 1c, 2a, 2b etc.) throughout the length of the boat, so that they could easily be detached to stow extra cargo. The shipwright stopped work to question me about the *Sinar Bulan*; it seemed that this was the most exciting piece of news to pass up the Kapuas for decades.

When we got back to the *Raja Wali* the *kepala* (the village headman) was talking with the captain. Paul grabbed my arm as I jumped into the boat: "See that - he's got a 'Fat Willy's Surf Shack' cap on. I can't believe it ... From Newquay!" Here in the middle of Borneo was a vision of home.

Paul flashed the *kepala* a thumbs-up sign, beaming at his baseball cap.

"*Nomor satu!*" I shouted - number one!

Before he left the headman came over and shook hands with us. "I velly happy meet you." It was the first English we had heard since Sarawak. "You velly kind men."

At Selimbau that evening, in the cheerless driving rain, we said goodbye to Norman. It was sad to know that we would never see him again and the rain running under our collars stopped us from saying what we would have liked to say.

Stranded for an hour while the crew unloaded, we went to a greasy dockside bar. It was owned by an intimidating figure with huge forearms and the mashed nose of a fighter. We drank a couple of beers and listened to the rain hammering on the iron roof. Teli, the fighter, turned out to be a very amiable character; anyway, we decided, perhaps you should be less frightened of fighters with mashed noses than of those without.

The storm carried on late into the night and I sat in the wheelhouse with the crew, watching for floating trunks in the silver path of the spotlight. It was cosy and dry inside and the jags of lightning, reflected in the river and backlighting the ragged trees, were exhilarating. I wished that our voyage was not nearing its end.

The next morning the two 'girl-detectives' came over to me as I sat trailing my feet in the water. Their approach had the air of a showdown. Endang wanted to see *potos* of my wife.

"If I had a wife and two children why didn't I carry *potos*?" she demanded.

Kustinah didn't bother to wait for an answer: "How could I leave my family alone for four months?"

If we could have talked in private I would have liked to tell them the truth about how the lie was perpetrated. But I knew that I couldn't do that to Coolie, or (if I did not give names) to our wharfy friends in general.

I could only brazen it out and when I awoke from a doze later that morning I found out that they had left the boat at Jongkong knowing that we had lied to them. It was a poor way to repay the honesty and openness of these people.

We arrived at Putussibau ten hours later, with only the last remnants of our little group intact. The jolly Malay woman and her son had joined the *Raja Wali* at Sintang (after some complicated adventures with the other *Sinar Bulan* refugees on a bus). They were both relieved to be home at last.

It was already dark and we were grateful when the captain invited us to sleep this last night on the *Raja Wali*. We wandered in what we guessed was the direction of town to find something to eat, walking in the middle of the track with the swampy jungle croaking on either side of us. The rainclouds parted occasionally to allow us a moment's relief from the blackness, then after ten minutes we stepped onto a road and headed gratefully towards a light.

Here, in this unlikely location, we found what is almost certainly the *pinkest* restaurant on the planet. Everything was pink: pink walls, pink ceiling, pink plastic flowers in pink vases in the centre of shocking pink tablecloths. We ordered chicken curry. It was delicious but the vivid orange clashed horribly with the décor.

The boat remained moored against the riverbank that night and without the vibrations from the engine we slept comfortably. We cruised the last few hundred metres of our voyage sitting in the bows. Perhaps it was the uncertainty of what lay ahead that gave us an exaggerated sense of camaraderie with the crew. We nursed our *kopi* and peered through the patchy dawn mist, itching for our first view of Putussibau.

Putus' is the last stop for the cargo boats of the Kapuas. Although there were already several hundred miles of dense rainforest behind us we looked upon this as the gateway to the jungle. I was surprised and slightly disappointed therefore, as we chugged around the last corner, to pass under the only bridge that we had seen since leaving Pontianak. My guidebook billed this town of seven thousand as a 'remote outpost on the Kapuas' and somehow I had imagined that we were beyond concrete bridges and asphalt roads. It seemed that we were still a long way from the land of the nomadic Punan.

Losmen Harapan Kita (Hotel 'Trust Us') was a riverside boarding house with timber verandas and a greasy *rumah makan* (dining room). Each room was equipped with a slimy cell with tanks of cold water for 'scoop showers.' The rooms were also apparently impregnated with the acrid smoke of mosquito coils and, as an added precaution against things that go buzz in the night, a pair of happily chirping geckoes were supplied at no extra charge.

Not only do they eat mosquitoes (the most dangerous creature in Borneo) but also, across much of South East Asia, geckoes are believed to bring good luck. In Malay they are called *chin chock*. The name echoes their cheerful call whilst at the same time reminding one of their good intent - *chock* means luck.

As we lay on the damp mattresses watching these little squatters (so transparent that I could see their hearts beating) we discussed our next move. Paul's immediate vote to 'keep pushing forward' seemed logical. It was the old hitchhiker's adage: just keep movin'.

I had hoped that in Putussibau we would find the guides who would be able to lead us south over the Müller Mountains. It was simply a matter of being patient and letting word get around.

Back in England I imagined that (if I was prepared to wait long enough) a Punan would come strolling up a street that looked something like Dodge City. He would swagger into the saloon where I slouched drinking Bourbon: "Hear ya bin lookin' fer me" he'd say, and our success would be assured. Putussibau was not unlike Dodge in the rain, but the rest was pure fantasy. Bourbon makes me sick.

Trying to reconcile the positioning of villages and rivers between the maps in my collection was a confusing exercise. One map even placed the whole Müller Mountain range sixty miles too far north.

The map that showed the area in the greatest detail was my *Tactical Pilotage Chart* - a veritable work of art. It showed the terrain in clearly defined relief up to the southern edge of the mountains. Then everything faded along a line that was marked 'Limits of Reliable Information'. Further south, there was what Conrad called 'a blank space of delightful mystery – a white patch for a boy to dream gloriously over.' This void held attractions and promises that the cartographers will never be able to depict. It had obviously been a torment to their ordered minds and they had neatly positioned a small box in its centre: 'Owing to inadequate source material there may be significant positional discrepancies in detail over the area of this chart.'

Their predecessors were more imaginative - 'Here Be Dragons' is the stuff of real adventure.

There are not many of these blank spaces left on the world's maps. But there are a few - and they still hold the same power that fascinated Conrad. I loved that map, but I had to leave it behind. This decision was made in the light of experiences in areas where travellers with large-scale (military-style) maps are not favourably received by frontier guards; I was not anxious to gamble our only map in testing the sensitivity of the Malay/Indonesian border.

The guidebooks said it was relatively easy to hire guides in Putus' who could lead one eastward over the mountains to the Mahakam River of East Kalimantan. George Müller, a Dutch colonial official, first explored this route in 1825. He never made it: the Dayaks took his head and the mountains took his name.

We wandered over the rotting boardwalks, on which the whole greasy conglomeration of riverside Putus' sways, and headed towards the market. We bought a thousand local Gudang Garam cigarettes, two hundred Marlboro (a gift for the *Raja Wali's* crew), five tins of condensed milk, five of Milo, five bags of *kopi*, four schoolbooks (to use as diaries), five reels of strong thread, rice, sugar, salt and more colour films. By doing all this shopping in one place we hoped we would be able to haggle for a good price from Tomas, the smiling Chinese storekeeper.

The last things we needed, and by far the most exciting, were our jungle knives. It was impossible to buy complete *parangs* in Putus' but Tomas showed us a bundle of used blades and said that we would be able to get handles and sheaths made upriver.

We haggled down to what still seemed an excessive price but then deduced that as all these things had travelled upriver in the cargo boats they would necessarily have become much more expensive. Tomas smiled even more as he placed our money in his home made till . . and we re-deduced that we had just been ripped off.

The till was a standard up-country design: a metal box suspended from the roof beams by a string that was weighted on the far end. Tomas gripped a tassel underneath the box and tugged it down - bells, tied along the string, tinkled their alarm. He held the tin down on the table whilst he sorted our change.

Three lads were waiting for us in the *rumah makan* when we got back to the 'Trust Us.'

"What news?" they asked, in the usual Indonesian greeting.

"Good news," we answered, as expected.

They were enthusiastic to lead us on a weeklong trek to the Mahakam via the rapids where Müller was murdered. Their enthusiasm was due mostly to the extortionate price (by local standards) that they asked. It was a sign that foreigners are fast becoming a legendary source of income in the Kapuas Hulu.

About the route south over the central Müllers nobody in Putus' was able to tell us anything. So, due to 'Limited Reliable Information', we decided to pin all our hopes on Gunungberuwang - a village shown on my map as lying twenty miles north of the Müller Mountains. I assumed that it must be named after a nearby peak (*gunung*).

Depending how you emphasise Gunungberuwang, it can mean Bear Mountain or Rich Mountain – I was happy with either, both smacked of adventure.

I wrote a letter to our sponsors telling them that we had arrived at our last point of communication until we emerged on the far side of the mountains.

Although foreigners do pass through here occasionally on a recognised trail to the east, the locals cannot remember anyone ever going south to the Müller Mountains. The planning and speculation have brought us as far now as it was ever hoped

that they could and, if we wish to go forward, we can only
step off into the abyss, over the hazy line into what has not
even been guessed at back home. Here it feels that we really
are on the verge of "the heart of darkness.

Paul was leaning over my shoulder: "C'mon Geezer. Wrap it up. Let's go!"

He had been to deliver the Marlboro and one of the *Raja Wali's* crew had offered to take us to visit a local longhouse. Ishmael was waiting downstairs and within minutes the three of us were whining over the bridge on his motorbike.

The longhouse was twenty minutes from town, on a dirt track that cut through a plain of padi fields fringing the local airstrip. A stand of palms hid the structure partially from view until Ishmael skidded the bike to a halt in an unnecessarily sensational cloud of dust. Here and there amongst the trees were rough-hewn carvings of toothy ogres and leading down to us from the structure's centre I was gratified to see a 'notched pole.' The books I had read before leaving England had been peppered with the words 'notched pole' and they had began to epitomise Borneo for me.

This pole was about ten inches in diameter and ascended in ten hacked-out steps to the grimacing 'figure-head' that crowned it. I wobbled to the top, arms outstretched for balance, and placed a relieved hand on the head of the effigy – polished through the generations. Kicking off my flip-flops I saw that the covered gallery stretching along the front of the building was deserted. Only a scraggy puppy snapped at a butterfly at the far end of what passes for 'Main Street' in a longhouse community.

Traditionally each family is responsible for the upkeep of its own apartment and, by extension, the platform directly in front of it. As the *kepala* will live in the central apartment so the least prominent and poorest families will live on the ends. This often means that walking away from the smooth hardwood boards outside the headman's *bilik* you pass over progressively worse flooring materials until eventually you find yourself trying to levitate across flimsy bamboo strips at the far end of 'Main Street.' This longhouse, however (perhaps because of its proximity to timber yards and easy access by road), was sturdily built all down its length.

We had come here on the pretext of buying *tuak* (wine made from the fermented sap of a palm tree) and I felt uncomfortable about treating the headman's apartment as a sort of off-licence. But the birdlike old lady who opened the door seemed almost to be expecting us and, with a toothless smile, she ushered us inside.

The headman's *bilik* was wallpapered with a garish floral print. A long chipboard cabinet was the room's only embellishment – it boasted a hi-fi, brass-framed photos, ceramic knickknacks and a cut glass sherry decanter (empty). There were none of the exotic accessories that I had imagined we would see in a longhouse: no weapons or hunting equipment hung on the wall, no hornbill-feather headdresses or animal skins. No trophy heads. There was a stack of woven mats leaning against the wall. The old lady gave a shrill call towards the back door and she was unrolling some of these mats when the headman came in. I guessed that the old woman must be his mother.

"Selamat datang" – Welcome. He gave us a bleary smile, shook our hands and gestured towards the mats. He had obviously just woken up and scratched himself absent-mindedly under his string vest. His thin moustache had long tufts at the ends and his dark eyes blinked continuously. He said something to his mother in

their own language and she tottered out through the back door.

I flipped a packet of Gudang Garam out of my top pocket and placed them in the centre of the mat where the two Indonesians could help themselves. The old lady returned with a loaded tray and the headman silently filled four tall beakers from a plastic jug.

"*Tuak*." Ishmael leaned forward in anticipation. "Taman tribe make best *tuak* in Kapuas Hulu."

"*Selamat minum*," said the headman raising his glass.

The *tuak* was cream-coloured, thick and slightly clotted. It tasted bitter but did not give the impression of being incredibly potent. I had the feeling that it would have been much better if it were chilled.

As I lowered my own glass I noticed that the headman's was already empty. I glanced around quickly and was relieved to see that both Paul's and Ishmael's were still half full. Our host refilled his own glass and waited politely to do the same to ours. Then he dispensed our second dose. "*Selamat minum.*"

How long had the Taman lived here in this longhouse, I asked the *kepala*.

"Built ten year only," said the headman, "But *orang taman* live here always."

The Taman has been one of the Dayak groups that have integrated most successfully into the *orang melayu* society and they have managed to do so largely without sacrificing their own identity. Several people from this very longhouse had graduated from university and others worked in the civil services. Although they no longer lived in the longhouse they had donated towards its building and upkeep.

"We have lived in Kapuas Hulu since before anybody can

remember," the *kepala* continued proudly. "We were only tribe to trade with *orang iban*."

The Iban's ferocity and hunger for heads had made them the scourge of Borneo. Although the Taman occasionally took heads themselves, they were no match for their warlike neighbours. Instead, it was their craftsmanship that allowed them to live in guarded proximity to the Iban. It was the Taman who forged plundered metals into Iban *mandaus* and served as an outlet for the fine Iban textiles amongst the other, more timid tribes.

We finished our third glass and the *kepala*, hearing that we had never drunk *tuak* before, stood up and beckoned us through the back door. We followed his slouching figure through a darkened room, furnished only with rattan mats, and onto a narrow veranda. Two scabby hunting dogs lay panting in the shade and the headman's fighting-cock strutted and preened in a bell-shaped basket.

Along this platform women were hanging out washing, slopping out dirty water and beating mats. Until the men returned from the padis, and the social life moved onto 'Main Street,' this was the hub of the longhouse's activity.

The *kepala* pointed to a metal cone embedded near the top of a palm tree. "In five days this *tuak* will be ready," he said. I wondered if patience was considered a virtue in the preparation of the famous Taman tipple.

There was a storage room built off the back of the platform, and we went inside. Beside the door was a large plastic butt. The headman lifted a plastic plate off the top and a cloud of tiny flies erupted like a puff of smoke. This was where the *tuak* was stored. I felt my stomach give a slight gurgle and tried not to think about the personal habits of those thousands of flies. Paul glanced at me worriedly and I knew he was thinking the same. But the *kepala* was already ladling our lumpy *tuak* into a plastic shopping bag.

There were rapid footsteps on the platform outside and a lanky man bounded into the doorway. Bahat was the headman's brother and he was as frantically energetic as the older man was lethargic.

"Take *poto!*" he chirped, hauling his brother and chief into a reluctant pose as Paul obediently raised his camera. Bahat was a *potografi* fanatic and after he had hurried Paul around, showing him what to take pictures of, he shot back into his apartment and reappeared proudly carrying an old Nikon. Paul made approving noises about this piece of equipment and loaded one of our colour films into it.

Thus armed Bahat shot along the platform snapping *potos* of a fleeing hunting dog, somebody's washing line and a small child as it screamed in terror at his sudden appearance. He swaggered back with the camera swinging around his neck, oblivious to the whimpering infant and the cooing of its mother.

Dubiously I watched him scoop a yellow plastic jug into the *tuak*. He took a swig, wiped his mouth on his arm and I watched the jug start off on a tour around our little group.

"Wan' go see *orang amerika?*" asked Bahat. Why should we want to meet Americans, I thought. I nodded an excited affirmative - his energy was contagious.

"*Orang misionaris,*" he clarified taking the plastic bag of *tuak* out of Paul's hand and hanging it on a hook under its attendant cloud of flies.

Sam and Sally lived about twenty minutes further up the dirt track in a neat timber bungalow behind a papaya orchard. They seemed genuinely pleased to see us and were equally enthusiastic in greeting our Indonesian friends. They were Protestant missionaries from Florida and had been living amongst the Taman for eighteen years. 'Telling the Lord's words in the people's own language' was how Sam described their mission and as such they were probably the only *orang barat* ever to learn to speak Bahasa Taman.

Sally poured us a chilled glass of papaya juice and apologised that she could not stay to talk. She had a bible class to teach – four girls were waiting, giggling self-consciously, on the other side of the fly-screens.

I hauled my now crumpled map out of my shorts and began to talk to Sam in Indonesian so as not to exclude Bahat and Ishmael. I was relieved when he switched us back to English - it would be easier for me to pick his brains about our proposed route and I was glad that Paul could listen in.

"All that area is Dayak Da'an territory," said Sam. His finger traced a circle around the Mandai River and 'Bear Mountain' - the whole area north of the Müller foothills. He had never been up the Mandai but he knew missionaries who lived in one of the lower villages. "If the locals don't go that way by habit" - his finger sliced south - "you'll have a hard time convincing them that they should guide you." His outlook was bleak but with his baggy, bright-eyed Walter Matthau looks (and my own skinful of *tuak*) it was difficult to feel discouraged.

If it is indeed necessary that traditional communities should receive their first taste of the modern world from the mouths of missionaries then I wish that they could always be as sensitive, caring and intelligent as Sam and Sally appeared to be. Unfortunately it is not always so as we were soon to see.

When we were leaving Sally came out from the back room to wish us luck and say goodbye. In a few days they were both leaving for a long-awaited three-week break in Singapore. "Gonna enjoy that aircon," she said.

The *tuak* slopped out of the plastic bag all the way back to Putus' so that by the time we arrived at the boardinghouse all three of us had a sticky mess down our right legs.

We planned to have a celebration on the hotel's balcony and we were disappointed when Ishmael declined our invitation to come up. His Muslim sensibilities forbade him from drinking 'in public' - even in the relative seclusion of the second floor.

We had special reason that evening for persevering with our noxious tipple. Paul and I are devotees of the San Fermin fiestas, annual celebrations that take place in Pamplona, northern Spain. At midday on the sixth of July (7.00 pm in Putussibau) a rocket is fired to launch the town on a bout of glorious carousal that lasts, unchecked, for nine days and nights.

An hour after sunset, with the Kapuas rushing chunks of jungle towards the South China Sea, we saluted the start of the fiesta. It was difficult to imagine the frenetic activity that would be erupting at that moment in the narrow city streets on the other side of the world.

The *tuak* (now decanted into my water bottle) was going down only with determination. I had a feeling that it would be a taste that we would be forced to acquire before the end of the trip - and it was unlikely that we would ever have the opportunity to see if it was more drinkable chilled.

Some time later Paul was swaying against the balcony's railing, trying to swat a monstrous moth that was flitting across his forehead. He leaned far, dangerously so it seemed to me, out over the edge and shouted to a figure in the darkness below: "Hey Ahi! C'mon up!"

Ahi was one of the crew of the newly arrived *Teladan Star*. He had been at our party on the *Sinar Bulan* and it took him only a moment to appear, with his perpetual grin, at the top of the stairs. "What news?"

"Good news."

"*Ngiropai!*" The grin widened and he raised the proffered bottle to his lips, "*Enak*" – delicious.

To Paul's groaning disapproval I spread my map once again across the coffee table. I was prepared to keep asking until I found optimism . . and Ahi gave it to me.

"*Orang dayak da'an* on Mandai River go over the Müllers." He shrugged. "I have relatives in Nanga Raun - number one Da'an village. You stay with them!"

We ordered fried rice in the *rumah makan* and Ahi talked about the Da'an on the Mandai River. We could stay with his grandmother and he was confident that we would be able to hire guides in Nanga Raun. In fact he had a friend who would be keen to lead us over the mountains. This was the first time that we heard the name Kolop.

Ahi just wished that he could afford to come with us himself. Just for the trip. "I'm *orang punan*," he said, "and the big river is a sad place for a Punan."

We had not mentioned the Punan and Paul and I were astounded by this coincidence. Things had happened almost how I had imagined they would; except that our Punan guide had trailed us all the way from Pontianak and that we never got to toast the success of our trip with Bourbon.

Tuak also makes me sick.

Chapter Three

The Search for Guides

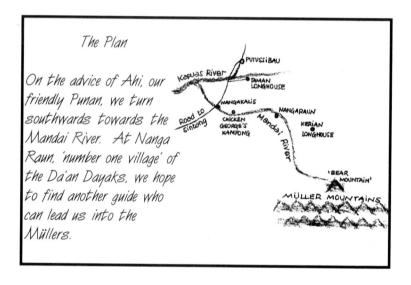

The Plan

On the advice of Ahi, our friendly Punan, we turn southwards towards the Mandai River. At Nanga Raun, 'number one village' of the Da'an Dayaks, we hope to find another guide who can lead us into the Müllers.

PUTUSSIBAU

Kapuas River

TAMAN LONGHOUSE

NANGAKALIS

Road to Sintang

CHICKEN GEORGE'S KAMPONG

Mandai River

NANGARAUN

KERIAN LONGHOUSE

'BEAR MOUNTAIN'

MÜLLER MOUNTAINS

Early the next morning Ahi jumped ship. He shrugged when I asked about his fee so I offered him what I had been told was the going rate: covering him also for the return trip and promising a good bonus if everything worked out well. We would pay his travel costs, his food, supply his cigarettes and I advanced him enough money to buy some boots. Whilst he dashed off to the market Paul and I stayed behind, battling to force as many of our provisions as possible into our packs.

Western style clothing has almost totally replaced the home-woven Dayak cloth. Shorts and tee shirts are everywhere and nylon swimming trunks are *de rigueur* in the jungle. Women wear cotton dresses or sarong-skirts and bras. The fact that our Punan guide needed new boots to go into the jungle somehow offended my sense of romance, but I recognised that it would be obscene to make Ahi go barefoot merely because it was more picturesque.

Ahi, in his enthusiasm to appear dedicated to his new employment, must have run to the market because within ten minutes he was back.

"Whooeeeh!" whistled Paul as the door swung open. "Look at the Punan!"

Ahi, grinning happily, raised one foot - proudly displaying an ankle-high, white canvas club-crawler, emblazoned with the words 'Sport Falcon.'

Ahi's suggestion was to take a mini-bus south to Nangakalis along the road that leads (after a further hundred and fifty miles) back to Sintang. From Nangakalis we could take a motorboat upriver to

Nanga Raun, the main village of the Dayak Da'an. Until Sam had mentioned this group I had never heard their name and when, months later, I returned from Borneo I was unable to find a single reference to them anywhere.

Nanga Raun did not exist either in my guidebooks or maps. But it was one step closer to Gunungberuwang: the solitary beacon in the darkness of my 'Limited Reliable Information'.

The absurdly attentive Ahi tied our *barang* (baggage) to the swaying heap on the bus's roof. In Nangakalis we would have to take time to get him to relax, to make him feel that although he was on the payroll he was on an equal footing with us. What we really needed now was an older man for our second guide: somebody whose experience would balance Ahi's youthful exuberance.

Before leaving England we had discussed the role of our guides and had decided that we did not want porters: each man in the team must carry more or less the same weight and do his share of the work. We did not yet appreciate how quickly the jungle could sap our strength and that the only flaw in this idealistic plan would be our own weakness.

Somehow the mini-bus driver figured that he still had room for more passengers. We sat cramped and sweating for over an hour before, dangerously over-loaded, we hauled a cloud of yellow dust across the bridge and out of Putussibau. We picked up speed on the downhill swoop past the airstrip and soon the truck was roaring along an embankment above bubbling black swamps.

The forest was peppered with 'No Trespassing' signs. This land was the property of large timber concessions and I was surprised at how untouched it appeared to be. In this imperfect world access is the biggest single deterrent to deforestation and I had imagined that most of the land, not only along the Kapuas, but along this main highway would long ago have been deforested. Later, in Central Kalimantan, we were to see the real horror of vast wastelands where until recently virgin rainforest had stood.

There were very few bends in the road, but the driver - foot to the floor - was invariably surprised by them all. Once he lost control and careered into such a wild, tyre-screeching zigzag across the road that it was an absolute mystery to me how we missed an on-coming car. I felt a cold tingle on the back of my neck when I imagined the scenes inside this crowded bus if we had swerved just two feet further to flip onto our roof in the swamp.

Nangakalis's primary purpose was as a trading station, connecting the villages of the Mandai Hulu with the only long-distance road in West Kalimantan. It was a ramshackle collection of eight small stores, a school, a post office and a police station. There was an army barracks across the bridge on the other side of the Mandai River but, since the town was out of bounds to the troops, 'Kalis had retained its sleepy ambience.

We climbed stiffly out of the bus outside a Chinese store by the bridge. A motley group sitting in the shade of the store's veranda told us that the boat to Nanga Raun was not likely to leave for at least an hour. So, heaving our packs onto our shoulders, we staggered back down the road to what appeared to be the only *rumah makan* in 'Kalis.

An adorable old woman ladled out watery vegetable *sop* and fortified it with instant noodles and poached eggs (the sort that are dropped into a pan of boiling water and emerge looking like failed test-tube experiments). She was tall and graceful and her silver hair was scraped back into such a tight metallic bun that her cheekbones and almond eyes seemed also to be swept upwards. Paul wanted to take her photograph and he tried to work up the nerve to ask her - but somehow she was just too regal. We could only imagine what immense beauty she must have had in her youth.

There were nine other people waiting for the boat: three school kids, a young couple returning from their honeymoon, a middle-aged couple with a little girl and Chicken George who was returning to his village with his victorious fighting-cock.

Whilst the cock strutted around beside the platform searching for cockroaches the old man kept a besotted eye on it. Occasionally he would scoop it up to re-settle a wing feather that had moved out of place. Twice during these affectionate administrations he licked the cockerel across both its eyes.

I reminded Paul about a cock-fighting tournament that we had once stumbled across whilst hitching through Southern Thailand. We had wandered into a crowded room at the back of the miniature bullring-type stadium. There, where in a real bullring the butchers would have been hard at work, the scene was not dissimilar.

We watched the cock-handlers 'operating' on their birds between bouts. They would put their mouths over the birds' heads and suck out blood clots to allow easier breathing. I had been sickened to see one man push a wet tail feather down a bird's throat and drag out a mess of internal haemorrhaging. Occasionally the cockerel would flap or kick its legs in distress or pain and licking across its eyes appeared to calm it or, more accurately, somehow to mesmerise it. A few deft stitches prepared it to re-enter the arena to fight again - this time perhaps to the death.

Chicken George was obviously very proud of his bird. "Champin," he said as he picked the fighter up again and held it tightly to his bony chest.

"Rocky!" said Paul as he snapped their picture. The old man beamed delightedly.

The boat left two hours later and we passed the time on the veranda in front of the store. We talked to Chicken George and made eyes at the pretty Chinese girl behind the counter. The fact that she was too cool to care only made her seem more attractive.

The *speed* that was to take us all up the Mandai River was twenty feet long and was fitted with low narrow seats across its whole length. It was manned by a crew of two; the driver was at the back with the outboard motor and his mate sat in the high bow scanning for obstructions. There was a constant danger from floating logs.

We had only just got under way when I saw what appeared to be a black stick dipping like a fishing float in the surge of the boat's wake. Just as I realised what it was and was about to point it out to Paul it ducked out of sight. It was the pointed snout of a large soft-shelled turtle.

We had seen many turtles for sale in markets in Sarawak (sometimes up to two feet in diameter). Later in Nanga Raun we saw some smaller turtles being fattened-up in a water butt. Soft, pouting lips belie the power of their jaws and I reached into the butt to lift one out.

Our host quickly pulled my arm back. Then he took off his rubber sandal and put the tip of it into the water. Instantly there was a splash and when he pulled it out I was amazed to see a neat V-shape cut out of it. These turtles have a long snaky neck that allows them to strike forward with their powerful bills to kill the waterfowl on which they prey.

Chicken George and Rocky were the first to get off the *speed*. The old man had waited for almost three hours in 'Kalis to make a forty-minute boat trip. We were getting deeper into the *hulu* and now the only way to travel through the dense jungle was by river.

Our sense of adventure increased as the jungle closed in around us. The wake, fanning out at our backs, washed ever-bigger clods of soil off the bank as the river narrowed. The wooden shacks that seemed like - and in a sense were - the homes of frontier settlers were now spaced further apart. We were deep in the interior: this land would remain a frontier forever.

Four hours after leaving 'Kalis we were flagged-down by a woman, waving to us from a huge floating log that was moored to the bank. She wore a richly embroidered Balinese sarong and a white blouse. The lobes of her ears were distended and she had a yellow flower in the wide hole through her left one. She had the most infectious smile that I had ever seen. Apparently overjoyed to see us, she went all along the side of the boat shaking everyone's hand: "*Selamat datang. Selamat datang. Apa kabar?*" – Welcome. Welcome. What news?

Now that we were closer we could see what made her smile so striking. All her teeth were capped with gold.

Nodding towards a gold key that was hanging on her neck Paul whispered, "Ask her if that's for the safety deposit where she keeps her spare set of choppers."

By now she was involved in rapturous conversation with the boatman: yes, yes, of course he would be delighted to deliver this monstrous, rotten catfish head for her. *Tidak ada masalah*. No problem. Nobody could refuse her anything.

"Oh please, no charge whatsoever," the boatman was saying as we sped away from the bank, leaving her waving. I almost expected her to blow us a kiss.

Everyone was happy again. The newly-weds had regained the cheerful grins that had been subdued by the increasing discomfort of the hard, cramped boards. But as we puttered back into mid-stream the stench of putrefying catfish (for what purpose it would be used we could not guess) wafted back along the boat. Everybody groaned and spluttered and pinched their noses. We stopped in the middle of the river and the lookout heaved the head backwards, I stood up to take it from the man in front and passed it back over the heads of the school kids to the driver. The children giggled and the little girl held her nose and groaned the Indonesian equivalent of "phwooar!"

It was only when the boat took off again that I realised that Ahi was still leaning over the side, retching.

Paul noticed at the same instant. "I don't believe it!" he laughed, "The big bad Punan's blowing his cookies!"

Our affection for Ahi had just multiplied a hundred-fold.

"We've got to take him into the jungle now," I said. "Even if you have to carry him over the mountains on your back."

"Stick with us, Punan! We'll make a man out of you yet." Paul slapped him heartily on the back.

"Blaaagh!" said Ahi, splashing water on his face and giving us a sheepish grin.

Six hours after leaving 'Kalis we were the only passengers left on the *speed* and we were intensely relieved to see Nanga Raun.

We climbed cautiously onto a bobbing pontoon made out of four tree trunks. The boatman heaved our baggage over to us and revved his motor up for the long run back. Under all this weight the end of the pontoon slowly began to sink - with the clear intention of depositing the three of us gently but unceremoniously into the Mandai.

We grabbed our *barang* and scrambled along the platform towards a small wooden cubicle that was now rearing up above the water. By the cunning strategy of panicking when we got close and running halfway back again we managed to stabilise the pontoon.

We stood gripping each other, hardly daring to breathe as the water lapped over our feet. Slowly we turned and craned our necks up towards the village. There, twenty feet above us, at the top of the riverbank a small crowd had gathered. 'Indiana Jones, I presume,' was what they were thinking.

The only link between them and us was a thirty-foot notched pole. These gringo-traps are laid all over Borneo. They are the access both into the village from the river and into the houses from the riverbank. There is no way to avoid them.

Had this particular notched pole been laid flat on the ground I would not have been confident about my chances of traversing it without mishap. It was not flat on the ground but was leaning at an angle of sixty degrees, with its lower end secured to a bouncing pontoon. I looked towards the disappearing *speed* as the thought crossed my mind that this was perhaps a set-up and when I looked back Ahi was already moving towards this perilous-looking piece of apparatus. My estimation of him increased with every confident step he took.

Later we were to see women skipping up this same pole, two steps at a time, carrying a child on one hip and a bucket of water in the other hand.

There are two schools of thought on the best way for a heavily laden *orang barat* to approach the legendary notched poles of Borneo. I managed to analyse both of these in astounding detail in the few moments that I delayed my own attempted ascent. (The possibility of avoiding thirty feet of splinters collected in an uncontrolled backward banister-slide seems to do wonderful things for focussing your concentration).

The first option is the death-or-glory method; with your pack firmly fixed on your back, from where it is unlikely to slip . . even if you should lose balance and plunge into the swift brown current.

The second, more faint-hearted approach calls for the pack to be swung over one shoulder so that, if you do fall, it can be easily (though unheroically) jettisoned. The disadvantages of this method, however, are that you have only one fully effective arm with which to balance and you run the risk of the pack slipping at any moment and knocking you off the pole.

Weighing up these options, whilst still trying to appear unruffled, I decided on method two. The fact that (*if* successfully executed) it would have the added benefit of looking supremely casual - perhaps even debonair - swung the decision in its favour.

However we appeared to that mercifully small crowd of fascinated Da'an spectators it was *not* debonair. Each 'step' in the pole was a plateau about half the size of a saucer, and the key factor to a successful ascent - the alternative is too hideous to consider - is to keep moving at all costs. Stop and try to balance, let alone attempt to grip the pole, and you might as well jump.

I covered the last fifteen feet with the profound concentration of someone walking over hot coals. As I took my first grateful breath I looked up at the smiling faces around me. There was a ragged welcoming chorus and about fifteen people, in sarongs or shorts and tee shirts, watched me with an air of expectation. Aware that Paul was now dashing up the last stretch of the pole (I didn't watch in case I unwittingly provoked a speed-wobble) I looked towards Ahi for a cue. He was studiously analysing the clouds that were gathering for nightfall.

The villagers were waiting patiently for something to happen and the smiles, though still essentially warm, were now becoming slightly strained.

"Ahi, is your grandmother here?" I asked pointedly.

But Ahi was suddenly fascinated by the river - on which he had spent the last six hours.

The silence was becoming uncomfortable. I tried to think of something to say, but what? – 'Take us to your leader.' Then my eyes alighted on a wooden object that a small boy was holding. It was a spinning-top, and one of typically lethal South East Asian proportions.

We had seen these tops in Sarawak and had been impressed by the violence of the game; the way that these 'toys' are hurled into combat, or come flying back out of the 'battle' is terrifying. Carved from a solid hunk of hardwood into a pumpkin-shape that often weighs as much as two kilos, they are more than capable of breaking bones.

I had found it impossible to get sufficient speed out of the whiplash momentum of the string to get them spinning properly, but for this moment it was just what was needed. I held out my hand and the boy unhesitatingly handed me the 'weapon.' Some of the spectators, seeing what I was about to do, fled giggling, to a safe distance. Others prepared to leap into the air to protect their ankles.

The string was already tightly wound around the top and I threw it at an angle towards a flat patch of ground, at the same moment whipping back as hard as I could on the string. The top took off at a terrific spin exactly where I had aimed. One of the bystanders cheered, several clapped gleefully and I said "Bloody Hell! – Didya see that?"

Two small boys, taking up an irresistible challenge, hurled their tops into the battle. Even Ahi relaxed although he still showed no intention of leading us to his grandmother, or anyone else. The boys were showing us how well they could spin their tops and Paul was snapping photographs when a young man tapped me lightly on the arm and, silently picking up one of our bags, led us towards the nearest hut.

Like the other huts in the *kampong* it was raised on stilts eight feet above the ground and it was equipped with a wide working platform across the front. The steeply sloping roof was made from rectangular 'tiles' of bark and was obviously designed to deal with heavy rainfall. This was a typical Da'an *pondok*.

We climbed the mercifully short notched pole onto the platform and, kicking off our shoes, we stepped into the darkness. With a formality that hinted at his position as the village's future *kepala* the young man, Maximus, welcomed us to Nanga Raun. He apologised that his father was out in the padi fields but assured us that he would return very soon. Maximus had an open, honest smile and a thick shock of curly hair.

I was glad to hear that we were in the headman's hut because, not being sure of customs (and getting very little help from Ahi in this direction), I was anxious that we introduce ourselves officially as soon as possible.

Whilst we drank *kopi* Maximus told us about the Da'an. As Ahi had said, Nanga Raun is their 'number one village' with a population that hovers around seven hundred. They had always lived in the Mandai Hulu but had only moved this far downriver during the last century. The Iban believed the Mandai River to be the location of the spirit world and would never have dared to venture up the valley. This fact meant that the Da'an were perhaps the only tribe in the Kapuas Basin to escape the terror of Iban headhunting parties. Although headhunting was never a tradition amongst these people the Da'an were the living inhabitants of headhunter heaven.

The tribe now numbers about two thousand people, living primarily by farming rice and hunting. They sell their surplus harvest to traders downriver, along with a small quantity of rattan crafts and *gaharu* (aloeswood). This is the diseased wood from a certain type of tree. It yields a valuable and increasingly rare incense favoured by the Chinese, Indians and Arabs and its collection from deep in the jungle forms an important part of the Da'an revenue. Maximus seemed convinced that amongst the *gaharu* hunters we would be able to find experienced guides who could lead us across the Müllers.

As he talked I glanced around the *pondok*. It had a dividing wall between the kitchen and the main room, and two small sleeping rooms to one side. The only furniture was a rough, homemade table bearing a huge stack of magazines (American, I noticed later) and, in front of it, a heap of rattan mats. A carefully folded fishing net was hanging from a hook on the wall next to some tattered soft-focus fashion shots torn from a 1987 calendar and a framed photograph of President Suharto. Propped across the roof beams I could see three patterned backpacks made from stained rattan cane. On nails beside the front door hung two sheathed *parangs* and a long-bladed pig-hunting spear. The spear had a steel crosspiece at the top of the shaft to stop a boar's charge.

The *kepala* came bustling into the hut. He was still dusty from his day's work, and Maximus gave him time to untie the *parang* from his belt and hang it on the wall before introducing him.

Pak Rejang ('Pak' is a term of respect - equal to something between our 'mister' and 'sir') was shorter than his son, almost bald, and through his threadbare shirt the muscular chest and shoulders of forty-five years of hard work stood out. There was something instantly likeable and welcoming about him but as the Da'an's first headman he was very busy and, stopping only to change his shirt and give Maximus instructions to make us comfortable, he dashed back out.

"*Mau mandi?*" asked Maximus.

After a long hot day on the river a *mandi* was exactly what we needed and we followed Maximus out of the back of the village to a small brook. We washed in the unexpectedly cold water that had cascaded from the tabletop mountain. Paul was attacked by tiny stinging ants that swarmed up his legs from the bank. Ahi, still in mid-stream, had an attack in sympathy, and splashed around slapping his legs. Then he left his underpants hanging on a branch and had to go back for them.

We arrived back at Pak Rejang's *pondok* to find the headman relaxing after the labours of the day. He was playing with a tiny ginger kitten. It chased a shred of cloth that the *kepala* was dragging around. A small bell tied around its neck tinkled as it scampered.

Maximus's wife was sat against the wall nursing their baby. An attractive, sultry young girl and an older woman (they were never introduced) sat either side of her. The older woman (Pak Rejang's wife, we guessed) smiled hazily at our greetings, showing a mouthful of scarlet juice and the blackened stumps of her teeth. She chewed betel nut almost constantly. The effect is only very mild but every time we saw Mrs Rejang she seemed to be obviously and contentedly stoned. Every so often she would keel over onto her left side to squirt a jet of scarlet juice between the floorboards. (Once, when my pen dropped through the same way, I had to make Paul promise to give me prior notice of Mrs Rejang's slightest list to port before I attempted to make the dash through the black slime between the *pondok's* stilts.)

The young girl seemed not to notice us at all. The smooth brown skin of her jaw flexed rhythmically as she shifted her own wad of betel nut and she stared straight ahead, unseeing - or all-seeing. She was fascinating and she became unfairly but indelibly fixed in my mind as the Beautiful Zombie.

We distributed some gifts from our *barang* - sarongs and sewing kits for the ladies, waterproof torches and packs of Gudang Garam for Pak Rejang and Maximus. We had no idea what would be deemed acceptable as repayment for our lodgings. However, we had come up here in the hope of finding our guides amongst the Da'an, however, it seemed that a preliminary step towards achieving this could be to earn a reputation for generosity with the headman of their largest *kampong*.

We - the men - ate in the 'kitchen': a room furnished with a huge hearth and a stack of firewood. Against the back wall were two monstrous baskets made from rattan strips. They were burnished to a dark gold by years in the smoky kitchen. Between them they held more than a tonne of rice – Pak Rejang's security against a bad harvest. We sat cross-legged on rattan mats and although they offered us spoons we ate, like our hosts, with our right hands. A huge bowl of boiled rice was the bulk of the meal and to it we added small quantities of boiled fish, boiled fern tips, instant noodles and tinned sardines.

We ate in silence. Dinnertime was obviously not a social affair in this household. Pak Rejang finished first. He swigged a glass of water and rose unceremoniously to return to the other room. We took our cue from Maximus and made our own exit a moment later.

I realised then the reason for our haste: it was only now that the women could eat.

Paul showed Pak Rejang and Maximus our *parang* blades. They were typical Malay *parangs*; thin near the handle, they leaned over backwards and spread into a wide chopping face that came back together into a corner rather than a point. They were unlike any other that we were to see in the *hulu*.

A good Da'an *parang* is in design almost identical to an Iban headhunting sword: long and straight, with very little widening in the middle and ending in a definite stabbing point.

Pak Rejang offered to carve the handles and led us into the kitchen where the fire served as a forge. We were delighted that our knives were going to be prepared by the Da'an's most influential leader.

As I described our plans to the *kepala* he hacked out the handles with his own knife. Using it also as a model he checked our grip to estimate size. The handle was turned down at the end to prevent it from flying out of a sweaty hand.

Pak Rejang had heard reports of Punan living in isolation in the Müller Mountains. He also warned us to be very careful because there were many *orang penjahat* (evil people) living up there. We already liked and trusted these two men and with Pak Rejang's experience to guide us we would have felt confident that our expedition would be a success.

Maximus had been all the way up the Mandai and half way across the mountains but, like his father, he was too busy cutting *ladang* (clearing the jungle for rice padis) to be able to come with us. The timing of the rice season was vital and we would have to wait at least three weeks before anyone in Nanga Raun would be free to travel with us.

Ahi had been silent all evening and, although I had little confidence in his information by now, I wanted to bring him into the conversation: "Where does your friend Kolop live, Ahi?"

"You know Kolop?" asked Pak Rejang, shooting a surprised glance to where Ahi sprawled at the edge of the fire's glow. The Punan nodded lazily and the older man turned thoughtfully back to the fire where he was heating our blades.

"Kolop, maybe in *rumah panjang* Kerian," said Maximus, looking quizzically at Ahi.

"Where's that?" I asked, translating excitedly for Paul: "*Rumah panjang* means longhouse."

Kerian was the Da'an's only longhouse and was a four-hour hike along a logging track on the other side of the river. This track was the only 'road' in the Da'an area.

We were welcome to stay as long as we wished in Nanga Raun. If we were lucky somebody may be free in a week or two.

Alternatively, Pak Rejang had a friend who was walking to Kerian in the morning. He would be happy to take us.

"People in Kerian don't rely so much on padi," said the *kepala*. "You can find guides there."

He turned back to the fire. The spike on the handle end of my blade now glowed a dull red. He held the blade in a pair of pliers and the metal burnt, hissing slowly, into the newly carved handle.

It took only a moment to discuss the matter with Paul. We were both excited by the idea of visiting another, more isolated longhouse. Besides, we felt that we should take every possible opportunity to keep edging closer to the Müller Mountains.

Paul, Ahi and I slept comfortably on a double layer of rattan mats in the main room. There was no door on the *pondok* and before I fell asleep I saw, among the silhouettes of the trees, the ghostly swoop of a hunting owl.

Maximus's wife, coaxing the fire back to life, woke me just after dawn. The ginger kitten swatted its tiny paws at a swirling piece of ash and I enticed it over and tickled its belly whilst I considered getting out of my sheet sleeping bag. It was impossible to tie up our mossinets in the *pondok* and we used these cotton bags as some protection against mosquitoes.

We had carefully researched the wealth of contradictory and fickle advice on avoiding malaria. The sources agreed on only one point: don't get bitten and you won't get malaria. Long cotton clothing, repellent oil, mosquito nets and coils, 'repellent impregnation kits,' Tiger Balm, ultrasonic repellents and diets of vitamin B, garlic or cream of tarter were some of the suggested ways to avoid getting bitten. We embraced many of these precautions and before we left England we had done our utmost to impregnate everything we came into contact with and considered ourselves possibly the two most repellent explorers ever to set foot in Borneo.

On the question of malaria prophylactics the experts were further divided. The recommended pills for Borneo were Chloroquine (weekly) and Paludrine (daily). Over long term or frequent travelling, however, there is a danger of side effects from the former, whilst mosquitoes quickly build up immunity to the latter.

Later, in the south, we met *orang barat* from a fair spectrum of society (missionaries and Australian gold miners make up, if not a representative section, a reasonably diverse group) and asked them about malaria prevention. The general advice (personal and official) was not to take either of these prophylactics for a long period. Both groups considered it a social obligation not to be responsible for the immunisation of the local mosquitoes to Paludrine.

I had also developed a phobia about poisonous centipedes being attracted to warm nooks in a sleeping body. I shared this fear with Paul: "How do you keep your nooks cold?" he asked.

My own nooks had been distinctly warm during the night and I moved tentatively as I eased out of my sheet. I walked out onto the bamboo platform. The river looked chilly and the first rays of sunlight were just beginning to show themselves over the mountains. It was a quarter to seven.

"*Sudah mandi, Pak Mark?*"

I turned to see Pak Rejang, towel over his shoulder, climbing the notched pole.

"*Selamat pagi, pak.*" I greeted him, and parried his question with my own: "*Dingin?*" - Cold?

"*Tidaaak! Tidak dingin*," he grinned, lying through his chattering teeth.

Pak Rejang preferred to *mandi* in the main flow of the river rather than the brook. There were three floating pontoons in Nanga Raun and morning and evening there was a constant flow of humanity along the riverbank. Like holiday campers - in happy gaggles with towels around their necks, clutching toothbrushes and soap - they trooped down the notched poles. The upriver ends of these pontoons were reserved for *mandi*-ing, dishwashing and water collection. On the lower end were the timber cubicles, coyly named the *kamar kecil* (little rooms).

There was a rough hole hacked in the floorboards inside these cubicles and through it one could see the hungry fish, struggling stubbornly against the current. Any matter whatsoever that fell through these holes would be redistributed and recycled before it had travelled two metres downstream by these super-efficient little sewage workers.

From our *own* personal preference we chose to *mandi* in the brook. This decision was based on the bowel-loosening fear that the thought of a return trip (this was the best synopsis) along that notched-pole-from-hell caused.

But by mid-morning we had accepted that, short of living the rest of our lives in Nanga Raun, there was no way to avoid it. We said our goodbyes and prepared for the descent back to river level. As I approached the halfway point on the pole my concentration was broken by something rubbing against the back of my knees. Pak Rejang's dog was trying to overtake me. I tried to shoo him away, slipped and, by some miracle, managed to ski down the last ten feet on one foot.

"Nice manoeuvre," shouted Paul, as I picked myself up. "The Rumanian judge gave you maximum points for that one."

Pak Rejang was waiting by the sinking pontoon ready to evacuate us in his dugout. He paddled swiftly, slewing sideways in the strong current, across to the opposite bank. We waited with our *barang* in the shade at the edge of the logging track and the headman, dog bouncing excitedly around his legs, went to find his friend.

Bayung seemed happy enough to have us along for the walk although he had very little to say. After a brief farewell with Pak Rejang we turned to leave. Bayung was twenty-three years old and had been into the mountains as far as the central Kalimantan border but he was a man of few words and I was unable to get any information out of him. He was wearing uncomfortable-looking, moulded-plastic trainers and his green trousers were tucked into long blue socks.

"Because of snakes?" I asked.

"Lintah" he said - leeches.

After about half a mile we turned off the dusty, sun-baked track onto an almost invisible trail into the thick vegetation. Bayung walked in front and hacked at the trail with his *parang*. He walked quickly and silently and I was content to save my breath for the hike. An hour and a half later we stepped back out onto the road. We were all sweating heavily and, with the exception of Bayung, we were limping from painful blisters.

Ahi had tried for the first half-hour to maintain the flashy whiteness of his 'Sport Falcons.' Now he complained that they were hurting him. He knew that we were carrying first-aid equipment and he simply must try some of it out before we went any further. Paul and I shot each other a worried glance . . . and decided that we might as well inspect our own stinging blisters.

We arrived in Kerian hot, dusty and hobbling (but without seeing a single leech) and climbed the greasy notched pole at the western end of the longhouse. We nodded to two old women who were chopping palm cores on the platform: *"Selamat pagi."* With the split bamboo flexing alarmingly under our backpacked weight, we tiptoed after Bayung, over a walkway toward the central apartment.

The Kerian longhouse was a tumbling timber structure that appeared to be three separate 'shorthouses' of three apartments each. I wondered if this was what the Da'an called a *rumah panjang*.

The whole structure was raised ten feet over the black, oily slime. Two rickety bridges, already under attack from a tangle of vines and ferns, connected the 'shorthouses.' Because of this riot of vegetation it was not until much later that we discovered the rotting posts that proved that Kerian had once been one continuous longhouse. What I thought were just connecting walkways were all that remained of four other apartments. It seemed that life in Kerian would be one long battle against the jungle.

On the gallery outside the central apartment we met The Dandy. Bayung disappeared without any further words and I assumed that this must be the *kepala's* son. At around five feet six he was taller than most Da'an, his hair was combed back and carefully oiled and his shirt was spotless and freshly ironed. He wore his steel watch loose so that it dangled from his wrist like a bracelet.

I spread out my map and explained our plans. The Dandy

flicked pampered fingernails across the Müller Mountains: "But there's nothing there!"

"There's jungle," I shrugged. "Have you been there?"

"No!" He was horrified by my assumption. "There's nothing there."

A burly older man had shuffled along to us on broken flip-flops. I nodded a greeting to him, and he shot back the dilapidated smile of a betel nut user. He seemed to be only mildly interested in the conversation and I turned back to The Dandy.

"Do you know where Pak Kolop is?" I asked, hoping to start afresh.

"Kolop? Maybe sleeping. Drank a lot yesterday!" He grinned at the older man.

Betel Mouth hitched up his sagging shorts. "Working on *ladang*. I take you," he said. I stuffed my map into my shirt pocket and we leaned our packs against the wall.

"Do you want me to come?" asked Ahi, rubbing his ankles.

"Yeah, sure we want you to come! You have to explain the plans."

This was the crucial moment when we were going to speak with someone who knew the route and I didn't want to risk any confusion arising from my bad Bahasa.

We followed Betel Mouth - with his shock of silver hair, flip-flops flapping and skin-tight pink nylon vest - back down the notched pole. At the back of the longhouse we crossed a stream, paddling up to our knees in the cool water. Ahi ran worriedly along the bank looking for a way to protect his 'Sport Falcons.'

We heard the buzz of a chainsaw ten minutes before we saw smoke rising through the trees. Five saronged women and a gang of young children were grouped around the campfire in a small clearing. As we walked out of the trees behind Betel Mouth one of the women said something to a small boy and he went running off up the hill towards the sound of the chainsaw.

There was a roughly built shelter made of leaves, behind the women and two blackened rice pots hung on a crossbar over the fire. We were to find out later that apart from two missionaries who visited several years before we were the only foreigners ever to arrive in Kerian. Yet nobody showed such bad breeding as to appear surprised at our arrival. It was almost as if we were expected.

At the womens' chirped invitations we sat down on a log near the fire. Ahi hovered nervously on the edge of the trees. One of the women shuffled forward with a tray holding a steel teapot and three enamel cups. Ahi drew closer.

"*Minum, pak*," smiled Betel Mouth - drink up.

"*Selamat minum*," I raised my glass. The women smiled.

The cloudy, off-white liquid was cooler and just pleasantly tangy this time. Paul was watching my face closely.

"Umm, like Chablis," I said. He looked tentative as he raised his own cup.

"Good *tuak*," I said to everyone in general, but it was not *tuak*.

"*Bukaaan tuak!*" said Betel Mouth drawing out the second syllable in the typical Da'an manner. "*Beram*."

Although *beram* often looks and tastes similar to the Taman *tuak*, it is made not from palm tree sap, but from fermented rice. It is essentially thick, cloudy *arak*.

There was the crackle of trampled undergrowth and fifteen men stepped into the clearing. The tallest one, wearing a blue baseball cap (peak backwards), seemed to be their leader and he smiled a welcome and said something to Betel Mouth in Da'an. Everyone laughed and their eyes were friendly.

The time seemed right to state our business and I nodded to Ahi. He looked away. I wanted our intentions to be clear and a 'local' who had already put his faith in the expedition would be our best possible spokesman. It seemed that now was the time for an official explanation – "Ahi!" The Punan stared sulkily at his soaking boots.

I swirled my cup, swallowed the last of the *beram*, and stood up.

"We're *orang inggris*," - pointing at Paul - "We've come to travel to the Müller Mountains. We want to go to Kal Teng (Central Kalimantan). We have one guide here – Ahi, *orang punan*." Everyone looked at Ahi. He shifted uncomfortably. "Now we need one more guide. We need somebody who has been to the mountains before."

"Nobody here has been there," said the baseball-capped man.

"Is Kolop here?"

He smiled and said something in the rapid coughs of Bahasa Da'an. He was making the unmistakable sign of the drunken raising of glasses. Paul and I laughed with them this time.

"*Minum, pak*" smiled the young leader, shrugging as if to dismiss the whole subject.

The old lady refilled my cup and I asked the man in the baseball cap about the *ladang*. It was on its first day of clearing and it would be about six months before the first crop of rice would be harvested. After two years this *ladang*, situated as it was on a steep hillside, would be washed clean of sufficient nutrients to grow rice and it would have to be abandoned. It may have to remain fallow for as much as fifteen years before it could again be cut, burnt and replanted.

One of the families at Kerian had chosen this spot for a new padi. It had obviously been cleared in the past but the trees were taking over again and they had begun to cut out sun so that the tangle of undergrowth was thinning.

The construction of the *pondok* was the first job to be done before the clearing of a new *ladang* could start. The family who had taken on the responsibility of working the new padis had to ensure that they had supplied enough food (rice and fish) and *beram* to sustain all the friends and neighbours who would come to help them. The women sat around and gossiped whilst they cooked and the men returned frequently to the camp for refreshments.

When the men left to go back to work we sat on at the *pondok*. I asked permission for Paul to take some photographs and, whilst he snapped away, I decided to head up to where the chainsaw was once again roaring. I was just walking away from the camp, on a roundabout route along the stream, when I heard one of the women hissing. I turned to see her wagging her finger at me.

I walked sheepishly back to the *pondok* and she scolded me through blackened teeth. As I was wondering if there was some special ritual that had to be performed before entering the *ladang* I heard a creaking noise. Then with a loud, crackling rumble a whole section of jungle came crashing down beside the trail.

The reason for this explosive collapse we saw when Betel Mouth took us up to the felling area by another, wider loop. The men were running around, stopping only briefly to hack at occasional trees with their axes. The man in the baseball cap, who was operating the chainsaw, only cut a wedge a few inches into each trunk. They seemed, at first, to be cutting absolutely at random but then I noticed that they glanced quickly at the high branches before they started on a tree.

The 'chonk' of axes echoed from all around us. After a few minutes of this hectic work there was a faint groan. As it grew louder the woodsmen retreated up the hill, checking overhead for more linked branches. They rushed out in a shower of twigs and wood-chips as the hillside itself seemed to keel over and crash into the valley.

The interlocking trees - their branches looped through each other like the arms of old friends – were steadily weakened until the weight of one dragged all the others down with it.

Betel Mouth offered to take us on to a more remote *ladang* where we might finally meet the elusive Kolop.

"I like the sound of this Kolop - sounds like my sort of guy," said Paul as we walked.

"Yeah. What do you reckon - a sort of Da'an Anthony Quinn? . . . or even Humphrey Bogart?"

"Knowing our luck, probably more like Ollie Reed."

At another leaf shelter we finally found Kolop. He was with half a dozen friends drinking *beram*. They were ragged and thin and looked poorer than the Da'an we had met so far. But they hid their surprise at seeing us here and slopped some harsh, lumpy *beram* into enamel beakers.

Kolop was smaller than I had expected. His features were clearly defined, exaggerated even, and on first appearance he seemed frail. Then you noticed the hard knots of muscle on his arms and legs and realised that the shredded tee shirt draping over his shoulders concealed a strong, wiry body. He kept a bright floral sports bag tucked close to his side and he had wonderfully mutilated toenails. His eyes which were incapable of focussing, due to the *beram*, were nonetheless bright and his narrow lips cracked readily into a contagious smile.

"Okay! Let's go to *Kal Teng*. We can hunt *babi* (wild pigs) with this." He shook his long pig spear. "Lots of *babi!*"

I was pleased to know that we were going to get meat without a gun that would be likely to scare away both wildlife and humanity.

"Pay whatever you think is right," he shrugged happily.

Kolop's reputation seemed to deserve some just recognition and so I offered him fifty percent more than Ahi was getting. I was confident already that he would be more than fifty percent more useful than our mighty Punan. But his eyes had clouded over and I wondered if he would remember our deal later.

"*Baik, baik,*" he grinned, perking up again. "Good, we'll go in two days. After the wedding. *Minum, pak!*"

Little did we know.

Chapter Four

A Dayak Da'an Wedding

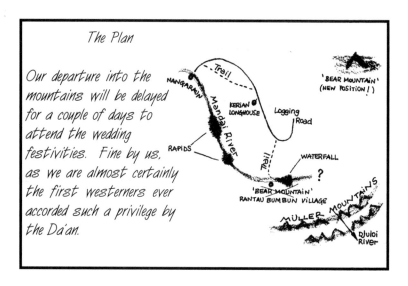

The Plan

Our departure into the mountains will be delayed for a couple of days to attend the wedding festivities. Fine by us, as we are almost certainly the first westerners ever accorded such a privilege by the Da'an.

NANGARAN

Trail

Mandai River

KERIAN LONGHOUSE

Logging Road

'BEAR MOUNTAIN' (NEW POSITION!)

RAPIDS

Trail

WATERFALL

?

'BEAR MOUNTAIN' RANTAU BUMBUN VILLAGE

MÜLLER MOUNTAINS

Djuloi River

By the time we got to the longhouse I had also learnt that Betel Mouth went more often by the infinitely more respectful name of Pak Tongkung. He was, in fact, the *kepala* of Kerian. Kolop talked incessantly as we walked back through the forest. He was from a village further back down the Mandai and he had come here for the party. We would have two or three days of partying to celebrate the wedding (he was too hyper to stop and tell me *whose* wedding). After that we could leave for the mountains.

Our *barang* had been moved into an apartment in the central 'shorthouse.' This was the home of the baseball-capped man and, since Pak Tongkung already had guests, this was where we would sleep. Our host's name was Dahing and I was already aware that, as the owner of a chainsaw, he was something of a leading figure in Kerian. Pak Tongkung didn't have any sons and it was generally agreed that Dahing was destined to be the longhouse's next *kepala*. Leadership of a Da'an community is considered to be a question of merit rather than inheritance, although it is usually expected that the headman's son is likely to be the best-prepared candidate.

I guessed that Dahing was in his early twenties although he was already father of the four children that kept his wife, Singkah, permanently busy.

The apartment was dark and smelt of a confusing combination of wood smoke and babies. Paul, Ahi and I were to sleep on mats by the front door and our host's family would sleep in the smaller back room that doubled as a kitchen. Two small 'serving-hatch' windows, which were never closed, allowed our hosts to converse with their neighbours and even for the neighbours to shout through to each other across Dahing's apartment.

We gave Dahing and Singkah a sarong, some cigarettes and some 'Loveli dan Glossi' shampoo sachets. The shampoo became such a hit that we had given away our entire supply by the time we left Kerian.

Out on the gallery there was already a festival atmosphere. We handed out sweets and balloons to the swarming children. The balloons had the unexpected benefit of providing Paul with some colourful and action-packed photo opportunities.

The youngest children had never seen an *orang barat* before but I could not understand why they were much more wary of me than of Paul. If I held out a sweet they would have to work up their courage to ease forward and make a grab for it before fleeing.

Paul could see that my feelings were hurt: "Don't worry. It's no more than their natural aversion to your hideous appearance. They'll get used to it."

He was right. These kids looked on my blanched, ghoulish appearance as if I was the stuff of nightmares. Okay, I hadn't shaved for a few days and I'm willing to admit I was no beauty, but this was a trifle harsh. To them Pak Tongkung's white hair was perfectly agreeable, but a young person with fair hair like mine (it had been bleached by the sun) had a terrible ghostly appearance.

I usually get on well with children and I worked hard to gain their trust. Finally I became, at best, 'Mark, the friendly ghost.'

We *mandi*-ed just before dusk in the swift, shallow river in front of the longhouse. I hoped that the chilly water was a sign that we were getting closer to the mountains. We skittered back over slimy logs that were laid end-to-end to form a rough walkway over the mud. Pigs and chickens bustled in the shadows under the building. Only when we were back in Dahing's *bilik* did I realise that I had lost my soap-dish. I had travelled a long way with that soap-dish and I went back to the river and spent the next forty minutes unsuccessfully hunting along the bank.

In his own apartment in the western 'shorthouse' Pak Tongkung poured out more *beram*. Paul was sitting next to Kolop, admiring the Da'an's jungle knife. The sheath was engraved with the words *Harimau Jantan Hutan*. The word *Jantan* makes it perfectly clear that this particular 'Jungle Tiger' was a male one. Kolop had a reputation to live up to: he wasn't about to let himself get mistaken for any wimpy tigers of unspecified gender.

An old man came silently into the *bilik*. His brown trousers and pin-stripe shirt were worn and dirty. Below his walnut-brown cheeks there was a tangle of grey-flecked beard – he was the only bearded Da'an we ever saw. Nobody spoke to the old man, or even seemed to notice him, and he addressed nobody. Treading lightly, he went from person to person (with the exception of Paul and myself) and placed the blade of his *parang* briefly into their mouth. They paused in their chatter only long enough to allow him to do so, and then he softly touched them on the head with his sword and moved on. He chanted quietly all the while.

When he had 'blessed' everyone in this way he took a shiny leaf from his pocket, threaded a piece of white cotton thread through its stem and wrapped it tightly around. Then he folded it up in a ragged white cloth and laid it by the fire. He left without having exchanged a word with anyone and his casual, yet obviously profound, actions made me think of Carlos Castaneda's Don Juan: *The bushes are filled with strange things.*

I wondered what secrets the old man might be able to tell and how deep his sense of his people's history might be. I promised myself that I would try to speak to him later but we never saw 'Don Juan' again.

A woman was trying to fill me in on the details of the wedding. Unhappily, she had already lost so many teeth to betel nut (and so much of her wits to *beram*) that I thought at first that she must be speaking to me in Bahasa Da'an rather than Indonesian. Why is it that whenever I attend a wedding I get latched onto by some relative with less teeth than marbles and a desire to impart information of apparently vital importance in Bahasa Da'an?

By the bottom of my fourth glass of *beram* the woman seemed far more coherent (and was even beginning to seem attractive). I had already been updated on all the wedding gossip: "It's Pak Tongkung's daughter, Anah, who's getting married. Nice girl. Done very well at school in Putus'. Then she went to Pontianak . . been as good as lost to her parents for some time. She had finally returned with her fiancé from the city – Abak . . Strange chap, Abak . . ."

I was getting restless. The reason for this was less my low resistance to the social graces of wedding conversation than my natural instinct for survival. In the midst of this little party Pak Tongkung, reeling slightly, had decided to play with his old home-made shotgun. From where I sat (and I had a better view than I wanted) the firing-mechanism appeared to be adapted from the ornate iron hinge of the proverbial barn door.

Paul leaned towards me. "If this thing goes off," he whispered, "I think we should try to be at the front end."

I was relieved when the Jungle Tiger (Male) - now lolling casually back behind the *kepala* - lurched to his feet, beckoned to Paul and me and stumbled towards the door. The gallery was crowded now and we smiled hazily at the people who greeted us as we hurtled along behind Kolop. Music was coming from the apartment next to Dahing's and the three of us went in. Someone slithered into the shadows near the back wall and hands reached up to haul us onto the floor. About fifteen people were seated, cross-legged, around a huge aluminium teapot. To our right, backs against the wall two men and a woman were hammering at brass gongs and another man was playing a *sapé* - a long three-stringed Kalimantan 'lute.'

Chipped tumblers were forced into our hands and, as I saluted and raised it to my lips, the chant of "Oih! . . Oih! . . Oih! . . Oih!" warned me that we were not expected to sip this one. The three of us lowered our glasses at the same time. Kolop smacked his lips and immediately refilled all three - "Oih! . . Oih! . . Oih! . . Oih!"

"What we have here," Paul shouted, above the din, "is a fair-dinkum Aussie cocktail party."

The teapot was dragged to the edge of the circle and from the way it slopped I could tell that it was still half-full. The clamour of the gongs vibrated along the floorboards and the swirling strains of the *sapé* cut through the jabber of conversation. Kolop made a grab for it, re-tuned, and began to sing in a quavering wail. He told me afterwards that it was a ballad of a traveller from Kal Teng who - in the way of travellers the world over – had left his girl behind.

"Oih! . . Oih! . . Oih!" The music and singing was just a counterpoint to the chant. A woman with a sarong around her waist and a black bra stood up and began to gyrate in the middle of the floor. Paul and I, pre-empting the invitation to join her, moved over by the wall and engrossed ourselves in trying to master the finer points of gong playing. It was thirsty work.

Waking in the early morning to the first ominous rumbles of diarrhoea I tried to distinguish dreams from reality. I could recall riotous laughter as Kolop tried to teach me to dance *Kal Teng* style. The smooth flowing motions and graceful crane-like struts had not looked so difficult, but they demanded total concentration and near-perfect balance: two faculties that are not renowned for their resistance to *beram*. There was also a dream-like vision of an old crone sawing the head off a brown hen whilst I held its jerking body, trying to aim the jet of blood through a gap in the bamboo boards. Paul verified that it was something less than ten minutes after this that I was last seen stumbling into the night.

Out on the platform I had struggled to fight the dizzying effects of the cool air and the multitudes of spinning stars. I didn't fight them for long. Sometime in the early hours Kolop had found me curled up on the bamboo slats, with a scabby dog sharing my body heat and a hundred mosquitoes drinking their fill. He dragged me to my sleeping-mat.

Early the next morning I was woken by Paul stumbling back into the *bilik*. "Uuh," he groaned, "my giblets are writhing in a state of heinous disapproval."

I battled across to the other side of the river to suffer my own intestinal disorders in relative solitude and as a result of this exercise I began to feel slightly better. Paul slept until lunchtime when Singkah prepared us rice and boiled fish. Ahi had still not reappeared.

We dosed intermittently through the afternoon heat until Kolop came to collect us in a great state of excitement: "We go watch them kill *babi*." We had been commenting drowsily on the possible reason for all the squealing that had been imposing on our siesta for the last twenty minutes and now we understood.

The pig had been putting up quite a struggle. One man was lying across its bristly flank, keeping the animal pinned down whilst at the same time trying to keep out of reach of the jaws that were rearing towards him. Another man, already pasted down one side by black slime, was trying to catch the pumping hind legs so that he could tie them. The toothless woman, now vulnerably bare-breasted with her sarong around her waist, ran around the wriggling threesome squawking advice.

These pigs were raised, free-range, under the longhouse where they were fed on anything that was dropped between the floorboards. It struck me as obscene that the other *babi*, though visibly shaken, were irresistibly drawn towards this life-and-death drama. Sometimes the woman would swing a kick - always misjudged - at their questing snouts.

Kolop roared with laughter. The woman shot us a black look and shouted something that sounded startlingly like "Wyduntjashaddap!"

The *babi* was eventually trussed around its hoofs and snout and hauled onto the platform to its destiny. Outside Pak Tongkung's apartment it was left beside another at the mercy of the hunting dogs. The scabby village dogs knew that *kampong babi* were out-of-bounds but they seemed to have an overwhelming, almost psychotic, hatred for pigs. Squeaking parades of piglets trotted busily underneath the longhouse, but if they so much as passed close to a dog its lips would ripple involuntarily into a sneer of intense loathing.

Pak Tongkung asked us, very politely, if we could spare some extra balloons for his wife to decorate their *bilik*. Paul dashed back to our *barang* to get some and to collect sarongs and a carton of Gudang Garam as presents for Abak and Anah.

It was only then that we realised that Abak was The Dandy.

The first part of the wedding ceremony took the form of a ritual raid on the bride's home. Abak was not from Kerian so Dahing and five other young men deputised as his family and formed the 'raiding party.' Armed with spears and swords they marched along to the *kepala's* apartment. The doorway had been decorated with flowers and balloons. The excited screams of women echoed from inside when they heard footsteps marching along the platform. Then from the *kepala's* apartment we heard barked orders in a man's voice.

The raiders forced the door open and six men from the bride's family immediately crammed into the doorway to prevent them from entering. There was a brief, clumsy struggle; one of the raiders got a dead-arm and two defenders banged their heads together in the crush. The groom, Abak, was wearing pressed trousers and a button-down shirt. His hair was immaculate and he stood behind his 'guard of honour' watching the performance with an irritatingly patronising air.

"Look at him," spat Paul, "How am I going to get any good photos if he's there all the time? Ask him at least to take that bloody watch off!"

Peace was quickly restored between the two 'warring

factions,' although the two protagonists of the collision still rubbed their heads and shot angry glances at each other.

Dahing knelt down to chop up a stalk of palm core that had been hung on the door as a symbolic lock. The agreement that had been reached through this scuffling was now announced. The cost of peace? - Anybody who wanted to witness the wedding ceremony had to drink a pint of *beram* before entering the apartment.

The crowd pushed forward once more to the beat of "Oih! . . Oih! . . Oih! . . Oih!"

An old lady was the first to elbow her way into the doorway. She was probably not yet sixty but looked far older and had fine silver hair. She gripped the battered enamel tankard in her spindle-fingers.

"Oih! . . Oih! . . Oih!" the crowd egged her on.

She slowly tilted her head back until she had swallowed the last lumps at the bottom of the cup, belched once, gave a black betel grin and passed the cup on. Then, just like any other old lady going to a wedding, she walked demurely into the apartment. Paul and I moved forward with the crowd, hoping that we could drain our own pints with as much style as the old lady had.

At the far end of Pak Tongkung's apartment four people sat facing the congregation. I struggled to distinguish their features through the stinging wood-smoke and then one of the gong players from the previous night's party called to me and forced a space near the front. Paul had already found a position near the other wall and was hurriedly reloading film.

Seated on four brass gongs (with our sarongs laid across the tops) were Anah, her sister, Abak and somebody who was standing in as his brother. The two girls were wearing thick, white headbands with tasselled fringes. The constant chant of the drinkers at the door seemed to strike nobody as irreverent and it continued throughout the wedding so that I heard nothing of what was said.

I had hoped to see Don Juan again but the *kepala adat* (literally, chief of ritual) was someone whom I had never seen before. He approached the foursome with a bowl, swilling with blood and a raw pig's liver. Among many Dayak peoples there is a custom that the future can be read in a fresh pig's liver and this ritual had already been performed in private.

From out of the gory mess the *kepala adat* lifted four cloth bracelets. These he tied onto the wrists of the four young people and then blessed them all with a *parang* in the same way that Don Juan had done. He passed a live fighting-cock over their heads, but the *beram* was already taking effect and I didn't see what happened to the cock.

With the noise of the chanting and the asphyxiating density of the wood-smoke my memories of the ceremony are extremely hazy. We were probably the first foreigners ever to witness a Da'an wedding and we were unable to explain afterwards our near total amnesia over the events inside the *kepala's* apartment. Paul took a lot of photographs. But unwilling to 'break the spell' he didn't use a flash and none of his photos came out. I kept notes, and I still have them, but beyond the first line ('totally bolloxed') they are indecipherable and only add to the mystery.

The ceremony must have lasted longer than we thought because it was dusk when we got back outside. A large glazed jar, relief mouldings of a dragon snaking around it, had appeared on the platform and from it the silver-haired lady was ladling *beram* into a motley collection of cups.

Several examples of these 'dragon jars' that are almost a thousand years old have been found in Borneo longhouses. They were sometimes believed to be the homes of dragon-spirits and have long been used as burial urns.

Dragon jars, brass gongs and antique pottery are frequently found in almost every Dayak community and yet there was never a record of any tribe ever manufacturing these things. They changed hands through marriage, *denda* (fines paid as compensation) or plunder but they all originated from Chinese traders as payment for the jungle produce that was, and often still is, so sought after in China.

In response to the old lady's summons I dutifully wandered over and another dose of *beram* was thrust upon me. I swallowed it and returned the cup. Bayung appeared, with a ghetto blaster on his shoulder, streaming out wailing Indonesian pop. Somebody grabbed my arm and hauled me into line. Others joined on behind and soon there were a dozen people in a shuffling, swaying conga around the dragon jar. Dahing had joined the circle and shouted something at me that I couldn't hear. Besides I was unable to concentrate.

"*Bagus, bagus!*" I shouted back, thumbs-up. Then, because obviously something else was needed, "*Enak!*" I pointed at the jar - delicious. Another cup was in my hand and the dragon-lady was waiting for me to empty it. I completed another couple of circles and then slid away and danced on my own down towards the darkness at the end of the platform – groovin' to a tune that only I could hear.

I had been handing out Gudang Garam from a pack in my top pocket and - purely as an excuse to hide for a moment - I went to Dahing's *bilik* to replenish my supply. Paul was already there trying, muddy-minded, to select a film from his pack.

I rifled through the *barang* box. "Paul, have you got the Gudang Garam in your pack?"

"Well, I've got one here." He dragged a crushed box from his shorts.

"No, I mean . . We're missing about a dozen packs."

"Well, I said Ahi could have one yesterday."

"That's fine but what's happened to the rest? We need them for the guides."

In lieu of cigarettes I grabbed a handful of Guatemalan bracelets and jammed them into my pocket. I once spent a few winter months travelling in Central America and, before leaving, I bought two huge woven bags and filled them with Guatemalan clothes, textiles and hammocks. I had sold most of these goods at a stall in Camden Market but one of the most successful purchases that I made in Guatemala had been two thousand hand-woven 'friendship bracelets.' When I gave up my market stall I still had several bunches of these left and I discovered that all over the world (with the obvious exception of Central America) there are few things that make a better low-cost gift than a Guatemalan 'friendship bracelet.'

We stumbled back outside and bumped into Kolop and Pak Tongkung. The *kepala* looked like he had just woken up and it occurred to me that I hadn't seen him for some time. With due formality I presented them both with a bracelet and we all trooped in a staggering band to the headman's apartment.

We were invited to eat - barbecued pork, rice, palm core and boiled chicken - in regal seclusion with Pak Tongkung's family, the newly-weds and Kolop. Kolop was continually breaking into his ready, happy smile: "Pak Tongkung's going to fix *parang*. Good, velly good." He had already set the *kepala* to work on carving our sheaths.

"No problem. Catch *babi* if you run fast enough Pak Bacoc!" laughed the headman.

I asked why he called Kolop Pak Bacoc and was delighted to hear that the (Male) Jungle Tiger's full name was Honorious Bacoc. I raised my glass – for the fifteenth time that evening - "To the Honorious Pak Bacoc!"

Back outside we tried to stay one step ahead of *beram* (the dreaded milk of amnesia) and shuffled our way as inconspicuously as possible into the dragon patrol. Being a foot taller than the rest of the conga (and not very inconspicuous at the best of times) it was not easy. We knew already, that alcohol was almost impossible to refuse; every ploy, from shaming and cajoling to haranguing and virtual force-feeding, would be levied at you until, intestines shrieking for mercy, you would have to give in. Our only chance of avoiding *beram* was to look like we were enjoying dancing too much to stop. But the dragon-lady was not about to let us get away with that!

I was woken, at 3.00 am, by a gong concert just outside Dahing's apartment and I staggered out bleary-eyed to have a look. Paul was already out there. We sat quietly against the wall, marvelling at the scene. At the far end of the platform Dahing, Bayung and some others were *still* dancing around the jar.

Some children were chasing each other in and out of the conga. They were playing a game of 'tag'; whoever was 'tagged' had to knock back a tumbler of *beram*. The dancers laughed blearily at their antics. I couldn't believe there could be any *beram* left in the entire longhouse.

The gong concert was hotting up - the beat getting faster and more demonic. A hunting dog that had curled for warmth behind one of the players decided that there must be somewhere quieter to sleep and moved away. It was not so easy for us, however. We'd been spotted and Dahing and his gang of raiders dragged us back into the realm of the dragon-lady.

I was again haunted by uneasy recollections when I awoke the next morning; I had keeled over somewhere, just managing to push aside a smoky rattan mat before I vomited between the slatted bamboo floorboards. What really worried me was that I could not remember where, during the endless night of *beram* and smoky rattan mats, this had happened.

"Don't worry about it," said Paul when I voiced my fears, "You were the personification of good manners. I saw Tongkung do the same thing."

We had not yet learnt that the only two valid reasons for exemption from alcohol abuse were religion or sickness (only if it necessitates the taking of *obat kina* - Chinese medicine). We spent most of the day trying to stay one step ahead of the dragon lady and her squadron.

Everyone was back at work in the *ladang* early the following morning and Kerian was once again as deserted as it had been when we arrived. Despite what Pak Rejang had told us, the Kerian Da'an still rely to a great extent on the rice harvest. The wedding was the excuse that they needed to let their hair down and forget about the work that was waiting for them. Now they would have to work doubly hard to make up for lost time.

Ahi was still missing and I was irritated that he had now been absent - whilst still on the payroll - for three days. Also, by a strange coincidence, I had met somebody during the party who had casually told me that he knew Ahi from a village further down the Kapuas. Our mighty Punan was nothing of the kind and had no jungle experience whatsoever. We already knew that he was responsible for our depleted Gudang Garam rations. Up here in the *hulu* we would have no chance to restock the precious supplies that would be needed firstly to lure guides and secondly as gifts when we made contact with the Punan.

When I eventually tracked him down, on one of the raised walkways later that morning, he put up no defence whatsoever and actually seemed relieved that he would not be coming with us to the mountains. The hike from Nanga Raun seemed to have more than quenched his thirst for jungle travel. I left him to worry for a while but in the end I had to pay his return fare to 'Kalis. The people of Kerian were far too hospitable – they might never have got rid of him.

That afternoon I paid Dahing some money for Paul, Ahi and myself. I was concerned that our store of goods was running short and decided that it would be best to pay in cash whilst we were still far enough downriver for it to be welcomed. Dahing thanked me and asked how long I thought we would stay. I returned the question by asking him when he thought Kolop would be ready to leave. I would be happy for Dahing to use his influence to get Kolop motivated.

"Pak Kolop pergi ke Kampong Lebangan," he shrugged.

Kolop had left. Just like that he had gone back downriver. Way, way back past Nanga Raun. His mother was ill and he'd had to leave quickly. Still I was surprised that he could not tell us before he went. Did he mean for us to wait here or was the deal off? Should we go on alone?

Instinctively we went to discuss our options with Pak Tongkung. It was odd how, like Pak Rejang, we had so quickly developed a deep respect for the headman's opinions and advice. The two men had radically different characters and these characters were oddly reflected in the temperament of their villages. Pak Rejang was as quick moving and busy as Pak Tongkung was relaxed and carefree. Both were obviously men of experience and worthy leaders.

We found the *kepala* outside his apartment chewing betel nut and watching his wife chop a palm core (a chore that she seemed to do endlessly). He had finished making the sheaths for our *parangs*. Two thin boards were carved to fit snugly around the blades and bound tightly with a red cord that was knotted to form a simple belt. Our jungle knives were ready – a joint effort by *two* Da'an headmen.

Pak Tongkung's advice was strangely similar to Pak Rejang's: there was a Da'an *kampong* further upriver where the people barely lived on rice at all. They lived only by hunting and fishing and they would be free to travel at will. So, we decided to go deeper into the *hulu*, to Rantau Bumbun, the last village. There we would either find guides or wait for Kolop.

I wanted to leave a letter for my parents in Pak Tongkung's keeping until somebody made the voyage downriver to the post office in 'Kalis and I was relieved when he said that he himself was going any day now.

The trail to Rantau Bumbun was hot and dusty and took us along the logging road in the company of two teenagers. Immediately on leaving the longhouse we had to wade across a small stream. The boys were wearing plastic trainers and simply kicked them off but Paul and I with our high-laced jungle-boots did not want to go through the rigmarole of taking them off at every little stream so we just walked through. This turned out to be the only water we would have to cross between the two communities and our blisters were needlessly aggravated. We were hobbling painfully when we arrived in Rantau four hours later.

Rantau Bumbun struck me as being more like a scene from a Tarzan movie than even Hollywood could conceive. We approached the village from the opposite side of the river and slid on our backsides down the muddy bank. Across the swirling current three huts nestled amongst the billows of a meadow. The sound of children's voices and a barking dog were the only things that betrayed the fact that the *kampong* stretched further up the river, hidden by the trees.

Our guides started hooting across the river for somebody to paddle across and collect us. They were very picturesque wilderness-type calls and I glanced at them to see if they really expected anyone to hear; I wondered if the cliché Tarzan-set had affected them too.

Paul scrambled down the bank behind us and gave one of his piercing two-fingered whistles. The echoes, swooping back to us, made me look up for the first time at the mountains surrounding the village. Immediately across from us squatted the awesome slab of Gunung Bumbun and to the right, contrasting with its solid bulk, the steep spire of Gunung Ngirol. Their power was emphasised by the flatness of the rainforest around them.

Looking back to the meadow I saw a white shape slipping down the grassy bank towards three dugouts that I had not noticed. As the canoe came towards us I realised that the 'ferryman', digging hard and fast against the current, was a girl in a white blouse. She was about fifteen and had the smooth complexion and 'page-boy' haircut that are the badge of her Da'an peers.

We followed the boys across the meadow, turned left in front of a large weatherboard building (we later learnt that it was a schoolroom) and walked through to the end of the village.

Apart from some small children who hid behind the stilts of one of the huts nobody betrayed any surprise. In the seventies a French surveyor had travelled through as far as the rapids above Rantau. According to the locals, nobody else had ever been here and many of the youngest children (who had never been to Nanga Raun to see the missionary) had never seen an *orang barat*.

We climbed a notched pole to a double *pondok* and, before crossing the flimsy bamboo platform, we gratefully unlaced our steaming boots. Within minutes we were, once again, passing around Gudang Garam whilst I spread out the map and began my now familiar speech.

The boys who had brought us from Kerian wished us luck and turned to leave. I gave them seven thousand rupiah each - a day's wages for a skilled labourer - hoping that some of their enthusiasm might rub-off on a would-be guide when they returned to Kerian.

I was determined to lay all our cards face-up on the table. The pain of my blisters (and the questions that they begged about my jungle-boots), and the boredom of trying to sound enthusiastic, made me sound brash and businesslike. I felt like I was trying to sell something.

Three sets of cracked, work-hardened fingertips moved across our map. One young man was listening especially attentively. His name was Pelaun.

"There are three people in Rantau who know the way to the border," Pelaun explained. "From there you just follow the Djuloi River down to Taj'ak Bangkan."

This was the first time I had heard of Taj'ak Bangkan and to hear such concrete advice was encouraging. My map showed the nearest village in Central Kalimantan to be somewhere called Kalasin but I was aware that this could be too far without collecting supplies en route.

I also checked on the whereabouts of Gunungberuwang and Pelaun admitted that, according to the map, we were not far from a village of that name: *"Tetapi bukan kampong, itu gunung."*

The 'last village' on which I had pinned all my hopes (and confidently pointed-out to our sponsors as 'the last chance to restock our provisions') was, in fact, not a village named after a mountain at all: it was the uninhabited mountain itself. Furthermore it was not where the map showed it to be but about twenty-five miles to the northeast.

Two more men arrived on the platform. They had their tee shirts pulled up in front of them and as they sat down next to us they carefully tumbled a pile of pink and white guava onto the floor. We ate as we talked.

Tani, was chubby and baby-faced. He was aware of this and had disguised it with a moustache that was unusually full for a Da'an. He was one of the three men who had been before as far as the border. The other two were away in 'Kalis.

"Beyond Rantau, eight days of paddling up Mandai Hulu until the foothills of the Müllers," Tani explained. "Then another week walking over the mountains before the trail dropped down into valley of the Djuloi River. Without a canoe it would take eight more days to walk to the trading town of Taj'ak Bangkan."

With a typical Da'an love for maps, Tani helped us to plot all these positions. He agreed that, from what he had heard, there are indeed self-sufficient bands of Punan nomads in the Müller Mountains.

Tani's friend Dujang was thin and had a gaunt, pockmarked face. One of his front teeth was missing and he had found this very useful; he would shove the filter of his cigarette into the gap so that it seemed to be stuck to his top lip whilst he talked. He had married a girl from the village seven years ago and moved up here from 'Kalis. He owned a chainsaw and an outboard motor and these treasures were enough to make him a powerful man in the *hulu*.

As I outlined our plan I had the impression that Dujang was setting himself up as Tani's agent. But Tani was nodding confidently: "*Bagus, tidak ada masalah.*" - Okay, no problem. So, cautiously now - teasing the hook - I detailed the pay: free cigarettes (what was left), food and bonus. Tani nodded decisively.

I breathed a sigh of relief, "Great so when will you be ready to leave?"

"Wah! Cannot! Have *kontrak* with logging company downriver for one month."

I made a supreme effort to control myself and picked out one of the sugar-sweet pink guavas.

Pelaun moved our bags into his *bilik*, a large single room, and there his wife, Andriatti, prepared us *kopi*. There was something in Pelaun's tranquil, silent posture that was almost monk-like. Although Rantau Bumbun did not have a formal headman we quickly realised that Pelaun was another one of those Da'an who had embodied the spirit of their village.

We stayed with Pelaun and Andriatti for three soothing days. But they were days that brought us no closer either to a guide or a dugout. Even in Rantau Bumbun, fringed with jungle that was plentiful with *babi* and deer and a river that was thickly stocked with fish, rice was the essential staple. To make the crossing on our own would be folly and possibly fatal – everyone agreed – but to try it in one of the village dugouts, unfitted for an expedition, was not even a possibility.

Eventually we had to face the fact that there was little likelihood of finding a guide in the Da'an territory for at least three weeks. Kolop knew where we were and if he did not approach us we could not very well go to find him at the sick bed of his mother. With bitter disappointment we decided to head back out of the Mandai and try our luck elsewhere.

Dujang owned the only outboard motor in Rantau and the trip to Nanga Raun would cost over fifty US dollars. Even given the high price of fuel in the *hulu* I argued that this price was extortionate. I figured Dujang for a mercenary who knew that without his boat we had no way to get back to Nanga Raun other than the blister-jarring two-day hike through Kerian.

I offered thirty dollars and Dujang refused.

So we separated: myself with the conviction that Dujang would decide that thirty dollars was better than nothing, and Dujang confident in his knowledge that we had nowhere else to go.

Chapter Five

We Beat a Retreat

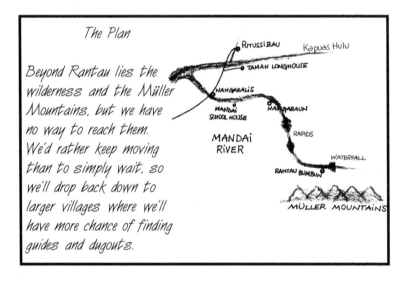

The Plan

Beyond Rantau lies the wilderness and the Müller Mountains, but we have no way to reach them. We'd rather keep moving than to simply wait, so we'll drop back down to larger villages where we'll have more chance of finding guides and dugouts.

PUTUSSIBAU
Kapuas Hulu
TAMAN LONGHOUSE
NANGAKALIS
MANDAI SCHOOL HOUSE
NANGARAUN
RAPIDS
MANDAI RIVER
WATERFALL
RANTAU BUMBUN
MÜLLER MOUNTAINS

Then Bilbo sat down on a seat by his door, crossed his legs, and blew out a beautiful grey ring of smoke that sailed up into the air without breaking and floated away over The Hill.

"Very pretty!" said Gandalf. "But I have no time to blow smoke-rings this morning. I am looking for someone to share in an adventure that I am arranging, and it's very difficult to find anyone."

The Hobbit, JRR Tolkien

I should have seen what was coming the moment we sat down in Dujang's fifteen-foot dugout and Tani passed back two plastic bowls. From the instant that the motor slackened-off as we swooped into the turmoil of the first rapids Paul and I bailed almost continuously. We paused only to grip the sides of the canoe to prevent ourselves from being thrown out, fighting the instinct that forces you to try to right the boat with your bodyweight as one rail after another plunges under the waves. To struggle against the rhythm of the rapids is to court disaster.

Twice we had to dismount and carry all our *barang* around the most violent sections. A hacked-out trail led for a quarter of a mile alongside the second of these cataracts to where Paul and I were to wait for the boat. Dujang and Tani removed the engine and tied it in the dugout's belly where it would be safe from the battering of the rocks.

We waited for twenty minutes on the gravel beach where the river widened. I was just beginning to wonder if the boatmen had given up and gone back to Rantau when the dugout came leaping and bucking out of the ravine. There was nothing in the misty gorge to give any idea of scale and at first I didn't notice them.

The boat plunged down and even Paul, balancing with his camera on a high boulder, lost sight of it. For several seconds it disappeared and we held our breath. Then suddenly it was surging back up on the billows, as if it was going to leap salmon-like into the air. The men were working frantically with their paddles, fighting to keep out of the worst of the turmoil. The bow went under and again it seemed that they were sunk, but it bounced back up so fast that most of the water was thrown back out and Tani almost went with it.

They exited the chasm backwards and dug their paddles in deep to battle their way across to us. With Tani expertly matching his own stroke to his skipper's they powered back on a wide sweep that would keep them out of reach of the clutching current.

These lads were risking not only their boat but possibly their lives in taking us to Nanga Raun and I was ashamed of haggling so hungrily to reduce what had seemed to be an unfairly high price. I could not even imagine how they would get the boat back to Rantau.

"Your friend was here yesterday," said Pak Rejang, shaking hands and giving us a typically welcoming smile.

"Ahi?"

"That his name?"

We realised with embarrassment that he had never met the 'Punan' before the day we landed in the village with him. In my stammering Indonesian I tried to explain our apparent rudeness when, on our arrival, we had simply waited on the riverbank in the belief that Ahi was going to take us to his grandmother's *pondok*.

I went along to the tiny store on the riverbank to buy a round of warm 'Stim Cola' and several bags of 'Choco Puffs.' This at least took the edge off my already suffering sweet tooth and Mrs Rejang (who also seemed genuinely pleased to see us) further helped by serving us *kopi susu*.

As we were saying goodbye to Dujang and Tani we were surprised to see a boy with ginger hair strolling towards us along the riverbank. James was thirteen and was the son of Nanga Raun's American missionary. Apart from periods away at school, he had spent his whole life in the *kampong*. He was talkative and happy, at times rattling away to Pak Rejang in what sounded to us like fluent Da'an.

James said that he had heard of my 'skill' with a spinning top. I told him that this was purely beginner's luck and was relieved that he didn't accuse me of false modesty and challenge me to a game. He invited us along to meet his father and we helped him carry the cans of kerosene (for the fridge-freezer) back to their painted clapboard bungalow near the brook.

Pak Harold and his family had been in Nanga Raun for seventeen years and they were among the few foreigners ever to learn Bahasa Da'an. Sam and Sally had explained that on arrival in West Kalimantan most Protestant missionaries spent several months in Pontianak learning Bahasa Indonesia. Only with this knowledge could they hope to learn the tribal tongues of the community with whom they would be living. Pak Harold had forgotten most of his Bahasa and we spoke English - to the exclusion of Pak Rejang.

We stepped through the fly-screen door and sat down on benches in the reception room: "Do you believe . . ." - My heart sank and, seeing the look on my face, the missionary faltered -

"Uh-hum, are you faithful to . . . Are you children of the Bible?"

"Well, no . . . I'm not religious at all" I said.

We both looked at Paul. He was studying a small gecko as it stalked a mosquito around the doorframe.

The conversation was getting off to a bad start. I explained what we were doing on the Mandai Hulu and the problems we were having trying to find guides and asked Pak Harold what he could tell us about the agenda of the rice season. In his experience did he think we could find a guide here now or would we have more chance back downriver?

In the busy years administering to his Da'an flock, Pak Harold had never had time to go to Rantau. He had once travelled to Kerian however, with a fellow missionary who lived downriver in Nanga Sarai. He seemed uninterested in the rice-cycle and had no idea at what stage the crops were at the moment.

"My mission here is to preach the Lord's words in the people's language." He quoted the party line. Unlike Sam's easy-going conversation, we were soon aware that Pak Harold's speech consisted solely of phrases and clichés straight out of the Good Book. He was unable to talk about anything other than his religion.

"How many souls are there in your flock?" I asked. Paul shot me a warning glance.

"There are seven," he said. "Many of the people here are Catholic."

Seven out of a population of seven hundred did not seem like great return on a seventeen year investment in the conversion business but I couldn't help being impressed by Pak Harold's unshakeable conviction that all would have been worthwhile if he had saved just one 'misguided soul.' I wondered if his church held the same strength of faith.

"Does anybody here still worship their animist religion?"

"The chief here - Daniel - he *says* he's Catholic but in reality he's animist like most of them." It was the first time that I had heard the *kepala*'s Christian name.

There has been a lot of pressure placed on tribes all over Indonesia to adopt one of the officially recognised religions. A great many people in Borneo have turned to Islam which, as already mentioned, effectively demands the almost total renunciation of Dayak identity. This idea is as unthinkable for the Da'an as would be the rejection of *babi* (pig meat is one of the Dayak's main sources of protein) and abstention from their *beram*, a focal point of their social-life.

In the case of Nanga Raun I believe Catholicism was a far more attractive policy than either Islam or life under the watchful eye of their resident Protestant missionary. I could never shake the feeling that Pak Rejang, though a leading member of the Catholic congregation, was first and foremost a very shrewd diplomat.

With a burgeoning smile Pak Harold began to relate what he considered to be a very amusing anecdote. He told us how he had tried, unsuccessfully, to convince Pak Rejang that it would be 'a sign of progress' if he and his people were to 'reform their toilet habits.'

"When they relieved themselves, rather than simply douse, I told him that it would be infinitely healthier if they were to wipe themselves with paper. I gave him a great pile of magazines."

The missionary roared with laughter as he related how Pak Rejang had tried several times but had eventually gone back to his old ways. "He said to me: 'You just don't understand how good it feels to lap that cool water up your ass!'"

I remembered Conrad's fictional league, 'The International Society for the Suppression of Savage Customs,' and tried not to picture the Mandai after seventeen years of Pak Harold's brand of 'progress.'

As we were trying to effect our escape there was the sound of footsteps on the veranda and I was relieved to see Pak Tongkung and his new son-in-law. The Dandy was dabbing some leech bites with a grubby handkerchief; it was heart-warming to see him looking so bedraggled.

Pak Tongkung withdrew my letter from the sweaty waistband of his shorts. He had guarded it there all the way from Kerian. Later I reopened it so that I could tell my parents of the honour that had been paid to their mail.

We sat up until late with Pak Rejang and his family. Huge moths made the lantern-light flicker and the dark square through the doorway was filled with the croak of frogs.

Mrs Rejang (blissfully stoned) and the Beautiful Zombie were sat by the oil lamp, their elbows jabbing shadows across the wall as they wove 'coolie hats' from palm fronds. Lounging on the stack of rattan sleeping-mats, I was struck with a powerful sense of wellbeing. We talked very quietly with long pauses and lazy half-sentences. Every now and then one of us would lean forward to bat the red balloon that baby Floretina was chasing. Maximus caught it and scrawled across it with a black marker: *HEPPY BRIDHAY!!!*

The Beautiful Zombie giggled behind a shapely hand and I wished that we didn't have to catch the boat in the morning. We had enjoyed our time in the Da'an villages and we were disappointed not to have found our guides amongst these warm-hearted people. Above all I had no wish to go back to 'civilisation.'

I sat next to Pak Tongkung in the boat and he chatted as we motored away from the shadow of the Müllers. He had a meeting at the high school in Putussibau – something about bad reports of a couple of Kerian's kids. I wondered what they would make of the *kepala* at the school when he strolled in with his silver hair exploding from under a torn camouflage 'beanie' hat. With his tight denim shorts and pink nylon vest ('7' stitched on the back) he reminded me of an overweight 1970's Aussie Rules player.

A little girl was leaving her village to go to school and she was travelling down the river with her father. As we drifted in towards the school's jetty, she began to wail. She was obviously horrified with the idea of leaving home.

"Mau pulang bapak. Mau pulang!" - I want to go home daddy!

Her poor father could do nothing but roll in the stern of the boat with his head in his hands. He moaned loudly as a woman teacher dragged his daughter onto the jetty and, bellowing angrily, hauled her towards the school buildings.

We could still hear the girl's screams as we puttered back into mid-stream.

Although we were travelling with the flow of the river it still took five hours to reach 'Kalis. We had thrown our boots in the back of the boat so that our blisters could dry out, but the flies bit painfully if we took a moment's break from swatting. I looked out for Chicken George's shack and the pontoon of the woman with the gold teeth but the river had risen with rainfall and everything appeared different to me. You have to be an old hand on a jungle river before it lets you into the secrets that are the key to its navigation and we were back in 'Kalis before I saw a landmark that I remembered.

We bade farewell to Pak Tongkung and Abak and unloaded our *barang* with the help of some naked children who were leaping off the riverbank. As we were doing so we realised that the schoolgirl's poor father was not merely distraught. He was absolutely paralytic - *beram*-ed to the eyeballs. What was worse: he had discharged a considerable belly-full of this beverage straight into Paul's right jungle-boot.

I waited, snickering happily, on the road whilst Paul rinsed his boot in the muddy current.

Then we headed for something to eat at the *rumah makan* where we had been so charmed by the silver-haired old lady. There were a dozen young men sitting around the front of the store but apart from Gudang Garam none of them seemed to be consuming anything. The old lady had been joined by a buxom and cheerful young woman. It struck me that in a non-abstemious town she would have made the perfect barmaid. It would not be long before we realised that this *orang melayu* village was not as abstemious as it outwardly appeared.

As we dropped our packs onto the veranda everyone turned to stare at us. There was such a look of expectation in their eyes that a simple 'good afternoon' seemed totally inadequate – rude even. We had either to enter with a whimper, or a roar.

"*Mau kake!*" I roared, rubbing my stomach. "*Tidak mau nasi, mau kake!*" - We don't want rice, we want cake.

The boys laughed.

"We want cake and fine wines," quoth Paul. "We want the finest wines available to humanity."

The *rumah makan* was typical of many in up-country Borneo. Shelves lined the walls from floor to ceiling and these we searched voraciously for an alternative to rice. The other customers became curious. Several came over to help us in our search.

There was an amazing array of soaps of differing properties - three of which were sold with a free glass beaker. A whole wall was stacked with packets of flavoured dried noodles. One of the lads pointed these out decisively: "*Enak sekali*," he pronounced - very delicious.

"*Enak sedikit*," I retorted - a little bit delicious.

The *rumah makan* was now filling with curious passers-by and a man came in from a back room to see what all the roaring was about. I started to spin a yarn about Paul being a world-famous English chef. He was in fact trained as a chef but as I got more and more carried away I began to build his reputation into a thing of eternal glory: "This is the finest European chef who has *ever* set foot in Nangakalis!"

This they were prepared to accept, and soon the mission was on to provide the ingredients for Paul to prepare what I clumsily translated as *kentang potong* (the epitome of fine English Cuisine) - Chips!

A small boy was sent running to buy all the potatoes he could find. He returned after ten minutes and proudly presented Paul with eleven (every *kentang* in 'Kalis). Soon Paul was stirring three spitting woks on gas burners in the steaming back room. He dashed out momentarily to grab another bottle of 'black beer' and ran back to his pots.

"No, but we don't need rice," I heard him telling the 'barmaid' as I drank my own warm, thick Guinness. This is the most popular beer in the *hulu*, despite the fact that it's almost undrinkable at forty-five degrees . . almost.

The result of this frantic effort was a groaning table loaded with corned-beef omelette, onion and garlic hash browns, fried eggs and, *piéce de resistance*, the first chips ever to grace 'Kalis. Everyone had to sample them and the population came trooping in. Most of them were polite enough to lie but the verdict was obvious: not nearly as *enak* as rice.

We soon proved ourselves such valued customers at the *rumah makan* that Yacob, the owner, gave us his room for as long as we stayed in 'Kalis. He would sleep in the storage room and Paul and I would take alternate nights on the mattress.

When I set off for my evening *mandi* in the river, the sky was just bruising its way into dusk. This is a process that takes about seven minutes in Nangakalis and happens almost exactly at six o'clock, at any time of the year.

I dawdled so much under the weight of our feast that it was almost dark when I passed the Chinese shop. I decided to go in. My pretext for doing so was the purchase of a soap-dish to replace my old one which may have already floated through 'Kalis on its long voyage back down to Pontianak. My real ambition, however, was an opportunity to talk to the pretty Chinese girl.

Inside the shop it was dark - the lamps had not yet been lit. I called out and, after a moment, the girl stepped into the doorway. I strained to see past the glare of her torch. A lantern in the next room backlit her curves faintly through a silky two-piece negligée. I knew better than to take her choice of eveningwear as a sign that she had any intentions of providing me with anything more memorable than a plastic soap-dish. Women in shops and *rumah makan* all over Kalimantan wear these filmy outfits almost as a uniform.

So we turned to the store's stock of soap-dishes and I - charmingly, I thought - asked her which one she particularly liked. Thus I ended up with a huge pale-green plastic box, stamped with a picture of a bear and a chubby dog holding hands in a field of tulips. It reminded me of my sixth birthday cake, decorated with mint icing to represent a football field.

I imagine her father was delighted when she told him she had finally sold that huge green box that had been cluttering the place up since Buddha was a boy – the one that looked like a birthday cake. As I paid for the soap-dish the torchlight glinted on some small gold-coloured boxes. Under a scrawl of Chinese characters were the words '*Minyak Angin*' - Oil of Air. I was fascinated. How on earth do you go about marketing oil of air? What sort of fool's going to buy it?

"What's this for?" I asked the girl. But her little brother had wandered in from the back room and was tugging at her top in his desperation to attract her attention.

"Shhh, there's an *orang barat* here," she told him.

But whatever he wanted was far too important for him to pause to listen to her.

"How do you use this?" I tried again.

She turned to answer my question but he was tugging at the filmy cloth.

"*Diam, ada orang barat,*" she told him again. He was still not listening, so she shone the torch on my face and I smiled down at the little boy.

He turned and saw my bared teeth and blond hair illuminated

by the torch. As I saw his little face crease into a mask of horror I stepped back and held up my hands to calm him. It was too late. He let out a blood-curdling shriek and I threw my arms across my face and reeled out of the door still clutching my *Minyak Angin*. (I had to return the next day – in broad daylight - to pay for it.)

Paul was already *mandi*-ing on the platform when I got down to the river. Despite the screaming, that echoed out through the night, he was whistling cheerfully.

"There seems to be a dedicated party attitude prevalent in this town," he said. "There are coloured lights emanating from every other building, surely there must be some music and a beer . . . What's all the yelling about? Sounds like someone's being murdered up there."

I shrugged: "Beats me."

We dived into the dark river to rinse the soap off, trying not to think about crocodiles. A truck rattled to a halt on the bridge. A row of red lights twinkled from the roof. "They even have mobile bawdy-houses here," said Paul. "We're lucky to get a fishmonger back home."

A moment later we were hailed from the darkness of the bank: "What news?"

"Good news!" we chorused as expected. I could just make out disembodied bleached jeans hovering above suspicious-looking white shoes.

"Where goin'?"

"We live here," I chuckled, "We're *orang indonesia*."

Paul towelled himself off with his sarong and wandered away, still whistling. A moment later I followed and found him on the road talking to the owner of the faded jeans.

"We know this fella from somewhere," Paul said, turning towards me.

The man and I started weaving around each other jokingly, like two dogs sizing each other up. At the same instant as the moonlight caught his face he saw the recognition in my own eyes - it was the Citizen Smith of the Dayak world.

He and two friends were trading their plastic goods and bottles between Putussibau and Pontianak. The Chinese girl (with the lunatic brother) had told him that two *orang barat* were bathing in the river. Although we were over three hundred miles away he had assumed that we were probably the two foreigners who he had shuttled into Pontianak almost a month ago.

After a few beers at the *rumah makan* Citizen Smith and his friends reluctantly departed to get back on the road. We spent the rest of the evening learning from Anih, the 'barmaid,' the correct way to prepare and take betel nut.

Betel nut comes from a palm tree and when chewed it produces the copious amounts of scarlet saliva that are responsible for the 'nose-bleed' stains all over the footpaths of South East Asia. To release the mildly tranquillising juice the nut must be taken with an alkali and it is the lime, most commonly used in this capacity, that causes the rotten teeth and blackened gums of habitual users.

Anih first placed a smear of gritty lime on a leaf and then folded two peanut size pieces of the dark brown nut into it. She held another chunk of betel on top of the package.

"Very good for toothache," she said tucking the whole package into her cheek. "Make-th th-trong teeth."

"What about the black, bad teeth some people have?"

"Wah no! Thath the lime!"

I accepted this explanation and refrained from pointing out that the lime is necessary to activate the betel juice.

Despite years of chewing betel the old lady had somehow retained a perfect set of clean white teeth. She maintained her regal silence and left it to Anih to educate us in the intricacies of the drug.

Anih was in her early twenties, wore her hair in a short bob and had extremely deep, bright eyes. Her husband was a long distance lorry-driver and they had two children. Their son, who was nine years old, already chewed betel nut at home although his school strictly forbade it. Anih and her mother were amazed that we don't have betel in England and absolutely scandalised that English girls are allowed to smoke. Only 'bad girls' smoke in Kalimantan.

Paul and I persevered with the betel but apart from almost uncontrollable quantities of a very bitter scarlet juice it had no discernible effect. The juice makes you sick if you swallow it, so you have to spit about every ten seconds. And if you spit every ten seconds for quarter of an hour you begin to feel sick anyway.

"I think I'm just gonna th-pit my wad and go to sleep," said Paul, dribbling. Some people have no stamina.

It rained heavily during the night and when we woke we were shocked to see the whole *kampong* under two feet of water. Only the main road rose above the water level and the luckier children were being shuttled from their front doors in canoes. Others had waded to the road and were now sitting on the steaming tarmac pulling on their socks and shiny black school shoes.

The river had risen three metres and was lapping over the veranda of the Chinese store. Most of the houses were high enough on their stilts to avoid being flooded but we were trapped for three days whilst the water level dropped.

Despite its lack of stores 'Kalis was a revelation for shopping. I found chocolate flavoured condensed milk, bubble-gum flavoured biscuits, sugared shrimp-puffs, and more exotic medicine. 'Four Seasons Medicated Oil' was sixty-seven percent peppermint oil and in four languages it promised to cure cuts, sprains, colds, fever, gout, toothache, seasickness, insect bites, vertigo and plague (for the latter take 3-10 drops in tea or hot water).

Everybody in the village knew us by now and we were greeted with shouted calls whenever we strolled down to the river: '*sudah mandi, pak?*' or '*mau kake?*' Once there was the novelty of a wonderfully mangled attempt at English: "'Ello John. What are you?"

Our days passed slowly. We used up our reading material sparingly, and I wrote my diary. In the evening I played badminton on the wood-chip court by the bridge with Yacob or the Chinese girl's teenage brother (he was very competitive and usually beat me). It was nice to see that her smallest brother was sometimes out playing. He was almost a normal, happy child again.

One afternoon, whilst Paul was dozing, I met Yacob on the pontoon having his afternoon *mandi*.

"What news, *pak?*"

"*Kabar biasa,*" came Yacob's customary reply – the usual news.

But it wasn't. As Paul would say, Yacob was nurturing a party attitude. What's more he had a plan to bring this end about and he wasted no time in roping me in. We would take his motorbike down to a longhouse he knew and there we would be able to buy *tuak*.

"*Diam, diam pak,*" he winked and tapped his nose – a gesture that seemed so out of place that I guessed he must have got it from the *televisi*. Unexpectedly he threw his head back and roared "*Banyak ramai!*" - making complete nonsense of his urge to secrecy.

"*Banyak ramai,*" I grinned trying to look as if I meant it. I was quite keen on this 'big party' idea - I just wished it could be done without being subjected to *tuak*. Yacob had been very hospitable, however, and I had no doubt who was being proposed as the sponsors of this little *ramai*. We couldn't refuse.

"What longhouse?" I asked.

"*Orang taman.*"

"Ah, I know them. We've been there."

Yacob seemed aggrieved at this - every Tom, Dick and Harry can get *tuak* these days.

Twenty minutes later I clung onto the pillion seat of Yacob's Suzuki as he went whining up through the gears and we left 'Kalis behind in a cloud of dust. Yacob wound the throttle back hard and the bike's thin tyres skittered on the loose stones. Even before we approached the first shaded bend I had the feeling that I was very much going to regret the absence of racing leathers during this trip. In only shorts, vest and flip-flops I was feeling extremely vulnerable. By the time we leaned through the second bend I had the large plastic petrol drum - the receptacle for our *tuak* - braced against my left thigh. I figured that any minute now it was this flank that would hit the road and I hoped to use the drum to take some of the force out of my first bounce.

Whenever we came to a curve Yacob would accelerate hard as if - *inshallah* - our momentum alone would carry us smoothly through any obstacle.

By the fourth bend I had my system worked out. Just as he wound the power on I would lean forward and yell some inane question into his ear. Fear taught me quickly how to balance the question so that it was just slightly mumbled. This cunning ploy made it necessary for him to slacken off so that he could hear. Of course it also made him turn around to look at me but (I weighed it up carefully) at least we would crash slower. A slow crash would be fine by me.

Incredibly we reached the junction by the airstrip and skidded onto the dirt track. On this last stretch Yacob took every bend at an angle of forty degrees on the single-lane track. The corners were continuous and he hurled the bike from side to side. In dread terror my mind simply refused to supply me with any more questions and I just gritted my teeth and hoped.

Shaken, dusty and thoroughly amazed, I arrived unscathed (at least externally) at the longhouse. I had some thinking to do though: I had just experienced what the sober Yacob (Dr Jekyll) was like on a motorbike. On the return trip I would be travelling with Mr Hyde.

The headman of the Taman was surprised to see me back and, as Yacob was obviously a regular customer, we partook of three complimentary jugs of *tuak* between us. Yacob showed not the remotest sign of refusing and . . well, I'm just a sucker for rituals.

It had been several years since I had ridden a motorbike and, as I plummeted down the notched pole in my hurry to get to the bike first, I was confident of no more than merely being a safer rider than Mr Hyde. I was piloting to the best of my ability - with lurching Yacob swinging three gallons of *tuak* behind me - when we came buzzing back into sleepy 'Kalis.

Paul was no more optimistic than I had been about the evening's debauchery, or our prospects for remaining in good health in the coming days. We started drinking at a corner table in the *rumah makan*. Our hospitable natures were emphasised by the huge quantity of this rancid beverage that we were faced with and we invited everyone who entered the store to have a drink with us. They all wanted to pose for a photo. Two old men, dyed-in-the-wool *orang melayu*, refused to drink and yet still insisted on being photographed raising their glasses.

Yacob decided to shift the party to, of all places, the Nangakalis Police station. There, all the revellers, except Yacob, Paul and myself were Javanese policemen. We drank in the secrecy of their 'barracks' despite the fact that everyone in 'Kalis knew what was going on by now.

The warm, carefree atmosphere of Dayak drinking in the *hulu,* was replaced here by a disagreeable furtiveness. The Javanese policemen, not much more than boys, missed their home and drank to oblivion. There was some mention of a karaoke but Paul and I pleaded ignorance, trying our best not to understand this word and we seemed to get away with it. After a reasonable time - in our opinion - we made our excuses and left.

But the damage was already done. I had already been to the river once with diarrhoea but whether the cause was *tuak*, boiled pink guavas, chocolate flavoured condensed milk or the confusing melange of all three I could not say.

Later that night the drunken policemen came to drag us away from our lodgings and frog-marched us across the bridge to the army camp. Most of the *kampong* was waiting on the parade ground for the rock band to start playing. The policemen, inspired by Yacob, began to circulate the rumour that the *orang barat* were all set to perform.

A uniformed official strode out of the guardroom straight to Paul and me and in a brisk, even slightly rough, manner ordered us inside. He searched frantically through filing cabinets and drawers. I wondered if he was looking for a gun with which to arrest us for some misdemeanour we may have committed, but he merely wanted us to sign the visitor's book. Paul signed in and I looked around at the photographs on the walls. There were parades, exercises, rifle ranges, drills, countless volleyball games . . and a snapshot of somebody getting a vasectomy.

An hour later an already sub-standard rock group hit the lowest point of their career when they accompanied Paul and me in a memorable rendition of The Righteous Brother's 'Loving Feeling.' I am sure that under normal circumstances we both know the words to this classic. Somehow, in front of sixty young Indonesians (and backed by a five-piece band who had apparently never heard the song) we managed to invent two completely new sets of lyrics. Then we each battled to prove, by volume alone, that our own was the original story line.

I like to imagine, looking back, that what we lacked in talent we made up for in enthusiasm and operatic posturing. That's what I *like* to imagine.

Chapter Six

Carry on up the Hulu

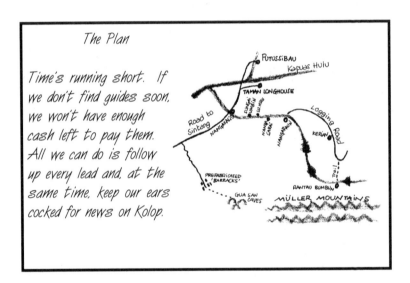

The Plan

Time's running short. If we don't find guides soon, we won't have enough cash left to pay them. All we can do is follow up every lead and, at the same time, keep our ears cocked for news on Kolop.

We awoke to the gut-wrenching pangs that are just another part of a *tuak* overdose. It helped to convince us that it was time to get back on the road. We had questioned everyone we came across in 'Kalis without finding out anything new about the Mandai Hulu route across the mountains. One of Yacob's policemen friends had, however, pointed us in the direction of some caves called Gua San. I tracked him down in his barracks and asked him to tell me everything he knew about them.

They were two hours from 'Kalis in the western foothills of the Müllers. Teams of men worked there, collecting edible birds' nests from the caverns in the mountainside.

"In Gua San you can find guides," the policeman said, "and maybe even a direct route into Central Kalimantan."

The *polisi* showed me his collection of 'confiscated' birds' nests. They ranged from small, almost transparent dishes to fluffy black cups up to three inches long. The smallest and cleanest are the most valuable made almost purely from the saliva of the brown-rumped swiftlet although it was once believed that the substance was dried sea foam which the birds collected during their migrations.

The Chinese have been trading for Borneo birds' nests for over twelve hundred years and the methods of collection in many caves have changed very little throughout this period. The collectors shin up to the cave's ceiling along poles made from interlocking bamboo sections which are secured with rattan guy-ropes. A rag tied between their insteps allows them to grip the polished wood and in this way they often work at a height of eighty feet. By the light of a resin candle they hack away at the ceiling with a long 'hoe' and chop down the tiny nests, along with baby birds and young bats.

I was struck by the Chinese talent for making *haute cuisine* out of such unattractive ingredients. In their natural state the nests are a haven for minute ticks and larvae feeding on the rubbery saliva and the droppings of the baby birds. I could have looked at these nests from now until Doomsday and never would I have said to myself, "Now these little suckers would make the chief ingredient in a very nourishing and flavoursome pot of soup."

The truth is that, on their own, edible birds' nests are neither of these things. They are entirely tasteless (if properly cleaned) and take on only the flavour of other ingredients. But the Chinese have invested birds' nests with fabulous curative properties, and the high prices (due to the dangers or difficulties of their collection) probably help to augment this belief.

It has been estimated that the swifts and bats in the huge cave at Niah, in Sarawak, eat (and recycle) between six and seven tons of insects a day. The collectors build *pondoks* covered with plastic sheets to protect themselves from the constant drizzle of guano. In the interminable darkness they share their homes with snakes, rats, bats, spiders, poisonous centipedes, hairy earwigs and huge cave-crickets with mandibles which are powerful enough to chomp through eggshells. Often the men will not see daylight for weeks at a time whilst, like Tolkien's Gollum, they hoard their 'precious treasure.'

In the most isolated caves the collectors work together for protection: in the dark lawlessness men are murdered for several months' gleanings. The trails to and from the caves are the haunt of bandits who are ready to relieve a homeward bound prospector of his harvest - and often his head.

The policeman gave me some parting advice: *"Hati, hati* in the caves, *pak.* Don't trust anyone!"

Arno, a friend of Yacob's, knew some men who were working at Gua San and kindly agreed to take me on his motorbike to meet them. I was glad that I would have an introduction but I memorised a list of inane questions to ask Arno on the way.

I never saw the caves at Gua San. They were several miles further into the forest from the collection of prefabricated huts where Arno skidded his bike to a halt.

We went up onto the platform of a long dormitory where a gang of men were lounging away the early afternoon heat. Many of them were wearing camouflage clothes. Arno introduced me to Onjei. Dressed only in ragged camo trousers, with an ostentatious bush-knife in his belt, Onjei looked like the sort of man who might not appreciate an enquiry into why he had 'Carwyn' tattooed on his fore-arm. Instead I passed around my Gudang Garam and folded out the map.

Everybody leaned in close and we quickly got down to business. Onjei had walked over to *Kal Teng* (Central Kalimantan) three years ago. He pulled at his moustache thoughtfully as I talked, but seemed enthusiastic from the outset about joining our expedition. I said that we would still need one more guide and was very happy when he suggested that Arno could come along. They accepted the same offer that I had made to Kolop and we shook hands immediately. I was surprised that it had been so easy.

Our new route would cut only across the eastern edge of the Müllers and I was disappointed that we would be compromising the expedition by starting so far away from the unexplored land that we had come to see. But as I would be paying Onjei and Arno by the day I might easily be able to convince them to lead us deeper into the mountains when we were already moving. If we were to contact the Punan it would only be by travelling slowly and I was very happy for our guides to stretch the crossing in their wish to earn more money.

I would go back with Arno to collect Paul and our *barang* and we could all leave in the morning. We leaned back in the shade of the veranda and chatted – we could discuss the finer points of the trip later when I returned with Paul. My questions about the birds' nests were coyly sidestepped and I steered to more general topics. With a feeling of impending doom I watched Onjei and Arno sidle quietly into the dormitory. After a decent interval I followed them casually.

Four armchairs and a coffee table seemed strangely out of place on the rattan mats. Arno rose to give me his seat as I shook hands with a hawk-nosed man and a pockmarked Indian. I realised that I had not sat in an armchair for over a month.

The jokes and light-hearted chatter were noticeably absent in here. I kept my smile, and asked the two older men if they themselves knew *Kal Teng*. They shrugged their shoulders, as if to say 'well, after all why would we?'

The Indian asked me how much I was paying his friends. As I answered I noticed Onjei shift uneasily.

"You forget," said Hawk-nose, mercifully avoiding the confrontation, "they will have *takut* (fear) to come back alone. You must have at least four guides."

"You mean I need two more guides to look after my original guides?"

"That's right."

"Wait," said the Indian, "there may be another way." He began scribbling numbers on a sheet of paper and we waited in strained silence for his calculations.

It seemed that the cheapest way for my guides to get home after the expedition would be to take a boat from Kalasin to Balikpapan on the coast and a ship from there to Pontianak . . via Jakarta, ". . and from Pontianak they can fly back to Putussibau," the Indian concluded happily.

"They can fly! Why can't they take the bus, or even a boat like I did?"

"Oh, okay. They can take a bus," he conceded.

I gaped in disbelief and looked at his calculations. By his reckoning the hire of two guides for three weeks would cost almost two thousand dollars.

Showing anger or impatience achieves nothing in Asia and I knew that there was no point in even haggling from this basis. So, after a moment of small talk, I got up to leave. It was partly a bluff - I hoped that they would reopen the conversation.

They didn't and Onjei acted surprisingly 'un-Indonesian' by refusing to shake hands when Arno and I left. I realised then that I had lost not only the chance of guides from Gua San, but also the use of this route for Paul and myself. I was not enthusiastic to be seen entering the jungle alone from this point.

That evening Paul and I discussed our options in depth. Things were looking bad. If we didn't find guides within two or three weeks we would be too poor to hire them anyway. Much as we had enjoyed our experiences with the Da'an it was awful to think of returning to England without even seeing the Müllers. Had it not been for the commitment that came with our sponsorship we would have been tempted to look about for some other adventure: perhaps a quick trip into the Apokayan region of East Kalimantan before lack of funds forced us home.

I believed that I understood the dangers involved in an unguided crossing of the Müllers and I did not want the responsibility of suggesting it. I was glad when Paul broached the subject: "Why don't we try to cross the mountains alone? It's got to be better than just going home without trying."

So we decided to take the *speed* back up the Mandai and try to buy (or commission) a strong dugout in Rantau Bumbun with which to paddle up the river. We had more than enough rice and we were carrying fishing equipment and snare lines with which, if necessary, we could trap small animals – maybe.

Our confidence would undoubtedly have been far greater had we been equipped with a GPS. Only one global positioning system on the market was powerful enough to receive satellite signals through Borneo's dense tree cover and it had been both too heavy and too expensive for our means.

Still, how hard could it be? You just keep paddling upriver and you have to arrive in the mountains, right?

Only time would teach us how naïve we really were.

Hating the idea of compounding our retreat, even marginally, we caught a bus back to Putussibau to restock our provisions. Wandering across the shaky boardwalks of the market I finally came to the conclusion that my British Army jungle-boots were a major weak link in my preparations for the trek. Even on the relatively short hikes between the Da'an villages they had quickly caused blisters which became septic within hours in the humidity. My Dayak toenail was uglier than ever and had now swollen so that it sometimes became painfully wedged under the steel toecap of my boot.

Before leaving England we had tried every old wife's tale in the book for softening leather, as well as those of a few veteran squaddies. Our boots had been through an adventure all their own by the time we limped onto the plane at Heathrow. They were determined never to forgive us.

In a fit of blind optimism, I purchased a rather nifty pair of Indonesian boots. It was the words 'Big Benz,' scrawled across their fake suede flanks, that swung the decision.

We went to see Tomas, our friendly Chinese trader, and bought another six boxes of Gudang Garam, some more *kopi*, condensed milk, disposable lighters, sugar, salt and the large plastic sheet that would be our home for the next few weeks. I asked Tomas, who was happier than ever, if any other *orang barat* had been through Putussibau since we were last here.

"No," he said, "but I heard that there are two in Nangakalis."

We paid Yacob for the rent of his room and I left my jungle-boots as a parting gift. As had happened with the pony-tailed Iban in Pontianak I was unable to refuse when he insisted on swapping shirts as a remembrance. I traded one that I had bought from a wily hustler in Tangier.

Just before the *speed* was about to leave Paul decided to post a package of fifty films, the entire harvest of the trip so far. The post office was closed, so we boxed them up and left them, and sufficient money, with Anih. The idea was that we would collect them from poste restante in Kuching. They never arrived and are possibly still in limbo somewhere between 'Kalis, Putussibau, Jakarta, Kuala Lumpur and Kuching.

We had decided to call at Kolop's home in Nanga Sarai to check with him before we left on our own. The water level had dropped again and when we reached the *kampong* we were faced with another spectacular gringo-trap.

I started up the notched pole confidently – perhaps too confidently. Halfway up I started to wobble. I windmilled my arms and tried in vain to regain my balance. The bank didn't look impossibly steep so I decided to make a run for it. The moment my feet hit the ground they shot backwards. A dramatic fall was only avoided by the fact that my legs jammed solidly between the pole and the muddy bank.

Only by wriggling did I manage to free myself and slide slowly and pathetically into the shallows of the river. "It's okay, I'm alright!" I shouted at the bemused crowd, peering over the ridge above me. Although they stared, wide-eyed, throughout this performance every one of them (with the notable and noisy exception of Paul) managed to keep a straight face.

The houses in Nanga Sarai were much more modern in design than those in the other Da'an *kampong*. They were bigger, had more rooms and were invariably fronted by a hillbilly-type veranda rather than the standard working platform.

We were quickly directed towards Kolop's ancestral seat. It was like the other houses in every way except that his family had acquired a surplus of paint from somewhere and the whole building was gleaming white. We kicked off our flip-flops and climbed the five white steps to the open front door. Three men were sitting in the middle of a bare room. We shook hands, saying that we were friends of Kolop, and went through the familiar procedure of folding out our map and passing around Gudang Garam. A woman shuffled in from the back room with a jug of *beram*.

Kolop was not in town. He was back down the river at a *kampong* called Sungai Umbin: we had probably passed him on our way upriver.

Kolop's mother lay groaning and coughing weakly in the next room. I asked tentatively whether she had medicine. I was reluctant to take on the responsibility of handing out drugs about which my knowledge was so limited but it was obvious that she was in a lot of pain and that we were carrying pills that could ease it.

I was relieved to learn that the *orang misionaris* (Pak Harold's friend) who lived here was coming to visit her regularly. He had a well-stocked medicine chest and was helping her as much as possible.

Like most Da'an men our three new friends were experienced travellers although they had all wandered to different regions. They were interested in our plans and had heard a lot about the high valleys of the Mandai and the Müllers. With a renewed thirst, we began to collect the information that may be vital for our own attempt on the mountains.

It was Kolop's brother-in-law who raised his voice loudest in offering advice on our route. "Wah! Don't go alone. Too much danger. Four, five men okay. Two never. Take Kolop and maybe Ajis."

"Yes, Ajis coming back soon. He'll go," said another man.

It was the first time we had heard of Ajis and yet they hit on the idea of his guiding us with such decisiveness that we wondered if Ajis, and not Kolop, was the natural conclusion to this prolonged quest.

The five of us sat in a noisy huddle around the map and, three hours and four jugs of *beram* later, Paul and I left with a sketched map of the Mandai Hulu. We were able to check this map later and even its scale was incredibly accurate – especially since the men were going only on information that they had heard from others who had been there.

Wayfarers from other Dayak tribes would occasionally pass through Nanga Sarai and the villagers were used to seeing visitors. There was always somebody sleeping in the *kepala's* 'guess-how.' This was the biggest house that we had seen in the Da'an villages and the 'guess-how' consisted of three rooms along a corridor leading to Pak Dakun's private *bilik*.

He was short, stocky and very friendly. His moustache and prolific tattoos gave him an appearance that was totally unlike a Da'an. The swirling tattoos had been collected during his wanders amongst the Kayan tribe of the Mahakam River.

The Kayan are the acknowledged masters of the art in Borneo. Even the Iban of Sarawak, famous for their tattoos, admit that many of their designs came originally from the Kayan. The Da'an in general dislike tattoos, labelling them barbaric.

That evening, whilst his wife prepared rice and fern tips for dinner, I asked Pak Dakun what he thought about our chances of crossing the Müllers alone.

"There are wicked people in the mountains," he warned us.

"Robbers?"

"Yes, and *orang pemotong*," he drew his finger across his throat and winked happily. "Very wicked!"

We went for a stroll along the riverbank. There was a small clapboard kiosk neatly positioned on the edge of a gravel volleyball court at the centre of the *kampong*. We bought cans of warm 'Stim Cola' and a packet of sweet shrimp puffs from the smiling kiosk owner. Merely with the thought of going to the mountains my chocoholism was beginning to rear its ugly head. Shrimp puffs were just not the answer.

"Just imagine," I said, inspecting the kiosk's meagre stock, "these kids have *never* eaten a Mars bar."

"Yeah, and never seen Baywatch," added Paul. "That's no way to raise your children is it?"

In deference to Kolop's reputation, we had decided that I should take a boat back down to Sungai Umbin to try to contact him one last time. If I was unsuccessful we would leave alone the following day.

The kiosk owner asked if we had met the *orang misionaris* yet and, with a sinking feeling, we agreed that it was something that we should do. So I settled on the plan that Paul could go to visit him whilst I went downriver to try to find the elusive Kolop. Paul settled on the plan that we would *both* go to visit the missionary and then *I* would go to find Kolop.

We followed directions through a thick stand of bamboo at the edge of the *kampong* and, stepping back out into the sunlight, we were greeted by such a cliché American scene that we stopped dead in our tracks. In the shade of a timber bungalow two fair-haired boys in cut-off jeans were shooting a basketball into a wire hoop. We called out as we approached and they looked back, shouted "Hi!" . . and then turned back to their game.

Luckily John, their father, heard our call and padded around the corner. He was a big man, broad-shouldered and sun-tanned. His blond fringe was slicked down with sweat and, as he held out a meaty paw, he gave the impression of a tough frontier-settler of the Wild West. And this, I suppose, is what he was.

"We don't see many visitors here," he said. "I'm glad you called. Dakun told me that there were some Brits staying with him."

Margie, John's wife, emerged from the kitchen with a warm smile and a chilled papaya. She had the same lithe, tanned appearance as her sons. "If there's anything you need while you're here just let us know," she said.

We didn't need a moment to consider and, whilst Margie rushed back in to dig out some reading material, we sat in the shade and listened to John's tales of the good life in Nanga Sarai. His conversation was light and amusing. I could just picture him sat on the back veranda happily munching his solitary durians – "Margie 'n' the boys won't allow them in the house on account of their smell, but I can't resist 'em. Trouble is, they don't do me any good – for a week after, when you go to the toilet everything stinks of durian."

"Awful things!" shouted his wife from the front room. John chuckled.

As far as the Da'an were concerned John displayed an obvious respect for their ways although he was obliged also to keep a distance between them. The 'familiarity breeds contempt' maxim seemed to be something that Protestant Missionaries in the West Kalimantan *hulu* are very aware of. There is very little danger that they are about to go native.

We spent a pleasant hour chatting to this happy couple. They never mentioned their religion once; perhaps they were sensitive enough to take their cue from us and we both liked them all the more for it. We walked away feeling relieved that our opinions of missionaries had been balanced and even with a vague envy of John and Margie's happiness in what would, for many people, have been a lonely life.

They had been living amongst the Da'an for thirteen years and I was intrigued by the fact that, at first, they had lived in Nanga Raun alongside Pak Harold's family. I found it inconceivable that the two missionaries, with such contrasting characters, could ever have worked together.

After seven years John's house burnt down whilst he and his family were away and they decided to resettle here in Nanga Sarai.

That afternoon I dutifully took the *speed* back to Sungai Umbin, two hours downriver. The return trip would be my fifth on this part of the Mandai and I hoped it would be the last.

Sungai Umbin seemed to be deserted except for a Chinese trader who told me that, yet again, I had passed Kolop on the river. He was with the other villagers at the *ladang* in Sungai Umbin Hulu. Oh well, since the sprawling metropolis of Sungai Umbin itself was a collection of six huts, *Upper* Sungai Umbin couldn't be very far away. Could it?

"No, not far," my adviser smiled, "Only two miles . . but only by river."

The sun was high and, apart from the trader and me, nothing but a few *babis* and chickens moved amongst the *pondoks*. The children were in school, the men were at the *ladang* and I was unable even to hire a canoe to paddle up there. The next *speed* would be by in four hour's time.

It was hot and Madiah, the trader, very kindly invited me to wait in his *bandung kecil*. This was a smaller version of the floating stores that we saw in the towns along the Kapuas. In appearance it was very like an English canal boat.

Madiah brought coffee, sarongs, shampoo, soap, books, coloured pencils, *Minyak Angin* (excellent for treating mosquito bites, he told me), sardines, Milo, instant noodles, fishing line and sweets to the *kampongs* on the Mandai Hulu. He returned with rice and the raw rubber whose stink had become forever ingrained in the timber of the boat. As we drank *kopi* I questioned Madiah about *bandung kecils*. I had seen an abandoned hull in 'Kalis and it had got me dreaming.

He figured that seven hundred dollars would buy a sturdy boat with a reasonable engine and that I could very easily hire skilled carpenters to help me fix it up. He passed me a cushion and I lay back with the scent of clove cigarettes, rubber and mosquito coils in my nostrils and day-dreamed about cruising the rivers of Borneo in one of these wonderful boats. I'd have a barbecue with a removable canopy on the large stern platform, my dining room would be on the roof, a mattress at the stern would be my bed and I would work on a fold-up writing desk in the bow. I'd decorate the walls with carvings, swords and sarongs that I would collect as I drifted peacefully among the *kampong* and longhouses.

By the time I heard the *speed's* engine my *bandung kecil* was halfway up the Mekong River, heading towards China.

As I jumped aboard the Muslim boatman jokingly asked if I wanted a job as his lookout, since I probably knew the river better than anyone else by now. Back, yet again, on the numbing seats I was less than usually receptive to the conversation of my fellow passengers - until I realised that one of them was called Ajis.

"The Ajis who is a friend of Kolop's family - who was in Putus' selling *gaharu?*"

"Same-same," said the lad next to him, "and he is going back up into the mountains now to collect more."

My conversation with Ajis was carried out almost exclusively through this talkative intermediary. His name was Addin and he was a teacher in Rantau Bumbun. I quickly found out much more about Addin than I could about Ajis and I was trying not to appear impatient when we pulled over to a rotting pontoon on the riverbank.

"What's here?" I asked Ajis.

"*Ladang,*" said Addin. If Ajis was a ventriloquist I wondered where his hand was.

There was a shout from the top of the bank, a flash of flowery sports bag and here was Kolop sliding down to us. "*Apa kabar, pak?*" he said with a grin.

"*Kabar baik,* Pak Bacoc - where goin'?"

"We're going to the Müllers aren't we?" It was all arranged. He knew very well that the *orang barat gila* were looking for him and he would be ready to leave in the morning. ". . And Pak Ajis is coming with us." He said.

I looked at Ajis in surprise.

"Of course!" laughed Addin. "It's all arranged."

I tried to find out exactly *how* it had all been arranged but my words were quickly swamped by Kolop's excited talk about the *ramai* we would have that night in Nanga Sarai.

Paul was also delighted to see Kolop and the three of us managed to have a brief, semi-private meeting in our room. I broke open the packet of sweets that I had bought from Madiah and was horrified to realise that they were durian flavoured. We gave them to Pak Dakun's children and they walked around for the next few hours with noxious durian breath.

Kolop and Ajis would combine the expedition with a *gaharu* -collecting trip and so we would have to carry sufficient rice to enable them to stay an extra two months in the mountains. We would need to buy a canoe in Rantau Bumbun and I agreed that when they returned Kolop could keep the canoe as a bonus and I would pay Ajis extra on his fee. The deal was struck and we strolled through the sunset to the kiosk and, although Ajis was absent, we toasted the success of our expedition with the kiosk owner.

Wavering Kal Tang melodies drifted off the platform of a large square *pondok*, down a set of steps and rippled across the volleyball court towards us. Kolop needed no further invitation and he led the way.

My eyes took a moment to adjust to the gloom. The *pondok* was already packed with sweaty bodies. A dozen people were dancing and ten more sat around the walls. Kolop was giving everyone his roguish grin and in the strips of sunlight slicing through the rickety walls I could see returned the gruesome gash of the betel users.

A wizened old woman in a rust-coloured sarong tottered over to us. She was struggling with a tray loaded with an enormous metal teapot and five enamel cups. She made her rounds at such a pace that we were offered a drink every few minutes and it was no wonder that most of the congregation was already *beram*-ed up.

I sat against the wall and chatted to an attractive young couple with a small baby. They were only mildly tipsy and I found refuge in their conversation from the more boisterous drunks in the place - for the time being.

When I next looked across the room Kolop was already grooving and Paul was surrounded by three ladies who, with great hilarity, were teaching him the graceful (not among Paul's many strong points) struts of *Kal Teng* dancing.

I was soon hauled to my feet and, as dusk came and went, - and the huge teapot continued to release its charge of goodwill - the party became increasingly surreal. The shiny, toothless faces leered and grimaced in the wavering candlelight and most of the male dancers had stripped down to shorts. The old woman was still delivering *beram* but she was stumbling and cackling to herself now. A lunatic cavorted violently through the crowd. People kept introducing him to me: *"Orang gila!"* and screwing their fingers into their temples. He guffawed and nodded his head vigorously.

The music blared out of a beaten old tape player but the door to its battery-compartment had fallen off. Its owner insisted that he had to dance with it on his shoulder and consequently every ten minutes or so the batteries would cascade out. Like some Da'an version of musical chairs everyone would stop dancing and crawl around on the floor, rounding up the missing batteries. But the *orang gila* didn't seem to notice that the music had stopped; he would carry on gyrating, ever more violently, taking advantage of the extra space.

I was disgusted to realise that I seemed to be noticeably worse off than Paul in the graceful department. I looked around for an escape and through the doorway I saw the cheerful young guy who owned the kiosk. He was watching alone from the darkness.

"What news, *pak*?" he smiled.

I had only ever seen him sitting in his kiosk, chatty and cheerful, and when I got closer I was shocked to see that he had no legs. They were missing from mid-thigh and the short stumps were thinner than my wrists. I went to fetch us both a cup of *beram* and we sat and swatted mosquitoes and laughed at Paul until Kolop came to drag me once again back to the dance.

Later that night, for no particular reason, Paul suddenly declared an irresistible appetite for fried eggs and we stumbled out into the blackness in search of chickens.

The rain was hammering down the next morning and the Mandai had risen considerably during the night. I sat on the veranda watching the muddy river and reading Margie's *The Secret Annie Oakley*, which had saved me from another reread of *Siddhartha*. But the weather can change in an instant in Borneo and the sun had burnt off the last of the puddles long before the sound of a motor droned up the valley. We had not been able to find Kolop or Ajis all morning. Knowing that it would do no good to chase them we were resigned now to leaving alone if necessary.

We left the pontoon at Nanga Sarai with a sinking heart and trepidation at the thought that now, against all local advice, we were going to have to attempt the crossing alone. As we rounded the corner a figure waved us down from the bank and, with his precious floral bag stuffed into a rattan backpack, Kolop jumped in. He was surprised that we had even doubted him. I was too confused by our constantly changing fortunes even to ask where Ajis was and we never saw him again.

At the last pontoon in Nanga Sarai (behind John's house) Pak Harold's three older children joined us. They were travelling back to Nanga Raun and, having heard that we were present at the previous night's debauchery, they were suitably icy. Kolop was obvious in his distrust of missionaries, which was in direct proportion to his appetite for girls and *beram*.

We were excited to see a pair of hornbills labouring up the river ahead of us. With their four-foot wingspans and huge beaks, their silhouettes looked like flying crosses. Kolop shouted that it was a very good omen for our expedition that they were flying from left to right across our path. Amongst most Dayak tribes birds are regarded as harbingers of good or bad luck depending upon their behaviour and hornbills are often worshipped as the earthly incarnations of deities.

Perhaps the hornbill appeals to the macho Iban in particular because of the male's habit of walling his mate up in a hollow tree whilst she incubates his eggs. He is then, however, faced with the formidable task of finding her sufficient food and pushing it to her through a slit in the 'prison walls.' If he should be killed whilst the hen is still incarcerated another male will take over his duty and look after her until such time as she can break out of the hole and find food for herself and the growing chicks. This form of 'adoption' is almost unknown in the bird world.

Despite the locals' religious convictions, the Chinese managed to instigate a lively trade in hornbill ivory. There are nine types of hornbill in Borneo and each gets its name from a description of the thick casque that branches from the top of its beak. This ivory was carved into anything from snuffboxes to combs and jewellery. During the Ming dynasty the horn of the helmeted hornbill (the only species with a solid casque) was worth twice as much as elephant ivory.

Pak Rejang seemed happy to see us back in Nanga Raun but

we eased our conscience at inflicting ourselves on his home so frequently by handing out as many gifts as we could spare. All being well we would not be coming back this way again.

Kolop insisted that there were some items that we had overlooked in our shopping and he took me to the *pondok* of a friend of his. His friend had all the equipment that would ever be needed for the Da'ans' hunting or *gaharu*-collecting expeditions. We bought a massive rice pot and a length of fishing net. Then we went to another house where they were carving a pig and bought some chunks of *babi* for dinner with Pak Rejang's family.

Behind the 'butchers' shop Kolop showed me a caged python. It was about six feet long and its skin seemed unhealthily dull, but perhaps it was just in the first stage of sloughing. In another cage, uncomfortably close to the snake was a Slow Loris. A ball of soft grey fur with huge black eyes and a moon face. Slow Loris is partly a misnomer; it is true that the animal climbs through the treetops so cautiously that its movements are almost unnoticeable but, when it comes within striking range of its prey, its powerful hand flashes out and another small bird has sung its last chorus.

In 1916 Robert W Shelford wrote in *A Naturalist in Borneo*:
On account of its very peculiar appearance the Slow Loris is considered by the Malays to possess magical properties, and they have many quaint recipes for employing various parts of its body for medicinal and magical purposes. A few of these may be quoted here.

The right eye dried and ground to powder and mixed with human or goat's milk and some sweet oil may be used as an eye-ointment which will make dim sight bright by the will of God. The left eye ground fine and mixed with rose water, honey and camphor (Sumatran) can be used as an eye ointment or eaten with 'sirih' [betel] leaf, the nerves of which meet together causes all who look on us to love us, and if given to a wild beast it will become tame. . . .

If its backbone is buried beneath the door of the house we can prevent thieves from entering. If the bone of its left leg be kept in the mouth during a conversation with a rajah, it will prevent his doing any acts of tyranny to us, and if we cook it with oil of snake or tiger or olive oil and rub it on the feet of a weak person, it will strengthen him. . . . If the liver be dried and a piece taken and rubbed up and given to a woman to eat it will produce in her feelings of love towards us.

Its tears, when applied to human eyeballs, are supposed to impart such clearness of sight that ghosts become visible. Its tears can be induced to flow by taking the Loris amongst a herd of cows, whereupon it will weep copiously: another plan, which sounds more reasonable, is to wrap the animal in a cloth and throw pepper in its eyes.

Loris is derived from *loeris*, the Dutch word for clown, but this specimen's vacant gaze of wonderment was replaced by a pitiful squint. One of its eyes was painfully septic, though its captors assured me that it was like that when they caught it. Even so, I hoped that it would not have to live much longer under the patient stare of the python.

The public transport system for the entire Da'an region was about to make its only trip of the week. This was the logging company's truck; as part of their contract, they were obliged to make one passenger trip every Sunday morning between Nanga Raun and the logging camp. En route the truck passed Kerian and a point on the Rantau Bumbun trail a couple of miles from the village.

Pak Rejang ferried us to the logging road and I was amazed at the size of the flotilla that paddled across the river to take advantage of this service. I wondered how everyone (and their chickens, *babis* and dogs) would be able to fit into the truck.

We waited for two hours by the sun-baked road. I went back to the shade of the riverside palms and sat with my back against the root-strewn bank to catch up with my diary. I was soon lulled by the lazy *kampong* sounds drifting across the river. Two women were scrubbing clothes on the pontoon below Pak Rejang's *pondok*. As they squatted side-by-side I could dimly hear their *omong kosong*. The cheerful gossip that accompanies every task in a Da'an village is known by this term which translates literally as 'empty chatter.' The importance of *omong kosong* is never underestimated.

The riverbank towered up from the pontoon and I wondered what the Mandai would look like in full flow. I could see dry, bleached driftwood and raffia-like flotsam hanging in the roots on the top of the bank and I knew that at this point the water level could rise twenty feet in a single night. We had to get moving now, whilst the water was low enough, if we were going to succeed in crossing the mountains.

A bell began to clang from Pak Harold's house. It echoed deeply against the looming hills and seemed so out of place that for a moment I had to struggle to bring my focus back to Borneo. I knew that the Protestant's call to prayer would go largely unheeded, however, in this village that was nominally Catholic, enthusiastically

Dayak and proudly Da'an.

When Kolop, Ajis and I had left the *speed* at Nanga Sarai yesterday, Addin had travelled directly to Nanga Raun. He came over now to complain about the lateness of the truck: "Some people say maybe three or more hours. Not good. Not good. So-o-o late. Maybe better we hire boat."

"It's a beautiful morning, Addin," I said, "there's no hurry." His face split into a huge smile and he waggled his finger, as he answered with the first English that I had heard from a Da'an.

"Time is money, mister Mark!"

Chapter Seven

The Edge of the Map

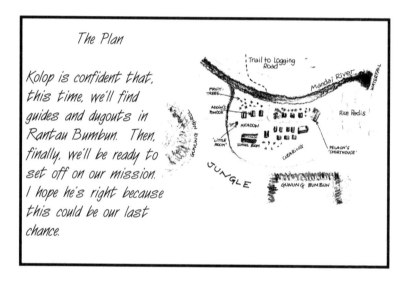

The Plan

Kolop is confident that,
this time, we'll find
guides and dugouts in
Rantau Bumbun. Then,
finally, we'll be ready to
set off on our mission.
I hope he's right because
this could be our last
chance.

The old Volvo dump truck lurched into gear. We scrabbled for a handhold and struggled to find legroom amongst the heaps of *barang*. There was no space for the passengers to sit and we lined the rim of the skip with our knuckles white on the rusty metal. We rattled along in this stance for two hours, bruised and battered as the truck bounced along the rutted track. The discomfort of the ride could not dim the Da'an good humour and *omong kosong* rebounded over the roar of the engine.

Kolop, however, was not his usual grinning self. He had crept out of the Pak Rejang's hut late the previous night. I feigned sleep as I watched him tiptoe across the bamboo platform into the darkness. Now, as the heat increased and the tipper got more crowded, Kolop's hangover was obviously becoming a torture. He caught my eye and shook his head woefully.

"*Sakit sekali*," he shouted rubbing his stomach - very sick. He grimaced as the truck rattled across a tree-trunk bridge.

At Kerian still more passengers boarded and, by the time we arrived at the junction near Rantau Bumbun, there were forty-five of us, swaying in the tipper, clinging to the roof or hanging from the cab doors.

At a point where a well-trodden track (at other times a stream) cut across the road we climbed down shakily from the Volvo's tail. Nine of us stood in the road and waved to the others who were going on to the logging camp. As the dust settled we hoisted our bags onto our backs and set off for the last two miles to the village.

"C'mon Pak Addin!" I yelled. "Time is money."

Within ten minutes my 'Big Benz' had aggravated my blisters and I was already hobbling. Paul was having the same problem with his jungle-boots and Kolop followed us at a distance in his melancholy self-pity. I turned around as we crested a low hill to see him heaving himself up the dusty track. We didn't look like three men who were out to 'conquer the wilderness.'

Addin began to sing quietly as we walked. It was a song that the Iban wharfies had sung on the roof of the *Sinar Bulan* and the tune had stuck in my mind. Addin taught me the words:

> *This destiny,*
> *To be a bachelor,*
> *Everywhere, all the people are content,*
> *Happy-hearted even whilst being poor.*

By the time we arrived at the river, and stared again at the picturesque scenery of Rantau Bumbun, we were all thirsty and caked with dust. Three dugouts ferried us across the river and we walked up onto the meadow where Paul and I turned left towards Pelaun's 'shorthouse.'

Addin grabbed my arm. "You stay in my *pondok*. My wife will cook dinner."

On Addin's veranda we unlaced our boots and breathed a sigh of relief as the pressure eased on our blisters. Strangely, Addin was the only Da'an who introduced us formally to his wife. Sriwahyuni was lissom and bright-eyed. She shook hands with a welcoming smile and went to prepare *kopi susu* and chunks of smoked fish.

We stayed with this blissful couple for a week and through them we came to appreciate the peace and contentment that was open to the villagers of Rantau Bumbun even more than the Da'an in other villages.

Rantau stretched in a band that was three buildings wide,

along the southern bank of the Mandai. There were ten stilted *pondoks*, two double-*bilik* 'shorthouses' and the weatherboard schoolroom. Four timber 'chalets' were positioned around the meadow and were responsible for the picture-postcard appearance of the village from across the river. Addin and his brother had partitioned one of these into two separate *biliks* for themselves and their families.

Rantau Bumbun also boasted the most amazing *kamar kecil* (little room) that I have ever seen. It was built on three-foot stilts, had a locking door, ventilation gaps around the top and a 'chute' that went down at sixty degrees into a ravine where the *kampong babi* congregated. It was technically a squat toilet but there was even a shaped and sanded seat raised four inches off the floor. Only the thought of what might live under this seat was enough to stop one from relaxing totally. Still, Paul reckoned that it was 'a real Sunday paper, cup o' tea and a packet of digestives bog.'

The tranquillity of Rantau Bumbun soothed us. Although we were aware of every dugout canoe and jungle-wise wanderer in the *kampong*, we soon began to forget our frustration and let the days slip by. The peace of this community was not the sort that luxuriated in idleness, however: it was a product of the constant though easy-going industriousness of the Da'an.

The old women would sit all afternoon on the working platforms, gossiping like old women all over the world (about the foibles of old men), whilst, with the dexterity of age, they split strands of green rattan to be woven into sleeping-mats. The numerous mats which they produced would gravitate freely to any *bilik* in the village that happened to need them. They passed their time like this primarily because they enjoyed doing so, and if they produced more mats than were called for they could be bundled-up and taken in Dujang's boat to be sold downriver. The proceeds would be used to buy ammunition, clothing or Gudang Garam for the villagers.

Addin and his brother shared a responsibility as the schoolteacher and each worked alternate mornings, teaching the score of children who were too young to go to school downriver. I was surprised to see that, even here, a strict code of school uniform was maintained. The kids would arrive in crisp navy and white uniforms, some even wearing polished shoes. Invariably they all arrived carrying some sort of vicious looking 'weapon' – sickles or old *parangs*. At mid-morning they would scramble out of the schoolroom and fan out in giggling groups all over the meadow to spend half an hour attacking the grass. It was through their daily toil that the meadow remained in such good condition.

The brothers decided one afternoon to tie their ammunition pouches to their waists, sling their homemade rifles over their shoulders and go hunting. Their motivation was obviously as much for fun as meat. Paul and I were very keen to join them but we were trying to let our blisters heal before we departed on our own journey. Kolop was strengthening the shoulder straps of his woven rattan backpack with new strands of cane and we sat in the shade of the veranda to watch him. The tall, rectangular basket had been decorated in star motifs, using strands of black-dyed cane.

The hunters were out all night and returned in the morning with their legs running with blood from leech bites and a dead *babi* slung between them. Word quickly spread through the village and children came running to collect a share of the pork for their families.

The rainforest, the river, the padi fields and the fruit trees were Rantau Bumbun's larder and anybody who collected provisions from it necessarily collected for the whole community. Nobody would think of climbing one of the coconut trees that leaned out over the river to pick nuts for himself alone. Pelaun climbed up and knocked down all the ripe nuts and Sriwahyuni prepared us delicious sticky rice made with sugarcane juice from the *ladang*.

One day two men arrived in Rantau from high up the Mandai with four huge fish in their dugout. There were three catfish and an awesome creature called a *salong*. It was a metre and a half long, weighed fifty pounds, and resembled a fat shark. Within ten minutes the *salong* was carved up and distributed evenly throughout the cooking pots of the village.

Back in England I was unable to find any reference whatsoever to sharks in the interior of Borneo but it seems most likely that the *salong* was a local, stockier form of bull shark. These sharks have been found in fresh water as far afield as Nicaragua, India and South Africa and one was once caught over a thousand miles up the Mississippi. The fishermen told us that the *salong* had been known to bite off a man's leg and recent studies have shown that bull sharks may have been responsible for many river mouth attacks that were previously attributed to great whites.

We were later to cross the pools where the *salong* was caught and the mystery deepened: that section of the Mandai is separated from the sea not only by four hundred miles but by three long rapids and a ten-foot waterfall.

The waterfall was a long step stretching right across from one bank to the other. It was just upriver from Rantau Bumbun and effectively separated the inhabited Mandai from the wilderness. We paddled up there one day with Pelaun and Andriatti. It was possible to climb carefully over the rocks at the foot of the falls where women and children were fishing with shrimp nets. This struck me as an unnecessarily awkward position to fish from and I noticed that their nets were bent double under the weight of the rushing water. Only when we got close did I realise that the nets were sagging under the weight not of water, but of hundreds of baby fish.

At the foot of the cascade was a shimmering cloud of sprats, leaping in their effort to get upriver. The near impossibility of any of these two-inch fry ever managing to get above the waterfall was evident in their mind-boggling numbers and in the mechanical determination of each individual. Scores of fish were flapping in exhaustion on the rocks at our feet.

Near the middle of the falls there was a rock basin, hollowed over centuries by the scouring effect of the river. I borrowed a diving mask from a small boy who was fishing with his friends and jumped in. It was eight feet in diameter and seven feet deep. The force of the current could not reach inside and below the surface it was relatively still. The water rushing over the top of the basin had formed a barrier that prevented the majority of the fish from escaping. It had become a cauldron of fluttering fish life. The water was so thick with fry – thousands of them - that they bunched against the mask and flitted all over my body. The physical density of the contents of the basin had been changed so that it was like floating in a great heap of brushed fur.

We helped the boys to haul out sagging bundles of this life force in their nets and they carried bucket loads back to share amongst the frying pans of the *kampong*.

The Dragon Jar at Kerian Longhouse

Climbing up the rapids - Mandai Hulu

A notched pole
in the village of
Rantau Bumbun

Narok
'The Ninja'

Kolop

Preparing to
cross the
Müllers

Paul, Bujang, Mark, Kolop, Narok, Bayung

First malarial attack

Paul's
leechbites

Hunting Dogs in Kampong Sopan

Paul & Narok - Djuloi
Hulu

Paulus' grave

Taj'ak
Bangkan

When we got back Addin and Kolop were in deep discussion. We noticed with trepidation that the word *beram* was never out of their conversation for long. Apparently this was one of the few things necessary to the Da'an *dolce vita* in which Rantau was no longer self-sufficient. They had run out of supplies and the beverage was perhaps the only thing that now changed hands for cash.

Luckily our old friend Dujang had reinvested the money that we had paid him for our passage back to Nanga Raun, and he was now the Rantau Bumbun *beram* baron. I gave Kolop some money and he went to visit Dujang whilst Paul and I went for our *mandi*.

There were no pontoons in Rantau. The Mandai here curved around in a wide sweep that had smoothed a narrow mud beach at the point where the *kampong* was built. At all but the highest floods the villagers could get down to the river in perfect safety; but getting back across the mud without ending up dirtier than you started seemed to be a practised art.

The two hours before sunset saw a constant stream of activity in the shallows of the river. People would call for their friends before coming down to the river so that they could combine their *mandi* with a pleasant session of *omong kosong*. Bathing was a social occasion here and everybody bathed together, although modesty was always observed and men wore shorts whilst women washed themselves under their sarongs.

Throughout the whole bathing period children splashed and fought excitedly under the eyes of watchful waves of adults. Whenever we swam out towards midstream the children would point to some imaginary ripple on the surface and do the ubiquitous 'Kalimantan crocodile clap' – a straight-armed scissors movement that unfailingly brings to mind huge slowly closing jaws. We would laugh and swim out just a little further. But the seeds of fear had been sown and we would soon be back in the shallows. Besides, we had carnivorous turtles and now the dreaded *salong* to add to our long list of things not to get bitten, stung, sucked, scratched, infected or hit on the head by.

In *The Field Book of a Jungle-wallah* (1929), Charles Hose gave some useful travel tips to wandering *orang barat*:

I once saw a crocodile seize a good-sized pig and disappear with it under water. Perhaps two minutes later, half the pig floated to the surface. In these circumstances it is hardly to be wondered at that swimming in the open river is not popular among Europeans, even in the heat of the day. The best that one can do is to confine one's self to the shallow water near the edge, with a boat moored a short distance out, in which natives sit, banging with their paddles on the side to keep the brutes away.

Due to a tireless war, waged wherever they are spotted, there are very few crocodiles left on the inhabited sections of Kalimantan's rivers. We did hear of a village on the Barito River where a woman was taken – mid-*mandi* – by a fifteen-foot monster, and an unlikely tale about a water-scooter rider in Kuching who had to make a hasty getaway when a 'floating log' suddenly reared up at him.

Over a few glasses of *beram* that evening I lost several games of chess to a young Sarawakian with a bushy hairdo and one extremely fat foot. He had been bitten on the ankle by a King Cobra a fortnight ago and for an entire week he had been in a high fever. He was now feeling better, but the skin was peeling from his bloated foot and he thought that it would be another week before he could walk on it.

The hated *ular hitam*, King Cobra, is the largest poisonous snake in the world and can grow to eighteen feet long. The Sarawakian considered himself lucky: "*Ular hitam* bite you – dead, twenty minutes. I was very worried. Wished Pak Kolop was in Rantau."

"Why?" I asked.

"You don't know? He has magic in his bag. If you're with Pak Kolop when a snake bites he can save you!"

This was the first that I had heard of any mystical powers or knowledge that Kolop possessed. Only then did it occur to me that he was more than casually watchful over his florid holdall.

There was the sound of footsteps on the veranda and Pelaun and three friends came in. He placed another two jugs of *beram* in the centre of the room and, with his smiling serenity, took a seat with his back against the wall. Merely because it is the only beverage that I have ever drank that is worse than Dujang's rancid 'milk of amnesia,' I started to describe the 'wiski' that you can buy in Thailand's Golden Triangle. The people of the hill-tribes believe that it is greatly fortified by the eight inches of pickled centipede - a creature which can nip you into a three-day delirium - that floats in the bottle. (Incidentally, the 'wiski' itself does a good impression of that same delirium but it is probable that the bite hurts less.)

Addin was visibly impressed, but then: "Wait, I show you something."

He went into the bedroom and returned after a moment carrying a large sweet-jar containing a liquid that looked like lumpy dishwater. He placed the jar on the floor and something pink swilled around in it. Unscrewing the top he lifted out what looked like a skinned Chihuahua; it was about a foot long and had grey bulges where its eyes should have been. It had tiny but perfectly formed hooves.

"What's that?" gasped Paul, instinctively reaching for his camera.

"Ginseng traditional," said Kolop, with a look that said 'you boys could be in for a real treat here if you play your cards right.'

Ginseng traditional consists of the foetus of a barking deer pickled in *arak* and it is said to give the drinker great strength. It is one of many ancient 'pick-me-ups' which the Da'an have copied from the Chinese – who else?

This brew had another couple of months to ferment before it would be ready to drink. We should be safely out in the jungle long before then.

Sriwahyuni carefully carried the heavy jar back into the bedroom and Addin, Kolop and some others started to play a complicated game of cards. The only obvious rule was that whoever was losing had to wear heavy batteries hung around his ears. After a time this became, according to Kolop, 'velly *sakit*.'

An hour later most of the *beram* was gone and Kolop was being reprimanded by the other players for cheating and moving his battery earring. Suddenly there was utter pandemonium in the room. Sriwahyuni went screaming towards the back door and two young kids dived to the floor with their arms protecting their heads. Paul and I imitated them instinctively and, noticing that everyone else was yelling, we yelled too.

Then we realised that a bat had flown in through the front door and was looping the room in desperate figures of eight, trying to find its way back out. Addin and Kolop began leaping like demented goalkeepers, trying to catch it. The rest of us jumped up to help and we all stumbled around, giggling and falling over each other. I took off my shirt and, in a clumsy *pase de pecho*, managed to trap the creature.

We manoeuvred the wriggling bundle into a corner and Addin courageously plunged his hand underneath and dragged the bat out. Whilst he was still searching for a grip on both wings the bat twisted around and sank its needle-like teeth into his thumb. There it stayed, snarling and spitting like a tiny demon whilst Kolop tried to release it by pulling its long ears. When it let go I cautiously took it from Addin, carried it by its outstretched wings onto the veranda and threw it up into the night.

Paul followed me out and, hypnotised by the incredible blanket of stars he lay down on the edge of the meadow. He was soon asleep, snoring heavily. An hour later Addin and I tried to move him but Paul was determined that he was comfortable where he was and sometime around dawn he found his own way in.

Kolop departed with his customary spontaneity at dawn the next morning. He left a message with Addin that he would be back in two days. He had a friend in Kerian who might come along with us and he believed that there might be a spare dugout in Nanga Raun.

We were as close to the Central Müllers as it was possible to get and if there was no help available we would try to make the crossing from here ourselves. But we would wait until we had exhausted all our other possibilities.

There were only two canoes in Rantau that were sturdy enough to tackle the highland reaches of the Mandai and neither was for sale. Their hulls were made from a tree trunk 'dug out' into a shallow dish. The sides of the boats were fashioned from carefully shaped planks curved around this hull and pegged into place with hardwood wedges. For a trip to Nanga Raun or above the rapids these sides had to be built up to double the height of the normal *kampong* canoes. Addin owned one of these 'expedition' dugouts and I spent a morning helping him to prepare it for his own shopping trip back down to 'Kalis. A boat like this could only be expected to last five years and this one was nearing its use-by-date.

He had collected *damar* (resin) as sap from a tree in the jungle and he dried it slowly until it was brittle enough to be pounded into powder. In this form, as long as it is kept dry, *damar* will last almost indefinitely. Naturally he prepared an extra large batch of powder and distributed it amongst others in the village whose canoes would soon need renovation.

Now Addin simply took three cupfuls of the powder and mixed it with boiling water and petrol and, as he stirred, it reverted to its thick sap-like consistency. A handful of kapok fibre bulked the resin up and formed a plug to caulk the larger holes in the boat's sides. Within twenty-four hours this natural 'fibre glass' had dried. The dugout was back in the water and Paul and I paddled it across the river to fish.

I have been fishing four times in my life and have never caught anything more impressive than an already-dead stickleback, which someone else had thrown back as being beneath contempt. Whilst it was undoubtedly the proudest moment of my fishing career, it had not been enough to foster an enduring love for the sport.

In Rantau Bumbun fishing was an altogether different prospect. It was effectively a matter of trading one grain of rice for one fish. This is a very attractive trade for anyone who is as heartily sick of rice as Paul and I were. As fast as I could fasten rice onto my hook - which if the rice is not exactly the right consistency is not really very fast - I could pull out another forkful of whitebait.

After half an hour Paul and I proudly presented Sriwahyuni with fifty sprats. Fried in flour, these made a very acceptable alternative to the boiled *ikan tupai* ('squirrel fish') that was the villager's fish of choice. Tasty as they were, these whitebait were not considered the product of real, honest-to-goodness Da'an fishing. Our hosts stubbornly refused to view our catch as 'real' food - which was why, after the novelty wore off, nobody had returned to the swarms at the waterfall. Fishing with a gill net was the way to catch 'food'; *pancing* (with a rod) was merely a hobby.

Addin was dedicated to *pancing*. At the rapids just below the village he could quickly catch more fish than he could eat in a week, simply by setting a couple of gill nets. Then, work over, he would return to the shady trees by the *kampong* and sit for two or three hours just to catch another four fish. He could often be found sitting quietly on the riverbank with his homemade fishing rod, waiting patiently for a bite.

He was always on the lookout for insects which he could use as bait. It was one of his less endearing foibles that he was never without some tortured creature squirming in the top pocket of his shirt. Cockroaches were Addin's favourite victims because, even with their heads and legs pinched off, they would still be wriggling hours later when he had time to go fishing.

We were once chatting in the shade of the veranda when a four-inch centipede came bustling along the corner of the step. Addin pinned it down and, avoiding its poisonous mandibles, casually nipped its head off with his thumbnail and dropped it into his pocket - all without a pause in his *omong kosong*.

One morning he decided to clear the area between the stilts of the *pondok*. He had to move some stacks of old roofing tiles (made of square-cut slivers of bark) and I stooped under the hut to help him. I should have guessed that bait-hunting was high among his motives.

It was very hot under the hut and we were both sweating instantly. Addin had to fend off the excited *kampong* chickens to protect his bait harvesting rights. I am no great champion of cockroaches myself but I refused to help in their mutilation, and so set myself up to be haunted by the sight of Addin's writhing pocket.

We were moving the tiles into a small hutch under the veranda and in doing so disturbed a nest of millions of minute ants. This spurred the scrawny chickens into an even greater frenzy. I hurried armfuls of tiles to the hutch and by the time I arrived my hands and forearms were smothered in the ants. They looked and felt like fur as they swarmed frantically, but they didn't bite. I dropped the tiles in the hutch, swiped off as many ants as I could before they reached the tops of my arms and my neck. Then I dashed back for the next pile. Meanwhile on our feet and legs the colony's defenders were left to run riot.

I picked up a bigger heap of tiles - keen now to terminate this awful job as soon as possible - and I was halfway to the hutch before I was aware of something wriggling under my middle finger. I shuffled my grip quickly and as I came out into the sunlight something fell to the ground.

I had been carrying a four-inch scorpion by one of its legs.

The hens were now in frantic pursuit of this succulent morsel and Addin was shouting at them, worried that one of them would be stung. He kicked them away whilst he trapped the scorpion under the corner of the steps himself.

"Have you got your knife?" he asked.

Reluctantly I gave it to him and, as I had feared, within two minutes the scorpion (lacking stinger and claws) was reanimating the roaches in his pocket. I had the horrifying impression that the headless cockroaches sensed what the newcomer to their prison was.

Addin returned from hunting one day, very happy despite several wasted hours on the trail of a barking deer. His only trophy was a present for his wife. Carefully he lifted a wriggling bundle of brown fur out of his ammo pouch. He called it a *tupai* (squirrel) and a long twitching snout identified the animal as a young tree shrew.

Sriwahyuni, laughing delightedly, took the *tupai* from her husband and started to stroke the back of its head soothingly. It calmed down almost instantly and arching its back - with its mustard yellow tramlines - it waved its thick tail and seemed almost to be purring.

"You name Charlie," Sriwahyuni murmured, with a curl of her lip.

Tupai are actually neither squirrels nor shrews. Nor do they spend much of their time in trees. They are primates and probably bear a close resemblance to a creature somewhere near the main trunk of our own family tree. They have an inconvenient blend of habits and characteristics that make them difficult to categorise neatly. However, the *tupai* don't seem interested in being categorised. Not only do they deliberately flout primate membership regulations by habitually giving birth to two or three offspring at a time but they have very mysterious nesting habits. The female leaves the nest that she shares with her mate to 'sneak away' and have her babies in a separate hidden nest. She then goes back to the male but appears to keep the location of the nursery nest a secret. She only returns to her babies once every couple of days to give them a dose of her rich milk.

For three hours Sriwahyuni comforted the *tupai* and two days later even her nephew, baby Agus, was handling it. With Charlie perched on her head and his bushy tail swinging down her neck she looked like Davy Crockett. Charlie was never tied up but he seemed absolutely content with his new life with Sriwahyuni and quickly grew fat on her cooking and crooning.

Addin and Sriwahyuni radiated a harmony that affected everyone who witnessed their relationship, and I noticed it most poignantly on the day they left us to travel down to Nangakalis: with typical hospitality they left their house open to us for as long as we wished.

Watching them disappear around the last bend in their dugout, perfectly matched stroke for stroke - the slim, pretty girl and the fun-loving man - we saw in them a carefree way of life which is now beyond the grasp of most of the developed world.

Kolop returned the next day from Nanga Raun in Dujang's *speed*. They were towing two big dugouts and had two younger lads with them. Narok and Bujang were nineteen years old and they were going to spend two months living in the highland valleys of the Mandai collecting *gaharu* (aloeswood) to sell in Putussibau. Kolop had suggested that the two expeditions should combine for added security.

Bayung (who had guided us to Kerian several weeks before) had arrived in the village earlier that morning. With his usual aloofness he had not told us that it had all been arranged with Kolop that he would be our second guide. After the crossing they too would stay on in the Müllers to prospect for *gaharu*.

Suddenly we had a party of six and two canoes. On top of our normal provisions we now had four extra sacks of rice that the *gaharu* hunters would live on. Much of their provisions would have to be hidden at the top of the river, eight days paddle away.

The weather was fine and the water level perfect. There was nothing to stop us.

"So we leave tomorrow?" I asked Kolop happily.

"Cannot," he shrugged, "Need paddles."

"We can buy here."

"Cannot. We have to make them . . . but first the wood must be dried."

After so long waiting already I found it difficult now to be impatient. It seemed that with the Da'an things miraculously came together if you were prepared to wait long enough.

Jurau came to visit us whilst Paul, Kolop and I were eating that evening. He was the local blacksmith and lived with his family in a ramshackle *pondok* on the edge of the village. We had already met him when we went to have our *parangs* sharpened.

He refused to eat but sat patiently and silently whilst we did so. As we pushed our empty plates away he leaned forward to invite us formally to eat in his *pondok*. Custom dictated that we couldn't refuse and he led us along through the darkness to more heaped plates of fish and rice. As well as numerous children Jurau had two pet leaf monkeys. A young one which he had only recently captured arched its neck and closed its eyes when I scratched it behind its ears.

I had just helped myself to the most minuscule ration of fish that I could get away with when a two-foot gnome, covered in scraggy fur, hopped in through the back door. Paul was staring into the fire and nobody else seemed to take any notice. In shuffling gnome-hops it moved straight past me and headed directly for the front door. I was dumbstruck.

As it passed me I could see the reason why it hopped (instead of walking like a normal gnome): its ankles were tied together and it was trailing a loose end of leather cord.

I was still watching in awe when it hopped into the moonlit doorway and I saw its beak. It was a large owl. Having lived with Jurau for most of its life it hopped with total confidence around the *bilik* between the dogs, humans and monkeys.

Headhunters from many Borneo tribes reasoned (not without a certain logic) that, since owls can turn their heads all the way round to look behind them, their heads must be less well connected than those of other animals. This lead to one of the strangest of Borneo's numerous bird omens: the man who saw an owl on the way to a headhunting raid was given a clear warning that his own head would not remain connected for very much longer.

Even before we had been in Jurau's *pondok* an hour, an envoy was sent from another shack to collect us and we were soon seated in a large circle around a teapot of *beram*. The party was roaring. Kolop started to play a *sapé* and the glasses kept being refilled.

One teenage lad suddenly fell over backwards out of the circle and vomited through the bamboo floorboards but in less than ten minutes he was back with us. The girl next to him was smoking and Kolop was turning on his charm. I remembered what Anih had said in 'Kalis - 'only bad girls smoke' - and I kept an eye on Kolop to see if it was true. He was generously handing out our Gudang Garam as if he had the greatest confidence in the truth of Anih's maxim.

The whole of our future expedition was here and Paul and I began to talk with Narok and Bujang. But to my right sat another man who, though he was too drunk to talk, kept grabbing my arm every time I looked away: "*Pak, pak. Tuan, tuan,*" he would say urgently, and then burp and slump forward again. This went on for ten minutes and although he was getting drunker I was still getting no more peace in my shouted conversation with the *gaharu* hunters. There was only one thing for it. I refilled our glasses and slugged three swift *berams* with the drunk in the hope that it would knock him out.

I never did finish my discussion with Narok and Bujang.

Kolop returned to Addin's *bilik* the next morning to announce unexpectedly that if we were ready we could leave that same day.

"But what about the paddles, Kolop?"

"Wah! No problem. We can buy them - only five thousand rupiah." - For less than three dollars each we had soon rounded up six paddles - "But we have to drink *beram* for luck!"

"Oh no, oh no. We'd love to but Paul and I must, absolutely must, go to visit Pelaun before we leave. Yes, we would certainly come along after . . . if it was at all possible."

Pelaun was with Jurau, sharing some mouse-deer meat. Of course, tradition must be observed and Pelaun brought out a jug of *beram* to wish us *selamat jalan*. We were prepared for our first day on the river and did not want to be disabled by Pelaun's hospitality even before we left.

Jurau had his baby with him and he was pulling off little shreds of meat for her. "Must eat before travel," he said, pointing at the mouse-deer.

"When we kill a deer," explained Pelaun as if to a child, "sometimes it has baby inside. We cook baby. Very good, make you very strong."

"It's barbecued mouse-deer foetus," I translated.

"Jesus, let's try it," said Paul, untiring even now in his quest for an alternative to rice.

We hid from Kolop and further *beram* abuse until the last possible moment and most of Rantau Bumbun waved from the banks as we paddled away. "*Selamat jalan!*"

In the first dugout rode Kolop and Bayung with me in the middle and in the other was Paul with Narok and Bujang. Paul and I watched carefully and timed our strokes against the man in front of us. A long deep pull was followed by a quick half-pull and we quickly picked up the beat - *Tak-tak . . . Tak-tak . . . Tak-tak* - as our paddle shafts clipped the hull. The dugouts sliced so smoothly through the water that it almost seemed that they were being sucked towards the Müller Mountains.

We all leaned forward as if anxious to see what lay ahead. The sound of Narok's chirped banter from Paul's boat was gradually swallowed by the roar of the waterfall. For at least three weeks we would be in unbroken and uncharted jungle. There was no more 'reliable information'. We were at the very edge of the map.

The *beram* and mouse-deer foetus gurgled in my stomach and I tried to force it from my mind.

"Strength for the journey," Pelaun had told us.

We would need every bit of it.

Chapter Eight

The River of Death

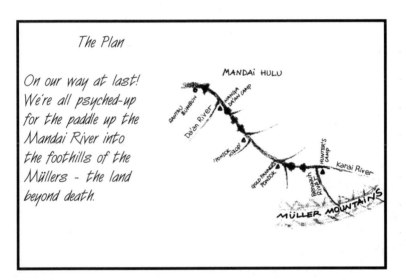

The Plan

On our way at last! We're all psyched-up for the paddle up the Mandai River into the foothills of the Müllers - the land beyond death.

MANDAI HULU

RANTAU BUMBUN

Dilan River

NANGA DAYAN CAMP

IPONDOK KOLOP

GOLD PANNERS PONDOK

HUNTER'S CAMP

Karai River

BUNGAN RIVER TRAIL

MÜLLER MOUNTAINS

In Iban belief, when a person dies his spirit crosses a footbridge called *Titi rawan*, the Bridge of Mourning. If his family and friends succeed in calling the spirit back from *Titi rawan* it will return to the longhouse and the person will live. If, however, the spirit crosses the bridge it is committed to a long and arduous journey through four stages: *Mandai rinyai, Mandai awai, Mandai ini* and *Mandai mati*.

Mati means Death and it lies at the beginning of the Mandai River.

We cut the canoes across the rushing current and drove them towards the gravel beach. Kolop barked *"Turun!"* - jump out - and Bayung and I flipped our legs over the side and the three of us shoved the boat out of the water.

It took us ten minutes to carry all the *barang* to the top of the falls. I noticed that the 'whitebait migration' was already over - there was not a single baby fish flipping on the rocks. Bayung was carrying a small black bantam cockerel and, although there was not much meat on it, I was pleased to think that we could eat fresh chicken further up the river.

It took the strength of all six of us to raise one canoe at a time onto our shoulders and struggle with it up the rock face. Narok and I climbed cautiously up the shallowest section, and when we were on top we pivoted the dugout on its centre point, then with the others pushing from behind we dragged it into the water above the falls.

We piled the *barang* back into the boats and Bayung decided that we would be better balanced if his scrawny bantam travelled in the middle with me. So he tied it by its leg to the rice sack on which I leaned.

We pushed the boats back into the tugging current, Kolop shouted "*Naik!*" (get in) and we sprang as smoothly as possible into our positions. I splashed the bantam with my wet legs and it ruffled its feathers and cursed me with its yellow eyes. We picked up our paddles and dug deep and fast to the rhythm that would occupy us for the next eight days. *Tak-tak . . . Tak-tak . . . Tak-tak*. It was pure hypnosis and neither Paul nor I ever felt tired when we were paddling.

We were now finally entering the 'unexplored' heart of Borneo. Only Kolop knew what lay ahead of us. The thrill was intense; we maintained our rhythm but dug deeper and harder with our paddles. We whooped and hooted with joy, and Paul and Narok traded shrill two finger whistles

There was only one way to celebrate this feeling. The boys learnt fast and soon all six of us were tearing along to the tune of 'Hawaii Five-O.' We raced the canoes, neck and neck around the wide sweep of the river, roaring like lunatics. "B-b-b-b-ba, baa-ba . . . Ba-ba, baa-ba . . . Dooo-do-do-do . . ."

Within ten minutes we reached the next rush of white water. Kolop gave his order to dismount and the three of us leapt as smoothly as possible overboard into the refreshing current. The other boat was right behind us and I heard Narok, the skipper, shout: "*Turun!*"

Without losing momentum we jammed our feet against the rocks and strained to haul the dugouts into, and then through, the cascading water. There was no time to take care over footsteps and I rushed to keep alongside my position in the middle of the boat, to be ready to spring in when Kolop called "*Naik!*"

In a week's time, still hauling up this river, we would be so exhausted that these twin commands, echoed from the second boat, would be the only words that we would swap for hours at a time. For now however the adventure was just beginning and we were exhilarated.

I was surprised how shallow the river was. Even on the deepest sections I could clearly see the rocks sliding back through the water and we never managed to paddle for more than twenty minutes before we would have to *turun* and haul. Kolop stood to punt us along with the end of his pig-hunting spear. Y-fronts were his standard attire on the river; he seemed to have a different colour for each day and every one of them was ripped along the elastic on the back.

In the early afternoon we stopped to camp at a point where the Da'an River flows into the Mandai. The Da'an people had emigrated from this region many years ago, attracted by trading opportunities that had opened up below the rapids. The Da'an River was extremely shallow and rocky; it would be almost impossible to traverse it   by canoe and it was probable that nobody but a Da'an had ever explored it.

According to our Da'an friends only the French surveyor who had visited Rantau Bumbun in the seventies had ever been as far as the *pondok* at Nanga Da'an (Nanga in Bahasa Da'an means junction). Hunting parties from Rantau often used this pondok, however, and it took the lads only a matter of minutes to renovate the rickety framework. Kolop cut a sturdy crossbar and lashed it between the two forked uprights. Then we draped our plastic sheet across and tied it out to springy saplings.

We collected wood and lit a smoky fire to keep the mosquitoes at bay. I killed two leeches that were looping excitedly towards us over the leaf-mould. They paused briefly to rear their pouting suckers as if sniffing the air, and then with renewed vigour began to flip end-over-end towards me. I was surprised - and vaguely disappointed - that none of us had been bitten yet, but there would be time later and plenty of opportunity.

The boys had each brought two nylon rice-sacks with the bottoms sliced out. Two branches were posted through the bags and then forced apart by 'spacers' with an 'L' carved out of either end. These firm mattresses were then laid in a row across two raised branches. Paul and I had brought specially made expedition hammocks but in an effort to cut down on weight we had chosen the design without side-sleeves. We could never find sturdy, correctly-spaced supports and invariably we woke during the night with our backsides soaking up the damp ground.

Kolop skewered three large *ikan tupai* with a green branch and then laid them directly on the embers. Cooked this way they were delicious; with crisp smoked skin and flesh that melted in your mouth like butter. We finished the meal with sweet black *kopi* and our last packet of biscuits. We all sat peacefully staring into the flames as night descended swiftly onto the river.

Kolop and I were still sitting by the fire long after the others had gone to sleep. We talked in whispers about what was ahead of us and travel in general. It was the creaking, croaking jungle that made us talk so quietly – the Da'an, like other Dayaks, don't whisper merely for sleepers.

Kolop had travelled over much of Borneo. He summed it up:

"Lots of pretty girls in Kuching. Wicked people in Pontianak. I want to travel much more. To see the world. But I soon come back to *hutan* (jungle). Here, in *hutan*, I feel best."

There was a widespread belief amongst Dayaks that the world is an island and the most developed places are just further down the rivers. From Rantau Bumbun through Nanga Raun, 'Kalis, Putussibau and Sintang the trappings of the modern world become more visible and more seductive. It therefore follows in this old tradition that England is just further down the river, somewhere beyond Pontianak, and that New York is nearest the river mouth. (I once met a mountain Indian in Ecuador who thought that England was a district of New York.)

Like most Da'an, Kolop was educated to a reasonable standard, and the wanderer's love of maps had led to an understanding of world geography. I got the impression that to him each stage downriver was a step backwards, away from his ideals. Only curiosity could lure him out of the Mandai Hulu. He had visited Pontianak only once, briefly. It was the only time that he had ever stayed in a hotel: if it was the Hotel Kalbar, then I could understand his distrust. I had the feeling that Kolop believed anywhere else would naturally fall far short of his beloved Da'an valleys.

"You never marry, Kolop?"

"Never. Like to travel too much. Like to go when I want to go."

"Same-same." I told him. We fell silent with our own thoughts. It was strange that though we came from such different worlds we were both prepared to make similar sacrifices for our way of life.

Apart from boiled *ikan tupai* and rice at five am, the next day started perfectly. As we paddled out into midstream, I became aware of a strange chugging noise approaching us from behind. Like a steam engine labouring up a one-in-three, it got louder and deeper as it approached us. *Hruumph . . . hruumph. . . hruumph.*

Two huge helmeted hornbills, as big as swans, with wonderful heavy bills, flew directly over our heads and laboured onwards along the river. *Hruumph . . . hruumph.*

The air pouches under their wings were responsible for the slow, booming sound. We watched them until they disappeared around the bend. Then we strained hard to listen to the last of their wing beats.

"*Bagus, bagus!*" Kolop shouted, when they had gone.

"Number one good luck!" beamed Narok.

In *Natural Man, a record from Borneo*, Hose reported on the hornbill guardian of the Punan's own spirit world:

A huge helmeted hornbill sits by the far end of the bridge across the 'River of Death,' and with its peculiar noises tries to terrify the ghost, so that it may fall from the bridge into the jaws of a great fish which is in league with the bird. On the other side of the river is Ungap, a woman with a cauldron and a spear. Ungap, if appeased with a gift, aids the ghost to escape from the monstrous bird and the fish. To propitiate this friendly witch, pebbles or beads are put in the nostrils of Punan corpses.

From this point, until we arrived on the lower Djuloi River, we would be travelling where no westerners had ever been. We were now paddling deeper into 'headhunter heaven' and the fact

181

that this valley had historically been avoided even by the fearless Iban warriors made the trip seem doubly exciting.

Narok was the most cheerful of our companions and he was still chattering happily about the hornbills when we rounded the bend ourselves.

We were facing a low waterfall strewn with boulders. I scanned along the face of this fall but there was no way we were going to get up above it without unloading.

"*Turun!*" We dragged the boats into the rocky beach. Kolop heaved out his famous bag and headed directly towards the biggest boulder. Amongst the mysterious equipment in his holdall was a thick blue marker pen. With dignified formality, he started to write on the smooth rock-face: *H. Bacoc, Bujang, Bayung, Narok, Mr Mark, Mr Paul. Selamat jalan. Sampai jumpa lagi. Mentuju Kal Teng* - (Bon voyage, until next time. Bound for Kal Teng).

I was not sure about the aptness of our passing being commemorated in perhaps the only bit of graffiti in the entire Mandai Hulu. But it was gratifying to know that this expedition was an incident of importance in the lives of our Da'an friends as much as in ours. We celebrated with a photograph of our little posse draped around the 'memorial rock.' First however Kolop made a dive for a comb from his bag - refusing to appear in a photo until he had arranged his parting. Narok earned the nickname of Ninja for his habit of springing into karate poses whenever he saw a camera.

We all shook hands with exaggerated formality.

"Hey, I just thought," gasped Paul, as he heaved a rice sack onto his shoulder, "If we're the first gringos ever to come up here does that mean that we get our names engraved in the anals of history? . . . Isn't that how you say it?"

This was the first of three rapids that would force us to unload our *barang* that day and the tempo was set for the coming week. In Rantau we had drenched our hands daily with surgical spirits as insurance against blisters but the simple fact that we walked more of the Mandai Hulu than we ever paddled meant that our hands never suffered.

Sometimes there was enough water in the rapids to allow us to slide the dugouts through once their cargoes had been lightened. Sometimes they tipped under, so that the current swirled giddily into them and we had to bail out before we could reload. We quickly became more efficient at loading the boats and began to take a pride in our teamwork.

Once at a very long bend Kolop told Paul and me to walk across the rocky beach and meet them again as they rounded the corner. Removal of our weight alone raised the boats just enough so that they barely skimmed the rocks of the riverbed. Though we were anxious to do our full share of the work, we were also keen to let Kolop take charge of 'troop deployment.' So, we did as we were told.

It was easier to walk in the river when there was a boat to lean on than it was to stumble across the slippery rocks on already throbbing feet. My feet were already cut and bruised and my Dayak toenail had turned horribly purple.

As I could not expect my Big Benz to last through the days in the river I decided to travel barefoot through this stage and reserve my boots for the mountain crossing. Only Kolop was also barefoot. Although Paul was wearing some sport sandals that he had bought in Sarawak his feet were already bruised and battered. The other boys were all wearing moulded plastic trainers. Though they looked very uncomfortable we soon realised that they were the perfect answer on the river. Very soon we began to wish that we had bought some *sepatu plastiks* from Tomas in Putussibau.

Concentrating as we were on the shifting boulders we might never have noticed the snake if it had not moved. When we were just a few feet away it suddenly raised its head six inches off the ground, uncoiled to its full six-foot length and slithered rapidly towards a grassy island in the centre of the beach.

"Come on, let's get it!" shouted Paul rushing forward. He picked up a boulder and hurled it towards the snake's disappearing tail.

"Wait, what do you want it for?"

"I dunno," he said, as it disappeared into the tall grass, ". . We'll skin it - or something."

This snake was the *ular hitam* (King Cobra) about which I had been warned by the Sarawakian with the fat foot. From what he had told me I was convinced that, even with Kolop's magic to protect us, we really did not want to follow the snake into the tall grass.

It was always a relief to get back into the canoes, back to the hypnotic, almost restful, *Tak-tak . . . Tak-tak.* It was pleasant to get the cool timber hull back under our feet after the bruising that the rocks gave us.

"*Babi.*" Kolop pointed to a spot on the left bank where the ground was chopped up and a dark mulch heap formed a ramp from the water's edge. "Maybe thirty *babi.*"

Twenty metres further upriver, on the opposite bank, another mud slide showed where the pigs would enter the river in one hectic herd, swim quickly across the dangerous exposed channel, and then scramble back up the other side. Sometimes they didn't cross quickly enough: Kolop described how the Da'an will wait quietly and patiently under the bank to attack the herd with spears from their canoes when they reach midstream.

"But we cannot," he added unhappily. "Have one spear only."

I would imagine that a swimming *babi* would be just fast food to a fish like the *salong* that we saw in Rantau.

At midday, having travelled for about six hours, we stopped on a sunny beach and ate more boiled *ikan tupai* (far less tasty than the baked type) with cold rice from breakfast. I was having great trouble maintaining any interest in boiled fish but the *kopi* that followed was to remain one of the simple though invaluable pleasures that would sustain us throughout the expedition.

The river was often only thirty feet wide and its passage cut a flickering emerald tunnel through the forest. In places it narrowed and there were deep pools between metallic boulders. We would glide smoothly across a bottle-green mirror with only the rhythm of our paddles to break the silence. Very soon, however, the mirror would be broken by the rumble of rushing water. "*Turun!*" – and we would leap over the side onto the punishing rocks.

Kolop pointed through the trees to the rustic scaffold that would soon be converted into our camp for the night: "Pondok Kolop."

This camp was named by the Jungle Tiger himself when he and two friends had lived there for three months whilst they were panning for gold. Apparently the river had been flowing too fast and they'd had very disappointing results.

Pondok Kolop hadn't had boarders for quite a while and it

took the lads a few minutes to hack away the saplings that had begun their race to take advantage of the precious patch of sunlight. After camp was set up Paul cut down a sapling with his *parang* to make a fishing rod to catch dinner. Bujang and Bayung refused to allow his noisy optimism to dissuade them from paddling a short distance upriver and setting the gill net themselves.

We were at a point where a small stream poured its rusty waters into the Mandai. The banks betrayed the comings and goings of numerous *babi*. It is dangerously easy to lose your bearings in the rainforest and I decided to use this stream to lead me safely on a minor exploration into the surrounding jungle.

I left the black slime of the *babi* mud bath behind and soon smooth, silvery sand was soothing my lacerated feet. Kolop had once told me that wherever these compressed beds of silver sand were found one could also find gold and I wondered if he and his friends had decided to prospect here after a survey of this stream.

The jungle of Borneo is actually a lot safer than most people imagine: there are no large predators such as panthers or tigers, only the much smaller clouded leopard which is notoriously shy of man. Snakes and poisonous insects are very anxious to avoid a confrontation and you would be incredibly lucky to see an elephant or a Borneo rhinoceros - and consequently extremely unlucky to get trampled by one.

I took my *parang* with me anyway and, since being gored by a pig is not at all romantic (and very painful), I fantasised about being gently mauled by a sun bear. *Beruang madu* ('honey bears' in Indonesian) have long vicious claws, which they use for ripping open bees' nests. They are dangerously bad tempered and will often attack instinctively.

Half a mile up the stream I came to a steep waterfall. I managed to climb its slippery face by hanging onto the twisted roots. I wandered a little way further along the streambed between some large boulders. The sun was getting low and only occasional beams of light penetrated the canopy.

Suddenly a boulder by my right hand erupted in a cloud of flies. They had been feeding on something and when I peered closer I realised that it was a large mud turtle. It would have taken an extremely athletic turtle to have paddled all the way from the river, climbed the waterfall and finally leapt four feet up onto this convenient shelf. I couldn't find human tracks or any other clue as to how the turtle had arrived at its final resting-place. I assumed that the turtle must have been planted by a were-tiger.

Were-tigers are men who can change at will into invisible tigers. Naturally (being characters from Iban myth) they have a great hunger for heads. Their 'code of honour,' however, dictates that they cannot kill anyone who has done them no harm. So, to get around this irritating legal problem, they leave food in a conspicuous place on a trail and kill anyone who takes it. This turtle was clearly well past its use-by date and it was no great sacrifice to leave it in place for the were-tiger.

Halfway back to camp I cut a long sapling for a fishing rod and had just started to tie onto it some of the line from my survival pouch when I was startled by the sound of cruel laughter. I peered up into the canopy towards the source of this harsh *cack, cack, cackle*.

After a minute's staring, I managed to make out the shadowy form of a hornbill up amongst the leaves of the giant trees. It really did seem to be laughing at me, and for a moment I felt absurdly self-conscious. The bird seemed to be clearly aware of how much out of my depth I would be should I really need to provide for myself here. *Cack, cack, cack, cack-ack-ack.*

Feeling rather hurt I finished my fishing rod and went back to the camp.

Paul was fishing from the beach and furiously slapping at sand flies. He hadn't caught anything and was not feeling any more proficient at jungle survival than I was. We decided to take a canoe and paddle over to the other bank where the shaded area under the trees looked like good *ikan* habitat. In addition, we would also be safe from prying Da'an eyes until such time as we made the catch that would earn their undying respect and devotion.

After several minutes stumbling over the rocks on the opposite bank (only narrowly avoiding losing the dugout) we managed to get into a position from which we could start fishing.

Twenty minutes later, having cut myself with my Swiss Army knife and stuck a hook (an optimistically large hook) into my thumb I decided that the rice that we were using for bait was overcooked. There were a million sand-flies but you can never find a leech when you need one. I threw my new fishing rod into the river in disgust, packed the tangled line back into my survival pouch and swam back to the camp.

We all had a bad night's sleep in Pondok Kolop. Again there was not enough room to tie our hammocks so Paul and I slept directly on the ground, sweating under our mosquito nets. Kolop got up four times to put more damp logs on the fire to keep away the voracious sand-flies.

We ate breakfast on the beach at half past five, watching the sunlight hit the trees on top of the valley. I felt sick and strangely shaky. I couldn't face even a mouthful of fish and rice.

Kolop warned us that we were going to have a long, hard day before we saw our next *pondok* but we expected nothing like the pain and struggle that was our next eight hour stint up the Mandai. The rapids were coming ever more frequently and we were just grateful that they were never big enough to force us to unload the canoes. There were only brief moments of comparatively luxurious paddling now.

Twice during the paddling sections (the only chance we had to look around) Kolop spotted *babis* in the shadows along the banks and we dug our paddles deep and lunged towards the rocks. Grabbing our *parangs* we raced after Kolop as he leapt through the bushes with his spear raised to his shoulder, ready to throw or stab. Plunging through the first barrier of bushes I felt the immediate change in the consistency of the earth beneath my feet. The pigs had turned the soil over with their snouts to a depth of almost a foot and the soil felt light and rich.

It was exciting dashing between the trees in pursuit of some vague black bulk but, in reality, there was little chance that we would ever be able to run down a *babi* without dogs.

The day's work drained our strength alarmingly quickly and by midday there was no way we could join another pig-chase. Our journey up this part of the river was just a constant round of *Turun*! - hauling and groaning, stumbling and sometimes going right under between the dugout and the rocks. Then *Naik*! for perhaps only a dozen fast strokes, fighting the current before leaping out again without losing any momentum.

My feet were bleeding and the constant soaking was beginning to cause ulcers. I had sudden periods of light-headedness and others of incredible lethargy, and the scrawny cockerel gave me the evil eye all day.

The boats had begun to reflect the battering that we were taking: both of them had sprung leaks.

"We get *damar* tonight," said Kolop confidently.

He would occasionally stand up to punt us along with his pig spear - Oxford style, from the bow. I was jealous of his freedom to choose this apparently more comfortable position until I tried it a few days later and realised that I was unable even to balance in the boat's bow. Once he paused suddenly in his punting, straightened up, and pointed ahead. "*Ular hitam!*" he roared.

He swung the spear back into the canoe, rapping me painfully on the elbow as he did so, and grabbing his paddle set off in pursuit of the snake. I saw it up ahead, swimming gaily across the river, head periscoping eight inches above the water.

I sensed Bayung, behind me, dig his paddle purposefully into the current and the three of us charged with thrilling acceleration towards the unsuspecting reptile. Just as we came close it dived, near some slime covered boulders at the water's edge. Kolop grabbed for his spear again and started stabbing it viciously into the crevices, rocking the boat so violently that I grabbed hold of the sides. He obviously reserved a great deal of hatred for *ular hitam* and after he had spent some time stabbing he leapt onto the rocks and, from there continued his attack. Long after Paul and the others had arrived peacefully alongside us he was still smashing the water with the flat of his spear point.

I was shocked to see how worn out Paul looked. His skin and his eyes were an unhealthy yellow.

"*Pondok!*"

It was with deep gratitude that I heard Kolop's cry that afternoon.

Up on the riverbank above us there was a small bamboo hut, raised on stilts about six feet off the jungle floor. Kolop said that it was home to four gold-panners who had gone to Kerian.

It took all my remaining energy to help haul the canoes onto the beach. I couldn't face even the short climb to the *pondok* so I dropped my pack on the beach and lay down against the hot stones. I slept there for two hours.

I was wakened by the sound of splintering wood and raucous laughter, but I was far too exhausted to investigate. I learnt later that Paul had fallen straight through the bamboo platform but had somehow emerged unscathed from underneath the hut - much to the appreciation of the Da'an who found our colossal clumsiness too amusing for words.

I lay still, shivering now with the chill of evening but dreading the climb up the bank. Aching in all my joints I was struggling with an exhaustion that was totally out of proportion to even our day's hard labour (in fact compared with any exhaustion that I had ever known). I believed that I could only be suffering from the first symptoms of malaria.

I remembered Marlow saying in *Heart of Darkness*:

One cannot live with one's finger everlastingly on one's pulse. I had often "a little fever", or a touch of other things – the playful paw strokes of the wilderness, the preliminary trifling before the more serious onslaught which came in due course.

And come it would.

Weaving like a drunk - and in serious danger of falling backwards over the bank - I hauled myself onto the platform and stepped into the darkness of the hut. The boys had gone to hunt and only Paul was inside. He told me that he had been passing blood. He was weak and, even in the gloom, frighteningly pale.

I was gripped by a chilling fear that perhaps we were both suffering from some awful unknown tropical disease of which there may be as many in Borneo as there are insects. I flipped through John Hatt's *Tropical Traveller*, and decided to treat Paul for amoebic dysentery. I rallied my strength to mix him a re-hydration solution and then gave him a dose of antibiotics.

I rifled through my survival kit for Chloroquine tablets and carefully counted out four of them. Then I separated two each into two sealed bags. I was aware that in my hazy mental state I had to be doubly careful about getting the dose right. Ten of these tablets could be a fatal dose and if I went under the full effects of malaria I could not be confident that I would remember how many I had taken.

The nearest medical supply was back in Nanga Raun at Pak Harold's and the boys might have to rush us back downriver if we got really bad. It was entirely possible that neither Paul nor I would be conscious upon arrival. I prayed that Kolop would not merely keep us here and try to cure us himself with his great flowery bag-of-tricks.

With a powerful and very real fear that it might be my last coherent act I crawled out into the fading daylight to write a message to Pak Harold: 'Both Paul and I are very sick here and I'm writing this note because I don't know how bad it's going to get. If necessary this will be a description of our early symptoms and treatment . .'

Then with greater loneliness than I have ever known I went back into the hut and lay down.

It seemed like I had been dozing only a few minutes when I was woken by painful convulsions in my stomach. The wrenches cleared my head enough for an ominous doubt to fix in my mind. I crawled across the bamboo slats of the floor and poured out the contents of my survival pouch: fishing line and hooks, water purifiers, spare knife, candles, lighter, Chloroquine tablets . . . unopened.

In my confusion, I had dropped a horrifying hammer-dose of four codeine painkillers. Feeling wretched and desperate, I crawled out onto the platform and forced myself to vomit. Then I drank as much water as I dared without using up our purified supplies. I couldn't risk taking a Chloroquine dose directly on top of the painkillers and the malaria would therefore be left to run its course until the next day.

I awoke several times in the night, and each time I was surprised that I felt stronger. I checked on Paul and he seemed to be sleeping soundly. By morning we both felt strong enough to travel onwards but it was with trepidation that we set off to travel another day further away from medical supplies.

Kolop had somehow known all along that there was *damar* in the gold-panner's *pondok* and he and Narok had patched the dugouts whilst I was sleeping on the beach the previous evening. He had also found some ripe papayas near the hut and they had helped to revive us far more than *ikan tupai* ever could.

We were climbing higher up the river now and the frequent

rocky sections and falls were split by deep, beautiful pools. The trees met over our heads and only allowed the sun to dapple the water in the widest sections. Twice Kolop called a halt to fish. Bujang and Bayung slowly dragged the net from one end of the pool and the rest of us splashed towards them with Kolop rattling his spear into the roots along the bank. I prayed that we wouldn't trap an *ular hitam* or the shark-like *salong*.

There were only two rapids that day that were big enough to demand the unloading of our *barang*. On the first of these I lost my footing as I tried to beach the canoe, got swept over a falls, missed Paul's outstretched hand and paid for my carelessness with a dead leg when I thumped up against a boulder with my penknife in my pocket.

I clawed my way to the shore and answered Narok's amused comments - "*Hati, hati pak!*" - with a sickly grin.

On the second big rapids Paul barely managed to drop the sack of rice he was carrying before he pitched dramatically off a five-foot boulder into a shallow rock pool. He landed on his shoulder but miraculously got to his feet unhurt.

"I don't know how they never fall," he blustered. "This is starting to get right on my tits!"

Kolop patted him affectionately on the back: "*Orang barat gila.*"

Twice that morning we saw white snakes puttering across the river ahead of us. Kolop showed none of his hatred for these reptiles and dismissed them as *ular bodoh* (idiot snakes) because of their absurd head-bobbing method of swimming.

That afternoon, amongst the detritus of a deserted hunter's camp, Paul and I collapsed on our packs. We were almost instantly spurred back to life by vicious sand-flies and thousands of tiny, stingless bees. Attracted by our sweat they flew into our eyes and ears and forced us to keep our mouths clamped shut. They were so numerous that just by rubbing the sweat off your forehead you could kill dozens and mix them into a sort of gritty paste in your hairline.

There were also the giant ants that Hose had described:

. . . the Elephant Ant, a giant about an inch long, with a large head and strong jaws like pincers, will run over your arms and hands without attempting to hurt you; but directly you touch them or make them think you are going to harm them, they bring their nippers into play; and then you know about it.

I changed into my trousers and long sleeved shirt early to find protection from the sand flies and irritating bees and as I started to button my trousers I realised to my horror that I had scooped up one of the giant ants. I ripped my trousers back down - to the cheers of the Da'an - and, hopping around on one leg, I managed to flip a totally undaunted ant back onto the jungle floor.

I had once eaten shallow-fried giant ants in Columbia and I tried to convince Narok that, as a break from fish and rice, we should try some of the mighty specimens that were running around the camp.

"*Orang da'an kuat makan ikan,*" he answered pointing at his biceps. - Da'an people strong, eat fish.

"*Orang barat* eat one more *ikan, sakit* one minute!" Paul retaliated.

We were both feeling infinitely stronger than we had the previous night. I convinced Paul to take another antibiotic but I was now sure that in my case the 'playful paw strokes of the wilderness' had not been malaria after all.

We awoke as usual at half past five the next morning and were drinking our *kopi* as sunlight began to filter through the canopy. Paul, contentedly scratching his bites, stopped suddenly to point at something on the other side of a small stream. The bushes rustled and shook as if something large and extremely clumsy - perhaps a stray *orang barat* - was stumbling around in there.

The boys were instantly on their feet, charging wildly across the stream with their *parangs* raised. Kolop, holding his coffee cup, rose to his feet like a general watching the progress of his troops. Narok got to the thicket first and leapt in, bringing his *parang* down viciously at the same instant. He made another brutal chop and them leapt quickly out of the fray. The other two, conceding that this was Narok's kill allowed him to take his time and let the animal weaken for a moment before he went back in and finished it off.

He sauntered back proudly, carrying his victim by its thick tail, rinsing his *parang* as he crossed the stream: "One velly *sakit* pangolin."

"Yeah, Ninja!" shouted Paul. "Meat!" he grinned happily.

It was a pangolin, a scaly anteater, about three feet long from nose to tail. Covered in a thick armour of golden scales that made it look like a miniature dinosaur, this animal was going about its daily business of feeding on ants and termites when it ran unexpectedly first upon Paul's betrayal and then Narok's *parang*.

The pangolin has evolved the unusual ability to carry a 'packed lunch.' Having dug up an ants nest with its sharp scything claws - a good enough reason for Narok to have treated it with a degree of respect - it allows the colony's defenders to swarm under its triangular scales and then clamps them tightly closed. Later, feeling peckish, it will stroll to a favourite bathing place and open its scales to let its lunch float onto the surface where it can lap it up.

The body of the pangolin travelled in the belly of the canoe between my feet. The beady cockerel eyed it with the indignant glare that it had hitherto reserved for me.

We had reached a major landmark in our journey. The Mandai River is born at a point where the Bengauh flows into the Karai. We would meet a younger version of the Bengauh a week later when we were hiking up the flanks of the Müllers. For the rest of our canoe trip, we would be travelling up the Karai River – along what, in Iban belief, would have been the place beyond death.

Chapter Nine

The Fever Trees

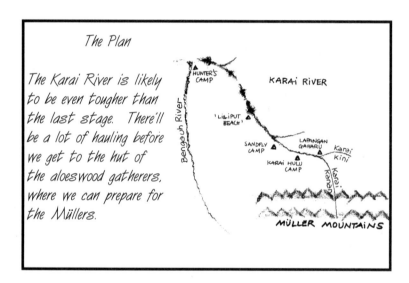

The Plan

The Karai River is likely to be even tougher than the last stage. There'll be a lot of hauling before we get to the hut of the aloeswood gatherers, where we can prepare for the Müllers.

HUNTER'S CAMP

KARAI RIVER

Bengaoh River

'LILLIPUT BEACH'

SANDFLY CAMP

LAPANGAN GAHARU

Karai Kini

KARAI HULU CAMP

Karai Kanai

MÜLLER MOUNTAINS

The river had got shallower, and so the restful spells of paddling became briefer. Often now when we *naik*-ed we could already see the spot where we would have to *turun* again.

That morning, after four strenuous hours hauling, we came to the longest and most violent rapid on the river. We had to carry the *barang* up over a steep boulder-strewn bank and onto a narrow track which lead for a quarter of a mile over knotted roots, under propped-up trees and across a rotten footbridge made of saplings. Kolop did a quick recce up the trail to hack away the vegetation that had invaded it since it was last used.

"Pretty damned *sakit* of this," grunted Paul, as we scrambled up the trail with our second load.

I was carrying a bag of rice on one shoulder and the pangolin in my other hand and I was not at all happy because it had just slipped and sliced my thumb with the sharp scales along its tail. "We'd be a lot better off without all this bloody rice."

I was also worried that I was getting ill again. For the first time since arriving in Borneo I was not sweating. My skin felt strangely cold and clammy.

It took all six of us to carry each dugout to the top of the rapid. Balancing them across our shoulders, we managed to lock our legs and clamber over the boulders and onto the start of the trail. Being a good foot taller than the Da'an, Paul and I complained that the others were just reaching up and touching the boats. Once I was literally underneath a canoe, with what seemed like its whole weight on my back, whilst we tried to slide it over a rotten tree trunk. It was all I could do to stop my legs from crumpling.

"*Orang barat* more strong if eat *ikan*," quipped Narok.

It took two hours to get the boats and all our *barang* back onto the water and we were relieved when Kolop called a *kopi-break* on the beach. We made quick work of collecting dry driftwood from the flood-line, keeping an eye open for the *ular hitam* who likes to build his nest in this part of the bank. Then we sat gratefully back on the warm rocks and tried to make the luxury of our *kopi* last.

Narok tipped the rice that was left over from breakfast into a plastic bag (he couldn't resist partaking of another plateful) and set a huge pot of water boiling to 'pluck' the pangolin.

The animal was too big to plunge into the pot so, curling it up so that its scales opened we began to ladle the boiling water over it. The scales and even the sharp claws came off easily and within ten minutes the pangolin was just a rubbery white corpse. Holding the end of his *parang* blade Kolop deftly gutted the animal in the shallows and carefully spilled out the contents of its stomach.

He was looking for a *bezoar* stone. These stones are highly prized in Chinese medicine; they are believed to be effective against asthma, stomach-ache and impotence. Usually they are found in the gall bladders of monkeys, but the rarer *batu landak* (porcupine stones) can fetch hundreds of dollars in Singapore or Hong Kong. Porcupine stones are found as concretions in wounds on the skin of the animal and are only discovered on one out of several hundred animals killed. As he gently inverted the stomach a black mass of half-digested ants poured out into the current. Intestinal *bezoar* are typically found in ruminants and I had a feeling that Kolop was being slightly over-optimistic in hoping to find a pangolin stone.

The icy touches of fever tapped me on the shoulder with such deliberation and unexpectedness that I straightened up and looked around in surprise. Almost instantly, I doubled over again as I was shaken by a spasm which seemed to knot all the muscles in my stomach.

By the time the butchered pangolin was stowed in the dugout I was crouched in the only patch of sun on the beach and I was being wracked by uncontrollable shivers. I staggered towards the canoe and almost fell onto the heap of provisions stowed in its belly. As we started to paddle into the stream my teeth chattered with alarming violence and the backstroke of Kolop's paddle sprinkled me with icy droplets of water that paradoxically seemed to burn where they landed.

Convulsions shook me so that I could barely even hold onto my paddle, and my stomach muscles twisted into such tight knots that I imagined they would tear. My teeth clashed together with a violence that I thought would shatter them. I clamped them tight and prayed for the momentary relief when the sunlight broke through a gap in the canopy.

I dreaded the next rush of white water where, at Kolop's command, I would have to jump overboard into the frigid river. I knew that it would not be far ahead. Sure enough, it took all my will power to force myself overboard when Kolop shouted. I clenched my fists and let the frosted teeth of the river bite into my legs.

"*Sakit?*" asked Kolop as we slid the dugout between the rocks.

"*Banyak demam,*" I stammered through chattering teeth – bad fever. He nodded. Fever was just a fact of life for the Da'an. It comes and goes.

The next two hours were a total blank. I ceased to register the misery and afterwards I remembered nothing. There must have been many more rapids and Paul told me later that I began to look better and had seemed normal to him.

Then we rounded a bend and over Kolop's shoulder I saw another wild white swirl. I dreaded the moment when I would be forced to jump out again into the numbing water. We ran the canoes towards a rocky beach and I managed to leap from the bow onto the shore without getting wet. I curled there trembling with my back to the sun-baked rocks.

Paul dosed me with the belated Chloroquine and then refilled and purified all the water bottles. The boys started to carry the *barang* around the rapids. I managed to stammer "*sakit sekali, Kolop, lima minit saja*" - very sick, just five minutes. But I knew that we couldn't stop here and it would take the strength of all of us to carry the canoes over the huge boulders.

Soon our bruised shoulders were back under the splintered hulls. I reeled like a drunk as we heaved and grunted over the rocks. I was convinced that any moment I was going to pitch over into the churning white-water twenty feet below. On the other side of the rapids we reached a few feet of precious sunlit beach and I found it physically impossible to force myself back into the glacial shade. I crouched there, feeling the sun on my back and yet still clutching my ribs to try to ease the painful shivers.

As I waited for the others - feeling thoroughly ashamed of myself for not 'pulling my weight' - I noticed a small waterfall. It was no more than a spout of clear water falling from the opposite bank but somehow it held my attention. Its very appearance seemed to quell the spasms in my stomach. As I watched, it stopped flowing, froze momentarily and then reversed and started slowly, then faster, to fall upwards. I forced all my concentration onto it. It was definitely flowing uphill.

My focus shifted suddenly to something else. A dark shape to my right along the riverbank became a large black jungle pig. It stood absolutely still and beyond it another and, equidistant from that, one more. Three identical black pigs, but diminishing in size like porcelain ducks flying up a wall.

"*Tiga babi!*" I giggled stupidly when the boys arrived - three little pigs. They looked where I pointed but were obviously unimpressed.

The afternoon passed in a haze of pain and exhaustion where I was only vaguely conscious of where we were and what was happening. I plunged frequently back into the agony of the river and tried my best to zigzag our canoe through the rare sunny patches. If I did manage to do my share of the hauling and the paddling then it was only because I was operating on a sort of 'auto-pilot.' Acceptance and continuation were easier than resistance.

I only drifted once more into 'consciousness' again when we arrived below another spectacular rush of foaming water and beached the dugouts. I realised that somehow I had fallen amongst the rocks. Paul helped me to my feet and, swaying uncontrollably, I stooped to pick up a rattan backpack and tried to haul it up the slippery root-ridden bank. I just saved myself from toppling backwards by grabbing a broken branch. I slid back to the beach.

"*Bawa barang sendiri!*" I heard Kolop bark.

My head spun: 'Jesus, he said, "carry your own bags."' - I realised instantly what this meant - 'They want to leave us here. No canoe, no supplies, no way back, no way over the mountains. This is it!'

I struggled into my own pack, picked the rattan pack up again and tried, with all my strength, to climb the bank.

Paul was at my shoulder. He too sounded panicked - "Mark, what the hell's goin' on?"

'He's sensed it too.' I thought, 'This is really it. They want to kill us here and no one will know. The *orang barat gila* just didn't make it.'

The river was roaring in my head. It bellowed once like a monster and then the roar became a pulsating chant. I dug my fingers into the bank and scrambled away from the noise. I dared not look behind me.

The next moment I was on top of the bank, running headlong into the jungle. I didn't notice the thorns stabbing my feet or the branches scratching me. I wasn't running from the boys anymore; it was the freight-train river that was trying to kill me.

My pack, somehow still on my back, snagged on a branch and I tried to shrug it off. I was caught fast and I could sense the river coming up fast behind me. I was almost crying as I struggled to untie myself. The pack dropped on the ground and, free now, I sprinted onward. I still refused to look behind me, not wanting to face what I thought I would see there. I knew instinctively that what I saw would terrify me so much that I would be paralysed – unable to escape.

Something chopped across the lower part of my shins and I flew forward and slammed my shoulder against a tree trunk. I closed my eyes, held my breath and waited.

But the river was no longer chanting and I strained to listen.

The forest was filled with the amplified buzzing and chomping of millions upon millions of insects. I have no way of knowing how long I stayed there but I know that my panicked heart-beat and heavy breathing slowed and I was able to focus my undivided concentration on the hideous feeding of those insects.

As I crouched there, with my head against the tree trunk, I saw with horrific - yet somehow detached - vividness exactly how my death would be. I knew that nothing specific would kill me; I felt cheated to think that a *glamorous* death by snakebite or large animal would be denied me. I would not even be allowed the dignity of a death by starvation. I saw the obscene but irrefutable truth that, alone in the jungle with just a pair of shorts and (I felt in my pocket) a Swiss Army knife, I was simply going to be eaten away, piece by minute piece, by those millions of chomping mandibles. I saw myself, oozing with sores and ulcers, stumbling in the undergrowth and I knew I would die without even the dignity of an animal.

My mind 'back-flipped' and an equal but opposite panic grasped me. My only hope was the river. I had to get there before they left without me. I span around and charged again in the direction that I had come from. I leapt through the bushes as I sprinted but my progress was again nightmarishly slow and I scrambled onto the slippery trunk of a huge tree and dashed along its length, grateful for the ground that it let me cover.

I heard the river calling me and slithered on my back down to the rocks. The cool billows looked enticing. The river would soothe my cuts and bruises, let me sleep away my exhaustion. Only with difficulty did I resist the temptation to slip into those welcoming sheets where I imagined I would be able to rest undisturbed.

When Bujang found me, I was sitting astride a boulder gripping it firmly with my knees and fingernails and trying control its violent rocking. I held onto his rattan pack like a drowning man as he led me to the clearing above the rapids. I was intensely afraid that he might walk off without me, not realising that in my intoxicated state I could now not even walk without support.

When we reached a clearing on the bank above the rapids the earth was heaving. I knew that this was merely illusion and tried to fight it. But it was too powerful, the ground buckled up towards my knees and I sat down heavily on a boulder. I put my head between my knees and dug my toes into the gravel for grip. My legs and arms were smeared with the dirt of the forest and my shoulder was grazed where I had crashed into the tree.

I heard voices and looked up to see Paul and Kolop. They had followed my trail through the jungle but had somehow overlooked my backpack. Paul said that when they came to the huge rotten log they had seen where I had run along it but had had great difficulty even in balancing along its length.

The lads went back to collect the *barang* and Paul hurried away to find my pack. I told him to take somebody with him. I was convinced that I had been offered a preview of what would befall anyone who got lost in the forest. I badly wanted to ask him not to leave me alone; I was not sure what sudden notions might send me hurtling back into the trees again.

But I couldn't ask, and when I was alone again I began to concentrate on the rolling motion of the ground. Out of curiosity I stood up. I braced my legs apart and stretched out my arms to fight the quaking. I looked towards the river and a gravel beach on the opposite bank attracted my eyes; it seemed to be shimmering and flickering like an out-of-focus television screen. Concentrating to clarify it, I brought into focus a tiny figure. He was wearing blue shorts and a white tee shirt and, though he was looking back across the river, he had not seen me.

Then I realised that each splash of colour was a minuscule figure – a Lilliputian, straight from *Gulliver's Travels* - each one the size of a tiny pebble. By association, the beach appeared to be a long sweeping crescent and the river a wide and incredibly beautiful bay. There were about two hundred tiny people on the beach. They wore colourful western beach clothes and here and there I saw the garish stripes of parasols.

I held my breath, literally spellbound, and glanced up at the trees looming over the 'bay.' They were fifty miles high and seemed to be swaying towards me. I looked away quickly, back to the happy scene on the beach. Some of the Lilliputians were playing with Frisbees, others beach tennis and many splashed in the water. The sounds of their laughter came clearly to me.

I was enchanted and looked around at my immediate surroundings. The slimy roots twisting out of the bank behind me became writhing masses of *ular hitam* and I jerked my head away again and drove the thought of snakes from my mind. Although I knew that all this was illusion, I felt that simply with my imagination I could have brought the trees crashing down or provoked the snakes to attack.

I was like the Solipsists who believe that life is merely a 'dream' and that anything that is not in your mind at any given moment simply ceases to be. By denying the looming trees and the snakes' existence in my head, they could not hurt me. I dared to look at them only for an instant and to dwell on these frightening things would lead me into a bad trip – in hippy speak 'a bum trip.'

The silver flow of the river caught my eye. Small rocks in the stream had become elegantly domed steel-grey islets. On each one I could clearly see two or three sunbathing Lilliputians. A sleek, bronzed beauty in a yellow bikini particularly attracted my attention. I was enjoying myself now and I let my eye roam onwards to the first ripples of white-water sucking into the rapids. Tiny dugout canoes with whooping holidaymakers were sliding into the churning water.

The sounds were so clear that I believe they must have been the 'real' sounds of some forgotten day at the beach in my early childhood, stored in my subconscious for that moment. I listened carefully to the laughter and shouts, and as I did so, I was aware that the general hubbub began to fade. One-by-one the Lilliputians stopped what they were doing. A man caught his Frisbee and turned to look directly at me. The girl in the yellow bikini stood up and shaded her eyes to stare.

There was silence.

Everybody was squinting across the sunny bay towards me. Then one voice somewhere in the crowd started shouting. Another joined in and from somewhere further along the beach still another. Suddenly I noticed a fat woman in a flowery swimsuit bellowing at me with unmistakable hatred. A ragged, ill-disciplined chant swept quickly through the crowd.

In the confusion of differing tones and volumes, I could discern individual voices - just slightly out of time. The girl on the rock was shouting so furiously, with such loathing, that her head butted forward as she spat out each word. I could clearly make out her voice but I struggled to understand the words. Then the chant became clearer and louder as it picked up tempo and soon the whole crowd was screaming hoarsely.

The meaning came to me with a shock: "Cut his throat! . . Cut his throat! . . Cut his throat!"

It struck me as obscene that all these people, a moment ago so cheerful, could have such a deep hatred for me. As with the giant trees and the snakes I was still confident that this was only an illusion and that I could come to no physical harm. After the first shock, I managed to calm my fear. The little people were my own creation and I was even aware that I had 'invented' the chant myself. I was sure that I could ultimately control all of this.

I concentrated and forced the Lilliputians back to what they had been doing. The chant started to fade. The normal laughter of the beach took its place and, apart from some mumbled complaints, they turned back to what they had been doing. I saw the girl on the rock shrug her shoulders, as if the thing that she thought she had seen was not there after all. She lay back down on her towel and picked up a paperback.

My knees buckled unexpectedly and I wobbled back to my seat. It seemed that the boys had been gone for hours and I looked towards the dark tunnel in the undergrowth from where they would emerge.

What would happen I imagined if, when they arrived in the clearing, I perceived them as some hallucinated beast? I might either run in terror or attack them - anything was possible now. It fascinated me to think that I must question everything before my eyes.

From where I sat I could no longer see the Lilliputians. I would therefore have relinquished some of my control over them and, the instant that I realised this, the ragged chant started up again.

"Cut his throat! . . Cut his throat! . . Cut his throat!"

I was intrigued by this bizarre power game. I was like some dictatorial god to the little people . . or a devil.

The chant was getting louder and I knew that, unseen - and therefore out of control - my tiny tormentors were creeping towards me from behind the rocks. They were now on my side of the river and crowding steadily closer. Although they were my creation, there was a point beyond which I would lose my control over them. I was like a rabbit in the headlamps of an oncoming car. I was too fascinated to be frightened.

But the illusion was becoming too real and I forced my mind in another direction. "C'mon boys, where the hell are you?" I shouted. The sound of my own voice worked as an incantation. Even so far from home the stock English phrase brought a note of reality to the situation that momentarily quelled the heaving earth and drove the Lilliputians back. They did not return to the beach but I had managed to hold them off for a while longer.

I heard them muttering in frustration and then the chant began to build again. "Cut his throat! . . Cut his throat! . . Cut his throat!"

I think the lads must have been gone for twenty minutes at the most but it seemed that I played this power game for hours. Sometimes I would tease the little people deliberately so that I felt that they were very close before I shouted: "What's keeping you, Paul?" Yet I was secretly terrified of seeing the first tiny heads appear over the rock in front of me. At that moment I would know that I had lost control of the monsters of my own creation. I was sure that I could maintain my power for some time but I felt that I only had a limited supply of incantations before the people creeping towards me would cease to take any further notice.

"All right Kolop, take your bloody time!"

I was elated to realise that the name of Kolop, known and respected all along the Mandai valley (as veteran jungle-man and party-animal), was in itself a deterrent to the little people. Surely, I reasoned, they would know about him.

The Lilliputians were very close and I sensed that my power was almost gone when Paul emerged from the trees carrying my pack. Bearded, dirty, limping and sallow-skinned he would have been a terrifying sight in Soho but to me he represented a pleasant vision from home – an all too rare note of reality. My attackers turned angrily and went back to their beach.

Strangely, neither Paul nor the lads had heard any of my calls.

At my beckoning Paul dragged me to my feet and held me up so that I could describe the miraculous view: "You've got to remember all this, Paul. It's amazing and I might forget everything . . there, see there, tiny canoes in the rapids . . all the people on that beach . . girls! . . there on that rock."

After all this time in the jungle, Paul was clearly slightly envious of this mirage: "I could do with some of what you've got myself."

Suddenly, boring up the 'bay' - as big as a destroyer - came a silver fish. A bow wave broke away from its scaly head and sent surf onto the beach. This too, I pointed out to Paul.

"It's an otter!" he said, wide-eyed himself now.

A Borneo hairy-nosed otter. This was an animal that I had particularly hoped to see on the river and, try as I might, all I could see was a monstrous silver *ikan tupai*.

The lads appeared on the edge of the rapids, fighting with the canoes and the otter flipped under the surface. The boys looked like hundred foot giants and I expected panic on the beach but the Lilliputians paid them no notice whatsoever.

I was still shaking too much to ride in a canoe and Kolop agreed to camp the night on the riverbank. The Da'an found my condition nothing more than mildly frustrating. Malaria was a common occurrence in their villages and never having known an *orang barat* they would naturally not realise that, lacking generations of exposure to the disease, we are more violently susceptible to its symptoms.

I changed into dry clothes, crawled under my mossinet and slept soundly for four hours when Paul woke me to give me two more Chloroquine tablets and some chunks of the rich, gamy pangolin meat. I sat shakily on the rocks to eat and saw that the little people were all gone. Where they had been I could see the different shades of the coloured stones that made up a small gravel patch at the bottom of the opposite bank.

I slept soundly that night. I kept my Dictaphone by my side and gave Paul instructions that if I awoke with violent (and interesting) hallucinations he would start the recorder before doing anything else.

The next morning I awoke feeling fresh and, although weak, extremely relieved. I dropped the last two Chloroquine of my hammer-dose and felt confident that the malaria was now under control.

We still had some papaya left from the gold-panner's *pondok* and, since the Da'an were not interested in eating anything that was not accompanied by rice, Paul and I polished most of it off ourselves.

The Da'ans' love of rice was a source of constant amazement to us. (Paul had gone so far as to christen it 'Da'an Diesel.') Not only did they have a greater penchant for packing the stuff away than any other people that I'd ever been in contact with, but they managed to exaggerate its nutritional value out of all proportion and place it on a culinary pedestal all of its own. We ate three times a day and our companions would regularly devour three heaped plates full at each meal. It worried them, that by their standards, Paul and I only ate tiny amounts and, as I was lying back on the rocky riverside digesting my breakfast, Narok suddenly reached for my hand and started bending my fingers back and fore.

"Must eat *nasi*," he explained patiently, as if speaking to a child, "If not all joints in your hands will soon stop moving."

A troop of gibbons was hooting in the distance when we paddled out into the river and they kept up their singing until the sun was high. The morning's travel was relatively easy due to the fact that Kolop fell over in one of the rapids and strained his neck. We stopped at midday to set up camp beside a rocky beach where the river swung a wide loop. This was our first camping sight where a *pondok* did not already exist. Nevertheless, it took Narok, Bayung and Bujang barely twenty minutes to collect the necessary timber and build a framework for the plastic sheet.

Kolop would not commit himself to predicting when he expected to arrive at the fabled *Lapangan gaharu* ('*gaharu* patch') which was the site of our last camp on the river. He was irritatingly elusive about our schedule and we had to content ourselves with waiting until the evening mealtimes, when he would answer questions specifically on the next day's travel. Perhaps he felt that it was unlucky to commit himself to predictions; perhaps it was just easier to take one day at a time.

We had been struggling with the river for six days now and it was getting so shallow that I found it hard to believe that it would not be quicker to walk from this point. But Kolop said, "Cannot. Two, maybe three more days with boats." He winked ominously, "Then we walk - lots of walk."

The early stop gave me the much-needed opportunity to catch up with my diary and Paul decided to test his culinary skills on the remains of the pangolin. He quickly became so bothered by flies that he made a 'tent' from his mossinet and we both sat inside whilst he carved. He made a tasty stew seasoned with an Italian spiced stock cube that he had guarded for precisely such an occasion. He was hurt that the Da'an blatantly let it be known that pangolin was more *enak* barbecued.

The meat helped to restore some of our strength. Paul was feeling almost fully recovered now, but I was still shaky and faintly feverish and my general weakness was evident in my wavering speech. It seemed that I could only speak from the very top of my throat - the slipping grip of my vocal cords. Often when I thought about my fear in the insect ridden jungle it seemed so real - a preview rather than a hallucination - that my throat ached and I could not trust myself to speak. My voice reflected the shaking that my soul had taken.

I figured out that I probably picked up my malaria in Rantau Bumbun. On the move in uninhabited jungle there is very little chance of catching the disease. The female *Anopheles* mosquito, the only harbinger of malaria, first picks up the virus from a person who is malarial. It then takes about nine days for the parasite to mature to a stage where it is again contagious to a human being. Most of the mosquitoes in the Da'an villages would be malarial but since they do not habitually travel more than a mile or two in the course of their lives there would be virtually no malaria deep in the *hulu*. Although our guides could infect the mosquitoes on our campsites, they would be unable to transmit the parasite to us as long as we never stayed in the same camp longer than a week.

There are three different types of malaria and a major difficulty in diagnosing them lies in the fact that the virus migrates between the liver and the blood. Whilst the virus is in the liver it is almost impossible to trace and so the disease can only be diagnosed at times when the patient is actually suffering from the fevers.

After I returned to England I suffered from malarial fevers (though without the hallucinations) every six weeks for five months before the doctors agreed with my own conviction that I was not suffering from common flu.

We all went to bed early but I slept badly. The gibbons that had cheered us from a distance for the last two days were resting in trees just over the river and kept up their whooping serenade well into the night. By then it had been drowned out by the gulping 'burps' of a thousand tree frogs.

We ate the last gristly lumps of pangolin for breakfast. As we were sipping our *kopi* and listening to the gibbons' renewed calls a huge black hornbill flew past. It had raised our spirits drastically by the time it had flapped - *hruumph . . . hruumph* - out of sight up the sun-flecked tunnel.

The river was becoming increasingly beautiful. But it was also becoming shallower with every hour and we now had less time than ever to enjoy the scenery. Three times we came to deep pools and the boys set out the gill net. We needed to stock up on the smoked fish that would sustain us over the mountains. Paul and I rested and checked the new slices on our feet as the boys took turns diving down to the net to emerge further down the river with a fish in their mouths, its tail flapping gaily even though its head was already crushed between their teeth.

After a week on the river our feet were bruised and lacerated and every step seemed to re-open old cuts. For two more days we clawed at rocks and shale with our fingertips, scrabbling out a channel that was just deep enough to slide the suffering dugouts across. We stumbled onward for hour after hour, calf-deep in the cold water, on bleeding feet. We managed to travel only five miles in those last two days.

I noted the eighth day in my diary: *so tough it was violent!*

The canopy over our heads was growing darker as we scrabbled at stones in the river that was now no more than a stream. Suddenly a piercing scream filled the little glade. It seemed to come from just behind my shoulder and I ducked instinctively and turned just in time to see three gibbons go swinging away from the bank. They were only ten feet away and seemed to be as big as chimpanzees. The boys, in a fit of illogical enthusiasm, splashed to the bank after them with their *parangs* aloft.

The gibbons were still laughing at us from their treetops twenty minutes later when Kolop pointed at a patch of sunlight at the end of the dusky tunnel and uttered the unforgettable words: "*Lapangan gaharu.*" We had reached the last camp on the river.

Chapter Ten

Crossing the Müllers

The Plan

Hope my malaria's under control. A few days rest before we head into the mountains will go down well. We're almost within reach of the Punan territory and looking forward to heading into the mountains. As Paul says, "This is what we came here for."

The *lapangan gaharu pondok* was a flimsy structure. It was raised three feet off the ground and the walls and roof were covered with sheets of bark, which had been buckled and twisted by the changing seasons. The bark around the inside of the *pondok* was etched with the names of Da'an *gaharu* hunters who had made it to this spot. It gave us a powerful feeling of achievement to see proof that to arrive at this isolated junction was a source of pride even for the Da'an. I used my *parang* to scratch our own names into a corner of the wall and in place of a Union Jack I pinned up one of our souvenir postcards of Tower Bridge.

The rivers of Kalimantan (the name itself means 'River of Diamonds') play such a central part in the lives of its inhabitants that I had decided to carry a pack of postcards so that I could show them our own river in London. The cards had become almost as popular as our Guatemalan friendship bracelets and I left almost our entire supply of both in the Da'an *kampongs*.

As night descended we were all grateful for the comfort of the *pondok* and the thought of two or three days rest for our feet before we started to walk. Paul was re-stitching his sport sandals with fishing line. Bujang and Narok were sprawled out, with their ears wired to the short-wave radio. Kolop sat in the doorway reciting mangled phrases from the dictionary that Paul had bought in Putus': "What costing taxi is here to town, please?" Bayung was turning the fish on a smoking-shelf over the fire and I climbed out to help him.

"I'm glad to meet you, I beg your guidance," chanted Kolop as I clambered past. "Gif more sugar to the coffee please."

Bayung was having more difficulty in relating to us than any of the others. He was naturally very reserved but his serious industriousness complemented Kolop's swaggering leadership. They had travelled together on several occasions but it was only as we flipped the blackened fish that Bayung told me the tale of their last trip together.

The two of them had travelled up the Mandai on a hunting expedition but the river was very high and for eight days they had struggled against its power. Having just made the journey in a company of six I couldn't imagine how they had managed to haul their dugout over the rapids.

Near the 'Lilliputian beach' the river had wrenched the canoe from their desperate grasp and hurled it back down the gorge. They lost all their provisions and it was only with grim determination that they had managed to reclaim the canoe and, after patching it with clay, started back down the river. Six days later they stumbled into Rantau Bumbun, half-starved and delirious.

Kolop stepped out of the *pondok*, still with the dictionary in his hand: "Your look's not fine today, Pak Mark. Have you visiting a doctor?"

He stared for a moment at the gathering rain clouds, asked Bayung to rig a plastic roof over the fire and leaned back inside the hut to tell Narok to prepare the rice for dinner.

It had been accepted by the whole team that Kolop gave the orders. Back at the worst sections of the river though, when my patience was reaching its limit, I had come very close to reminding him who paid the bills. I was glad, however, that I had not challenged his authority and perhaps upset the balance of our group. We all knew that without Kolop's knowledge and experience we may never have reached the *lapangan gaharu* with all our provisions and equipment intact.

I realised how foolish Paul and I had been even to consider attempting the trip alone. Our chances of getting this far would have been nil: our chances of merely surviving, very slim. It had taken the eight toughest days of our lives to get all the way up the Iban's valley of the spirit world. We had carried one small tin of beef rejang all the way from Nangakalis to celebrate the occasion. For the past few days neither of us had managed to stomach boiled fish at every one of the three daily meals and the fish that we were smoking was perhaps all we would eat during our crossing of the Müllers. With an attitude which we could applaud, even if we could not at the moment even remotely understand it, the Da'an turned their noses up in haughty disapproval of anything so unfresh that it came from a can.

Whilst we watched the beef cook it felt safe to voice the thoughts that had occupied us during the last three weeks that we had been in Da'an country: Bacon, Steak, Chips, Potato salad, Poached eggs, Macaroni cheese, Milk, Ice cream, Fishfingers (strange but true), Buttered Crumpets.

We carried our meals carefully down onto the beach and for twenty minutes the only sound was the reverent scratching of spoons against our tin plates. We chewed every mouthful in pure bliss and afterwards we sat in a profound silence: neither of us had the words to do justice to that tiny tin of unforgettable ambrosia.

A violent rainstorm descended on the Müllers that night. When it began to leak between the layers of bark Paul and I, being the tallest, fought under the driving rain with the flapping plastic sheet before we managed to haul it over the roof and secure it. There was just enough room inside the *pondok* for the six of us to sleep and for once we managed to tie our bunks comfortably. We secured them to the support posts and, although by morning the walls had bent in and our hammocks were sagging onto the floor, we slept well.

We camped for three days at the *lapangan gaharu*. During this time Kolop supervised the building of a small hut for storing the rice that would be needed for their return trip. We thought that he was simply going to hide the rice stores and make sure that it was covered with some sort of roof. We were therefore very surprised when we went along to see the finished 'hiding place.' They had built a miniature stilted *pondok* that was obviously well protected from the environment but immediately noticeable to anyone who walked along this section of the river.

It seemed that the very fact that they had taken so much care over their *nasi* supply ensured that a passer-by would be less likely to raid it. This theory apparently held true only for rice (sacred to the Da'an); the dugouts were hauled up into the trees and carefully camouflaged with branches.

Paul and I never strayed far from camp, hoping that our battered feet would heal as much as possible. Eight days travelling barefoot over the rocks of the riverbed had left me wondering physically how much more my feet could take. The cuts and grazes that had been ulcerating with the constant soaking were just beginning to dry and I hoped there would be time to allow my throbbing Dayak toenail to simmer down before I had to put my boots on. Nevertheless, we were looking forward to getting up into the mountains and not even Kolop's warnings about the difficulties that lay ahead could dampen our enthusiasm. The trail across the Müller Mountains was what we had come half way around the world for and our high spirits were returning as our strength grew.

Besides, we were convinced that whatever lay ahead would have to be easier than the Mandai Hulu.

It was with a powerful bond of comradeship that we lined up for a group photo outside the *pondok* on the morning of our departure from the river. Bujang wore multicoloured striped shorts and a black vest and Narok was dressed in shredded jeans and an amazing check shirt. This shirt had originally been brown and white check but it was so old that most of the white squares had rotted away leaving just a net of brown squares all up his back. Bayung made the greatest concession to jungle travel. He was wearing his green trousers with long blue socks, as he had on the day when Pak Rejang had introduced us, but now he was also sporting the orange pullover that he had worn all the way up the river.

"We can't have him in the photo," laughed Paul, "he looks like a bloody great tulip!"

Paul was going to leave *Siddhartha* in the pondok but at the last minute Kolop collared it and it joined the other mysterious and perhaps magical items in his floral holdall.

At *lapangan gaharu* the Karai River splits into what are logically known as Karai Kiri and Karai Kanan - the Left and Right Karais. We turned up the Karai Kiri until we reached a shallow section where we crossed before putting on our boots and starting a steady meandering climb up the rocky bed of its sister river.

My trendy 'Big Benz' were destroyed within two hours. Both soles were flapping and when the boys stopped to fish at the rare pools I hurriedly tried to stitch them with a whole reel of fishing line. The boys dragged the nets through two separate pools and caught nine big fish. I snapped three needles and my boots held together for a further forty minutes.

Leeches looped after us from all over the forest floor or stretched out from leaves and branches, rearing towards the heat of our bodies. The biggest were about two inches long. Paul and I passed the hours of hiking in keeping a running 'leech tally.' We must have sounded like some strange marching bingo game shouting out our personal count as we pulled another one off our legs.

Kolop showed a disproportionate amount of disgust whenever he found a leech on his legs and he would invariably stop to slice it in two with his *parang*. By the time our leech-counts had reached double figures we could no longer be bothered with even this small community service. There was no time to burn them off anymore and we would simply pull them away and roll them in our fingers to loosen their frantically searching suckers. Then we would try to flick them far enough so that the lads walking behind us would not collect them.

The place where you would least appreciate finding a leech is exactly where they want to go and it is frightening how easily they can get there without you noticing. Having found the spot where they want to feed they make a Y-shaped incision with their three circular teeth and pump an anaesthetic and an anti-coagulant into the wound. Often the first you would know of the leech's visit is a slowly expanding scarlet circle on your shorts or streams of thin blood running down your leg. The anti-coagulant works so well that even when a fat, well-fed leech has dropped off the blood continues to flow and perhaps helps to attract other leeches towards an easy meal. To counteract the loss of precious nutrients SAS soldiers are told to squeeze their own blood from a bloated leech back into their mouths. The only member of our team who appreciated this super-abundance of creepy-crawlies was Bayung's beady bantam who rushed around in a feeding frenzy during the occasional smoke-breaks that Kolop called.

By the time we had reached 'fifteen all' we were already getting used to leeches and, although we inspected our legs at every stop, we began to pay them little notice. If, however, someone felt a leech wriggling under his shorts the whole procession would immediately grind to a halt for as long as was necessary. Whilst the rest of us waited we would begin to get paranoid and start fumbling around in our own shorts. I was sure that, if it was to happen at all, it was at one of these times that we would finally bump into a Punan hunting party.

It was encouraging to realise that we were quickly gaining altitude. The trees were already dripping with cloud-forest type vegetation and their trunks were almost fully shrouded in mosses. When we were forced by a heavy rainstorm to make our first mountain camp, near the top of the now youthful Karai Kanan, the thunder echoed throatily through the trees.

By now my boots were held loosely to my feet only with a whole roll of heavy-duty sticky tape and the flapping soles probably aided me in recording a very respectable leech-count of twenty-two.

Although Paul offered, I was reluctant to use the already repaired and re-repaired sport sandals. I knew that he may have need of them himself before the hike was over. They were beginning to look like my only salvation, however, when I entered into a session of desperate haggling with the giggling Narok.

We both knew that my tender western soles would not last an hour over the rattan spines on the jungle floor and I was happy to pay an outrageous price for Narok's shoes. He knew this and although he was no mercenary he could not ignore the comedy of the situation. He was a born actor - alternately cursing, wheedling and playing aloof.

"But you not understand, Pak Mark. These *sepatus* very specials."

"No, no. These very old *sepatus*. Last one, maybe two days only."

In the end, with an exaggerated show of handshakes and bows we came to an agreement. I would pay him what amounted to three times the price of a new pair of shoes, merely to hire them until we reached the Djuloi River. And I was grateful for the privilege.

We watched Bayung's bantam cockerel strutting between the bunks getting fat on leeches and thought of murder, but Kolop had already explained that Bayung was carrying it over the Müllers to give to a friend. We could not find any dry fuel and dined only on cold rice and some greasy sticks of smoked fish.

Several times during the night we heard the crash of falling trees somewhere along the hillside where decades of root growth had been undermined by this sudden torrent. The Da'an, like many other Dayak groups, believe that merely to hear a tree fall in the forest is an evil omen. They mumbled amongst themselves and I was aware of their tension as we lay awake listening, breathlessly, for the first ominous creaks from above us.

The rain was still falling steadily the next morning. It appeared that we might be stuck there for another night and we were frustrated by this unwanted halt. But by eight o'clock the rain had eased and we started to break camp. Ten minutes into the climb, rays of sunlight began to glow in the canopy and we were cheered by a troop of gibbons, celebrating the end of the storm with their whooping. They followed us closely for the rest of the morning and there is no happier sound in the jungle than the call of gibbons.

I walked in line behind Kolop and hurried along, carefully watching his footsteps and following in blind trust. At times he seemed to dash through the trees and I stumbled desperately after him, occasionally catching the yearned-for glimpse of orange polo shirt or hearing a 'thud' as his *parang* bit into a branch that encroached on the trail.

Sometimes I would lose sight of him entirely and I would scan the area for signs of his passage, the inch-long flash of fresh wood that marked a decapitated sapling or just flattened leaves. Usually I would stop in frustration and Bayung would point the way as if it were sign-posted. Even when he'd shown me I could rarely see the trail until Kolop was back in sight again. It was at these times that I realised how inadequate we really were in the jungle.

As we walked, Kolop became, in my mind, a little holy prophet-pilgrim. His short craggy legs, sprouting out of the bobbing rattan backpack, seemed built for the harshness of the terrain as they pumped tirelessly up hills that left me gasping and clutching my thighs. His cracked, splayed feet carried him shoeless over rocks and swamp with a sureness that was almost mechanical. We trailed along behind this wandering poet-monk, with his baggy saffron-coloured shirt and the pig spear upon which he leaned.

We dragged ourselves grimly up one mountainside for over an hour. Hauling on one trunk at a time, we kept our heads down and tried to find some refuge in the rhythm of our breathing. I found some solace in day-dreams of chocolate binges.

Suddenly I was startled by a cry from above: *"Baru, baru duniaaaa!"* (the Bahasa equivalent of 'brave new world'). I looked up to see Kolop grinning down at us, spear held victoriously aloft. Narok yelled something back at him: I was too exhausted to register his words but I was sickened to hear how fresh he sounded.

As Paul collapsed onto his pack at the top of the hill he looked at me and shook his head: *"Nothing* ever needs to be this tough - this much of a test."

"When I arrive at Heathrow, I'm going to go straight into WH Smith's and I'm going to buy the biggest bar of Toblerone I can find - the white chocolate one - a massive bar of Galaxy and . ." I stifled a sob.

"Stop it! Why do you insist on torturing yourself?"

The Da'an took a ten minute break to smoke some Gudang Garam, then we started to slide down the other side of the mountain. It was frustrating to lose the benefit of the last hour's painful climb so quickly, only to know that we would have to regain it later.

There was never a half-hour stretch of jungle-bashing when either Paul or I were not providing entertainment for our Da'an friends by thudding spectacularly onto our back-packs or narrowly saving ourselves from a fall only by firmly gripping a handful of rattan spines. The little dances we performed whilst trying to extract the painful needles were apparently highly amusing. It was small consolation then to be slapped heartily on the back, tears of joy streaking our companions' faces, and, as the procession began to move again, to hear an affectionate chuckle . . *"Orang barat gila!"*

The chocolate deprivation that always plagues my travels became an absolute torment that day and as my exhaustion increased so the hallucinations became more real.

As we marched through the jungle I spent hours at a time in a dream-world where I remembered the pure decadence of life in London, the bliss of being able to walk into a shop at almost anytime and choose from a rainbow array of packaged chocolate bars. I pictured in minute detail the wrappers and their sensual descriptions: 'light fluffy centre', 'packed with fruit and nuts', 'thick milk chocolate.'

I once arranged to interrupt a trip midway through to meet a girlfriend in Mexico. Being a well brought-up French girl she knew the way to a man's heart. A girl who will set off on a two month trip with only a thirty-five litre backpack deserves respect in my book: when ten litres of that pack are jammed with chilled Mars bars . . well, I could have married her on the spot.

Luckily even I can only eat five Mars bars without pausing for breath, and by the time I'd finished my more sensitive urges were floundering in a seething morass of 'soft nugget and caramel centres.'

I passed the interminable hours of climbing in a dream world where I gazed with rapt attention at the chocolate counter of my local Shepherd's Bush corner shop or examined, in minute detail, the biscuit packaging in an air-conditioned Safeways. In my fevered state I even drifted sporadically into philosophy: is it not significant that the Swiss and the Belgians (the notable aficionados of the chocolate world) have never, so far as I know, been renowned for their exploration? 'Chocolate' they say, 'is a love substitute' and Henry Fielding quipped, 'love and scandal are the best sweeteners of tea.' Now, although I have taken these theories to heart and tried, at times tirelessly, to put them to practical use they have proved of little help. I have usually found that the substitutes are even harder to come by than the original solution to my craving.

The point of my somewhat hysterical harangue is this: when will the nutritionists admit that, for many of us, chocolate is a necessary part of our modern, western diet? These days, when we travel, we can supplement our original iron and vitamin supplements with royal jelly, alfalfa, 'ginkgo bilaba extract', guarana, 'devil's claw extract', ginseng (take your pick from Korean, Chinese or Siberian) and Icelandic sea kelp (with added calcium). Is it unreasonable to hope, one day, to be able to shuck off the burden of my pampered, twentieth century appetite like an overly cumbersome backpack and to stride off into the wilderness with total confidence in my Choco-supplement supplies?

Although none of this land had ever been settled or cleared we were now travelling through what was in effect secondary rainforest. The high rainfall and the steepness of the hillsides meant that, not only did the big trees fall more readily, but that when they did they took large tracts of forest down with them. Thus ground cover was very like the tangles of vegetation that shot up in a desperate race to occupy the precious sunlight in abandoned *ladangs* near the Da'an villages. Kolop was kept very busy, hacking the path clear with his *parang*.

We bathed that evening in a four-inch deep puddle that was

the source of the Karai. It was impressive to think that the water bubbling up through this rock shelf would eventually flow over four hundred miles - down the Karai Kanan, the Karai, the Mandai and the Kapuas - to the South China Sea beyond Pontianak. The next day we would be climbing up, up, up to a little over four thousand feet through the thick jungle.

After dinner I made the discovery that I hoped would ease me through the rest of the hike: *nasi inggris*. I coined the phrase 'English rice' in defence against the boys' balefully accusing stares as they watched me ruining perfectly delicious *nasi* by sprinkling it with sugar. Crystallised momentarily on the fire it made a fine dessert and was destined to be a massive contribution to the harmonious relations within our little group.

We all slept badly that night. It was so cold that Kolop got up about midnight and one by one we all joined him drinking *kopi* and shivering near the fire.

I awoke to the familiar clatter of the battered tin cooking pots and opening a reluctant eye I tried to make sense of the dancing shadows in the fire's amber glow. Slowly Kolop's squatting form detached itself from the darkness. He was offering his palms to the flames, lost in meditation, the glow of his cigarette, like a spark from the fire, hovered above his chiselled jaw.

His love of travelling had led him from his tribal homelands into Central Kalimantan three times before and he knew this route possibly better than anyone else alive. I wondered if he felt stifled with the responsibility of guiding two teenage *gaharu* hunters and two *orang barat gila* all the way up here into the wilderness.

"*Kopi! kopi panas!*" As I sat up and reached gratefully for the steaming enamel cup I caught sight of my filthy, dew-dampened shorts, hanging behind the fire. On the shredded right buttock there was a bloodstain about the size of a beer-mat where one or more of the tenacious leeches had managed to feast on me without being noticed.

It was supposed to be an easy day, mostly downhill, but in fact it was a horror. Over the last two days my Dayak toenail had become painfully septic, it was swollen to twice its size and the nail was already halfway off. I had to lance it every morning just to get it into Narok's shoes which were at least two sizes too small, and I spent the first two hours of each morning doped on Codeine painkillers. After this I resisted the temptation to drop any more pills but by the time the drug wore off I was almost numbed anyway.

A full day's hike downhill was far more painful than the uphill hike which at least took pressure away from my toes. I never removed my shoes during the rest stops, for fear of being unable to get them back on. When I carefully peeled my shoe off that evening, the end of my Tubigrip sock which did duty as a leech-guard was matted with blood.

The camp on the Bengauh Hulu was perhaps our most beautiful. It was situated on a rocky islet in the middle of a tumbling falls. There was a deep pool just in front of the *pondok* and after a swim we felt refreshed enough to do some washing. The smoke from our fire curled out of the sunny clearing and into the high canopy on the slopes where the leaf monkeys were defiantly shaking the branches at us. Despite our cuts and exhaustion everybody was in a cheerful mood that evening.

Narok and Bujang surprised us by going hunting along the

stream just as darkness fell. As a result we had a treat for breakfast; they had managed to supplement our ends of dried fish with a few boiled frogs. Paul and I, like true Europeans, ate only limbs and some shreds of meat that clung to the flanks but the Da'an wasted nothing - sucking every bit of goodness even out of the head.

We waded across the river and started to climb the hill. Kolop showed us where the bark had been shaved from a tree and the names of five Da'an travellers were carved into the wood. One was Maximus, from Nanga Raun.

We started to hear thunder at about eleven o'clock and under the thick canopy the jungle darkened dramatically. We were surprised when Kolop shrugged and said confidently that it was not going to rain.

We heard the rain battering against the canopy a couple of minutes before it actually broke through. Within ten minutes the whole mountainside was a rushing stream and we were all caked with mud.

I was already gritting my teeth against the pain of my poisoned toe. The codeine could do little to alleviate it. This was one of the 'hell-days' of the entire trip. Paul declared that it was the worst day of his entire life. I was too exhausted even to fantasise about chocolate and I just kept my head down and tried to plod automatically in the footsteps of the little pilgrim. We walked onwards through the torrential downpour in heartbroken silence. The rainfall brought the leeches out and by the end of that terrible day I had scored a leech count of seventy-two.

The rain had stopped by the time we arrived at a waterlogged clearing on the bank of the Kacang River. Paul and I shrugged our packs onto the ground and crumpled onto them ourselves. We had covered twenty-five kilometres through dense steep jungle that day and we were amazed at the resilience of our Da'an friends, as they bustled around cutting branches to build a *pondok*.

As I mustered the strength to peel the covers off my throbbing toe, I heard Paul begin to chuckle. In a moment he was holding his sides and roaring uncontrollably.

"This is totally, bloody ridiculous," he managed to blurt, shoulders shaking. "Why the hell did I listen to you?"

I looked up giggling too, infected by his laughter, but the hysteria in his eyes shocked me. We had been friends for a long time and had been through other trips together. I was surprised to see in Paul's face the marks of age – marks that I knew would be reflected in me.

It was exactly two weeks since we left Rantau Bumbun and without a doubt they were the toughest weeks that either of us had ever faced. Even without our illnesses the diet of fish and rice would not have been sufficient to keep us in good health throughout the ordeal. Neither of us (perhaps luckily) was clear enough in our minds to realise how ill we really were.

We forced ourselves to *mandi* in the muddy river and had changed into fresh clothes by the time the boys returned from their hunt. They had not found any meat but our spirits were lifted by the thought that we might be walking into the fruit season. They had found something called *prendit* which Paul identified as mulberries and *apel hutan* (jungle apples) which were like dry plums with scores of white seeds. These delights took our mind off the dried fish tails and bitter boiled rattan cores.

That evening whilst we sat watching Kolop fastidiously plucking his stubble with the tweezers, I asked him again about the

Punan. He told us that they lived more on the other side of the border, in Kal Teng, but there would surely be bands somewhere near us now. He explained that we would be unlikely to meet any but might see some of their fern messages on the trail. Nomadic Punan have to disperse widely across the jungle to find a living on the natural produce and they keep in contact by leaving messages for one another in prominent places along the trails.

Of course to an *orang barat* the trail itself could not be described as prominent, but whilst we might just trample straight past these signs Kolop said that he knew what they meant and would certainly notice them. There are signs that point the direction towards sections of jungle where *babi* are plentiful, where a certain fruit is in season or where honey can be found. He explained how *orang hutan* (nominally Dayaks make no distinction between 'jungle people' and the red ape - 'orang-utan' in English) make a rendezvous.

"Two *orang hutan*, Pak Mark and Pak Paul, want to meet here in five days. So they tie five knots in rattan strips to wear, same-same like belt. They untie one knot every day until meeting. But Pak Mark want to hunt for two more days - because he number one *babi* hunter - so he come here first, leave one piece of rattan with two knots. So when Pak Paul come back, he very happy. Pak Paul say 'Wah! Can have two more days to eat plenty *ikan* and *nasi*.'"

On the fifth day of hiking the trail was much harder to find. For the first time we saw Kolop backtracking, looking for old notches that marked the trail. When he found one he would hack his own sign: two vertical slices joined by a swift chop and three neat slivers of wood would fall away leaving a livid 'H': 'Honorious Bacoc was here.'

The old cliché is that sex is the ultimate motivator. I concentrated on fantasising about the nurse in Kuching. It worried me that I was unable even to focus. I tried to recall a sheer cheesecloth chemise sliding off sun-tanned breasts and I could not even form a picture in my mind. I hoped that this mental faculty was not destroyed forever. The breast connection led to thoughts of an old girlfriend (who worked in a patisserie in Hampstead Heath). This thought in turn led very naturally back to Black Forest gateau.

Just before midday we came out into a small clearing on a hilltop. The jungle had been driven back around a carved wooden grave marker. The area of the grave had been fenced with moss-covered stakes and resting next to the rotting marker was a beaten rice pot and a rusting hatchet. For a Da'an woodsman to be accompanied into the afterlife by his rice pot seemed to us highly appropriate.

Kolop told us that this was the grave of his old friend Paulus, from Nanga Raun. Paulus had been in the mountains six years ago collecting *gaharu* with a dozen friends when he was, with cruel irony, crushed to death by a falling tree. Kolop gently removed the fallen leaves and twigs from the grave and lit a cigarette for his friend before stepping back and saying a few quiet words in Bahasa Da'an. Bayung, Narok and Bujang then added a lit cigarette each to the rice pot and I left a couple of Guatemalan friendship bracelets as tributes from Paul and me.

It was a daunting thought that should any of us die here it could take weeks to carry the body to civilisation. This would clearly be impossible, and yet to be buried here in deserted jungle, miles upon miles from the sound of human voices, seemed to me to be the loneliest fate in the world.

This trip had been my idea. I had invited Paul. How could I ever be able to visit his mother and sisters in Cornwall to break the news to them that I had left him thousands of miles from home with only a carved stick and a rice pot for a tomb?

Paulus's grave marked the border between West and Central Kalimantan. We had crossed the Müllers into *Kal Teng* and we were at last on the downhill trek to Taj'ak Bangkan. The thought put a spring into our steps and we headed out of the clearing with renewed energy.

But we were now in dark and mysterious land to the Da'an. Kolop whispered a warning to the other Da'an to stay alert and I caught the words *orang pemotong* (literally 'choppers' - headhunters).

The walk was mostly flat now and although my poisoned toe was still throbbing I felt happy and incredibly grateful - even slightly surprised - that we had both made it here. From the top of a steep bluff we got our fist view in five days through a narrow gap in the trees and from down in the ravine we could hear the tumbling of the Djuloi River. Narok hacked all our names into a tree trunk on the edge of the bluff.

The band of gibbons that had followed us for most of the day deserted us and we whooped our own triumphant descent into the valley.

Chapter Eleven

Racing the Flood

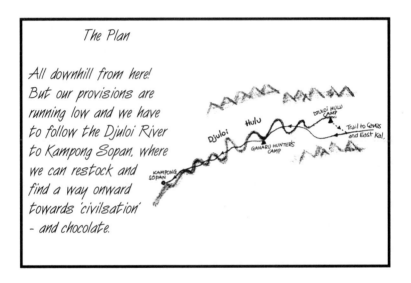

The Plan

All downhill from here!
But our provisions are
running low and we have
to follow the Djuloi River
to Kampong Sopan, where
we can restock and
find a way onward
towards 'civilsation'
- and chocolate.

Kolop said that it would take us about five more days to walk downriver to Taj'ak Bangkan and we would reach it via Kampong Sopan. I consulted my dictionary: '*sopan*, well-mannered; honourable; decent.' All in all, more than you'd have any right to demand from a collection of *gaharu* collectors' shacks in the middle of the jungle.

Kolop called a day of rest at our first camp on the Djuloi, citing as a reason: "Bayung, very tired. Need to rest." We found this puzzling because Bayung appeared no less dynamic than the other Da'an. Perhaps Kolop was just too polite to come right out and say that it was Paul and I who looked like we needed the rest.

Before he went hunting with the boys, Kolop took me aside and told me to keep our *parangs* close to hand and not to allow anybody into the camp on any pretext. I gave him my most grimly courageous nod and he turned and walked out of the camp, leaving me uneasy in the knowledge that I was going to let *anybody* into the camp on *any* pretext whatsoever rather than attack them with a sixteen inch jungle knife.

Our imminent exit from the jungle made us aware of just how desensitised we had become. We began to look at the things around us and to point them out as if we were trying to trap a few more of the images that had been lost to us because of our single-mindedness.

"It's scary how you stop noticing things when you're going through all that," said Paul nodding towards the mountains. "We must have been almost blind."

We lay on the narrow rocky beach and marvelled at the towering trees and drunken fluttering of butterflies. We tried to creep up on the leaf monkeys as they came down to the water's edge to drink.

That night, after (or perhaps because of) a meal of boiled frogs, I reached the climax of my chocolate-obsession. I fought sleep for a full three hours so that I could enjoy my hallucinations. I felt the cool air of a gleaming celestial kitchen and Formica under scrubbed hands that did not feel or even look like mine (perpetually scratched and dirty). I saw with tantalising vividness the creation of the king of all chocolate logs. It was enriched with brandy butter, clotted cream, blackcurrant conserve and cherries (all sampled during preparation). It was as thick as a man's leg: it would be a chocolate log which would be talked about for generations or at least *ad nauseum.* It was a phenomenal feat since in my present 'clear-headed' state I wouldn't know where to start making even a far less ambitious confection.

I never completed this delicacy because the next thing I knew the sky was misty yellow and the tall grass beside my pillow was sparkling with dew. I could smell the hot aroma of *kopi* in the air.

Up on the ridge the gibbon troop was greeting the new day. Their song had cheered us throughout our trail and I hoped that it would not be the last time that we would hear them.

We were just surveying our vacated campsite for any accidentally dropped items or litter when we heard another familiar sound. *Hruumph . . . hruumph . . . hruumph*, and two huge black hornbills, with four foot wingspans, wheeled around the bend and chugged onward down the valley.

When we turned to leave each of us was smiling.

From the southern foothills of the Müllers we would have to follow the Djuloi River down to the southwest, to where it meets the Barito River, as it heads to the Java Sea. So I was naturally confused when we strode off uphill and for the first hour climbed eastward, away from our destination and towards West Kalimantan. Kolop was characteristically evasive.

We heard a crack of branches and a heavy 'thud' on the hillside to our right. Narok and Bujang went leaping through the bushes towards the sound.

"Durian!" laughed Kolop. The boys carried back three of the spiky green 'coconuts' but they were not yet ripe and the flesh had the taste and texture of raw cabbage. Kolop warned that it would make us *sakit*.

The Djuloi River was well to our rear and I was biting my lips in preparation for asking Kolop for the fourth time why we were not going downhill when suddenly we stepped out onto a track. It was the first real, beaten path we had seen since leaving Rantau. I had a vision of a trail in one of the darkest corners of Hampstead Heath: Sunday strollers with Barbour jackets, all-terrain pushchairs and time for a pint on the way back home.

Kolop told us that this track led back into East Kalimantan, and the Southern Müllers, and westwards to Kampong Sopan. We stretched our legs as the path looped over the hillside, always dropping slightly, back towards the river. Here and there we spotted the signs of human passage: footprints, a spot of betel spit, a cigarette butt (I was so surprised that I picked it up and showed it to Paul).

Kolop pointed towards something moving down on the riverbank and we all craned our necks to try to make out what it was through the trees. There were two men climbing towards us leaning heavily on their pig-spears. Their rattan packs were stacked high above their heads so that they were bent almost double beneath the weight. With a feeling of absurd happiness I realised that we were about to meet the first people we had seen since we left the Da'an territory.

In a real wayfarer's meeting we stopped, mid-trail, to exchange Gudang Garam and news. The two men were Ot Danum (a tribe of hunter-gatherers, loosely akin to the Punan) and lived on the Barito River. It had taken them eight days to walk from Taj'ak Bangkan. The water level was very shallow even on the lower sections of the Djuloi they told us and there had not been boats running for several weeks.

Kolop spoke *Bahasa ngaju*, the lingua franca of *Kal Teng*, but one of the men spoke Indonesian and I asked them about their destination. They would spend the next two months - more if their rice lasted - collecting birds' nests in a network of caves, three days further up the trail in the Müller Mountains. Other than *gua sarang burung* (birds' nest caves) the caves have no name and they are almost certainly unexplored by anybody but the local Dayaks. Not only would it be fascinating to be the first outsiders ever to visit the caves but also I believed that they could make an ideal base camp for exploring the area and perhaps making contact with the Punan. However, as the Ot Danum said, living in the caves could be very dangerous. There would be no law and birds' nests are very valuable.

Kolop brazenly told the Ot Danum that we had run out of sugar and they instantly replenished our supplies. Wishing we had more to give I handed out our last two waterproof torches. I hoped they would be useful in the awful blackness of the caves. I also gave them two Guatemalan bracelets and their faces cracked into wide smiles when they noticed that our whole band was wearing them. We shook hands again and the Ot Danum turned doggedly towards their caves and we bounded onward, cheerfully now, chewing on a parting gift - some delicious chunks of *babi*.

When the path dropped down, into the chasm of the young Djuloi, it began to twist and turn so that I was very quickly struggling to get my bearings. Sometimes it doubled back on itself and we had to wade across with our packs on our shoulders, pushing hard into the current.

"Don't worry," said Paul, "if you lose your bearings in here they'll probably get washed up on the beach at Taj'ak Bangkan."

The vegetation was at its thickest along the riverbanks where the battle for sunlight was not limited only to the forest giants. As we wriggled through into the open forest Kolop stopped suddenly and waved his hand downward in a patting motion. We all crouched quickly to the ground. His head was cocked, dog-like, to one side. I strained my ears and peered through the trees ahead.

Kolop plucked a blade of grass, and I breathed a sigh of relief as I realised what he had heard. Carefully splitting the leaf's stem he was making a whistle to attract a *kijang* (barking deer). We had seen him do this before but had not been surprised at the lack of success since the ridiculous farting cough that he made sounded nothing like the bark of a *kijang*. Nevertheless, we stayed obediently crouching for about five minutes, grateful for the rest. Paul and I tried not to giggle whilst Kolop farted through the grass.

Then we heard a hoarse, dry cough and there, not fifty feet away, her sandy fur prominent against the trees, was a *kijang* doe. Looking at her, posing so prettily on a hummock of tufted grass, I was suddenly immensely pleased that we had not brought a gun. She twitched her ears and with a single bound and a flash of white tail she was gone.

Despite the increased signs of human presence, wildlife was far more abundant on this side of the Müllers. Before we had been walking again for ten minutes Kolop identified the cause of a clumsy thrashing in the foliage ahead of us as a fleeing *burung ruai*, an Argus pheasant. We had heard the distinctive *'ki-au'* call of the Argus often in the mountains but they are timid and, despite their flashy colours and long sweeping tails, they are very difficult to see. *Burung ruai* is one of Borneo's most universally revered birds - but it was not keen to bless us with its presence.

The stylised markings of the peacock-like 'eyes' along the Argus pheasant's tail are a common motif in Dayak (specifically Iban) tattoos. It is an appropriate symbol because according to myth the Argus pheasant was the first creature to be tattooed.

'Long, long ago,' - so the story goes - 'before any of the birds had colours, *burung ruai* and the common coucal decided to tattoo each other. The coucal did his best by the Argus and the results of his intricate and painstaking work can be seen today. But then it was the pheasant's turn. He was lazy and stupid and very quickly he got into a mess. Suddenly he made his loud, ringing *'ki-au'* call, warning that danger was approaching, and took off with his usual flustered flapping. As he escaped he knocked the pot of dye over the coucal. That is why, to this day, the coucal is stuck with a sticky mess of dark feathers over the top half of his brown body whilst the Argus pheasant is the most beautiful bird in the jungle.'

It was just after noon. We had been walking for five hours, crossing the Djuloi ever more frequently, when we were shocked by a deep growl. It was somewhere close to our left flank.

We stopped immediately and scanned the tangled undergrowth. Silence. Kolop lowered his spear slowly. Nothing moved.

We started walking and again there was the low roar, louder this time. We spun around. Kolop poised his spear again. It sounded so close that it seemed impossible that there was nothing to see.

"Kolop, what is it?" I hissed.

No answer.

"*Apa ini?*" I asked again.

"*Diam!*" - Quiet!

Whatever it was, it was stalking us. When we stopped, it stopped. I searched my memory trying to recall all the large animals that I had read about. I could think of nothing but tigers.

Supposedly, there have never been tigers in Borneo, but the point has always been somewhat in question. When the sea level dropped during the last ice age a huge expanse of rainforest known as Sundaland was formed connecting Borneo, Sumatra and Java with the Malay Peninsula. Borneo is the largest remaining piece of Sundaland and yet experts believe that tigers never followed the migrations of deer, pigs, orang-utan, monkeys, rhinos, bears and otters onto this island as they did throughout the rest of Sundaland. There are frequent references to tigers in Dayak folklore and numerous place-names bearing the word *harimau* – not to mention at least one *parang*.

"Kolop," I hissed, "*harimau?*"

"*Bukan*" - Not.

The creature bellowed and we swung towards the sound, expecting a charge. Some low branches shook violently but the animal was too intelligent to show itself.

Kolop moved away faster.

Then maybe a honey bear I thought. But this sounded far too big. Too big even for a clouded leopard, Borneo's biggest cat - officially. We hurried onwards, glancing back over our shoulders, and after a while realised that we had left the animal behind.

Still Kolop was unwilling to speculate on what had followed us. It was only later, when I bullied him, that he told me it was an orang-utan. Some Dayaks believe that they are humans, condemned to live a solitary existence in the jungle or that they are the re-incarnations of the dead. It was the only thing I could think of that would explain Kolop's stubborn reluctance to talk about the creature, particularly in its presence. I was amazed that such a ferocious roar would come from an orang-utan and at the same time I was disgusted with myself for not summoning the energy, and the nerve, to investigate.

We had covered, by Kolop's estimation, about twenty kilometres that morning. I had just figured out that (including the switchbacks of the Kapuas River) we were just about to cross the equator for the ninth time since arriving in Borneo, when we saw a man running along the opposite bank.

We waited for him as he crossed at a shallow section. He held a shotgun above his head and as he climbed onto the bank we could see that he was wearing cut-off jeans and wellington boots which were several sizes too big for him. He clomped over to meet us with a wide smile and shook hands all round.

Hopping around whilst he emptied the river out of his boots, he invited us to sleep in his camp, a couple of miles further downriver. He dashed along at such a charging pace that even Kolop, the prophet-pilgrim had trouble keeping up with him. He ducked and dived and weaved around and over obstacles on the trail like a bantamweight boxer. We limped along behind, tripping and getting our packs snagged on branches so that we were exhausted by the time we saw smoke rising out of the trees. A radio pouring music out over the hissing of the river seemed strangely alien.

The man was a *gaharu* hunter and he was camping by the Djuloi with four friends, building up the stake that would make them relatively well-off when they arrived back home. One of them had tufts of long moustache hanging from only the corners of his betel-blackened mouth and another had rough tattoos in his tribal language scrawled erratically all over his chest. They were all very short with knotted muscles and thick legs. Three of them were puffing fat, stumpy pipes and with their muscular necks and chunky features they reminded me of formidable Hobbits.

They were Dayak Memaruh from the Melawi River. This could be translated as 'half-dayak' but since the only alternative to being Dayak is to be *orang melayu* (Muslim) and therefore absolutely non-Dayak . . . well it seemed that 'half-dayak' would be an impossibility. I never did manage to grasp the meaning of Dayak Memaruh in this context and it is perhaps just another example of the confusion (for outsiders) in Dayak tribal identities.

One of the men was carefully dissecting driftwood-like lumps of *gaharu* into chips of matching shades. It is one of the world's most expensive spices and is graded according to its purity - the darkest being the most valuable. Best quality *gaharu*, almost totally black, can sell for hundreds of pounds per kilo - but, unfortunately for these men, not to the shrewd Chinese traders on the Melawi River.

There was obviously good money to be made here, however. The man laid his pipe aside and held up a bag of *kayu biasa*, standard grade wood. He estimated that it would fetch about 150,000 rupiah (sixty-five dollars) per kilo when he sold it. He passed me the hoard to me to inspect. It weighed about four kilos. They had been camping here for a month and figured that their supply of rice would last about two more months, but the river was stocked with *ikan tupai* and crayfish and they had two guns that kept them supplied with meat. They invited us to help ourselves to *kopi* and some hunks of meat that was slowly roasting on a shelf above the fire. There was some *babi* and some dangerously under-cooked *landak* (porcupine), which we, nevertheless, had to sample. Black and white quills were strewn about all around the fire attracting a buzzing cloud of flies so we plucked some stringy meat off a *landak* leg and went to sit with our hosts.

"*Enak!*" Paul waved the pink meat.

"More *enak*, yesterday," laughed the tattooed hunter pausing to puff his pipe, "*Makanan orang hutan.*"

"Jesus! Paul, they've eaten an orang-utan!"

Orang-utans are generally solitary animals but we couldn't help wondering if there was any connection between this killing and the ape that had followed us. We were both very glad that we had arrived one day too late to take part - or to refuse to take part - in the feast.

Clearly Dayak Memaruh don't entertain any fantastic notions about 'jungle people.'

We cleared an area and set up our camp next to the prospectors. It rained heavily all through the night and was still streaming steadily when we woke at dawn to drink our *kopi*. Kolop stood worriedly watching the river - it had risen by almost three feet during the night. He explained that we would have to cross the river many times before Kampong Sopan and that if it swelled much more we could be stranded indefinitely in the Djuloi Hulu.

Paul and I were anxious to get going. The thought of being stranded here, two days from 'Decency Village,' was intensely frustrating. But the speeding current meant that laying gill nets was already an impossibility. We had no more fish or meat, we had enough rice for only two more days and Kolop was reluctant to leave the security of the prospector's camp whilst the rain was still falling. He knew the reality of the situation better than anyone and we tried to wait patiently for his decision.

It came about seven o'clock: "We'll try."

The rain, though lighter now, looked like it was in for the day and we powdered and bandaged our feet and broke camp quickly. Then we said our 'goodbyes' and 'good lucks' to the *orang memaruh* and set off at a brisk stride.

Kolop said that we would be unlikely to reach the *kampong* that day but if we didn't make it the next day it may be too late. The river ran noticeably swifter throughout the morning and at times we dogtrotted along the banks. We crossed and re-crossed countless times with our packs balanced on our heads. The rain had brought the leeches out by the thousands but Kolop, running on points, seemed to pick most of them up before we got to them (I scored only thirty-four). When we stopped briefly to rest they were everywhere on the jungle's leafy carpet, flipping excitedly towards the warmth of our bodies.

We needed maximum concentration to battle across the floodwater - leaning almost our full weight into it, sometimes chest deep – and to dodge the obstacles as we trotted along the trail. But this kept us alert and, although the trek was a hard one, we began to enjoy ourselves.

Neither Paul nor I (and certainly not the Da'an) felt the strain of the pace. So, when Kolop called a break to cook up some 'Da'an diesel', we devised a plan. Paul managed to ease my alarm clock momentarily out of Kolop's pack and by the time we hit the trail again he believed that we had an extra hour of daylight. Thus, we just might reach Kampong Sopan that day - if we ran.

An hour later, with a belly-full of rice, we regretted our rash move.

We kept up our trotting pace through the drizzle. The river was getting visibly higher with every crossing. We were driven by the adrenalin of the race: it heightened the sense of adventure and combated the fatigue. We stopped to rest at two o'clock (really three o'clock) having covered thirty kilometres. In reality, we only had two hours before we would have to find somewhere to camp.

"Can we reach the *ladang* today, Kolop?"

"*Moga-moga.*" - Maybe.

We tightened our packs against our backs and ran at almost full speed now. But we ran with high spirits. Kampong Sopan was still eight kilometres away and the river was now so powerful that we had to pick our spots to cross carefully. We leapt across the streams that surged into the Djuloi. We laughed and joked as we ran - not feeling the pain any more. The blisters stopped hurting and we didn't even have to fight for breath. The joy of this rush through the jungle even eased the throbbing in my poisoned toe.

At one wide, muddy inlet (a typical *babi* wallow) I tripped as I lined myself up to jump and went careering down the slimy bank on the seat of my shorts. I stumbled towards the far bank and was trying to claw my way out when Narok, running behind me, misjudged his own jump and landed with a splash beside me. Giggling hysterically we fought to use each other as a prop to haul ourselves out of the stagnant grey ooze. Meanwhile, Paul and the others roared with laughter, well out of our reach up on the bank.

The path into the village was along three huge trunks, chopped down with almost scientific precision so that they had fallen end to end. The last was about three feet in diameter and formed a bridge, ten feet above a swampy stream.

As I jumped off the end of the log I became aware of some very poignant noises: a dog barked excitedly and a cockerel crowed. The sounds of a village carried an unexpected power.

Chapter Twelve

Out of the Darkness

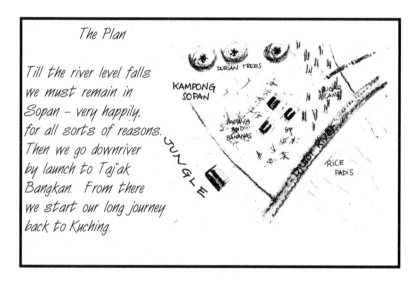

The Plan

Till the river level falls
we must remain in
Sopan - very happily,
for all sorts of reasons.
Then we go downriver
by launch to Tajak
Bangkan. From there
we start our long journey
back to Kuching.

DURIAN TREES

KAMPONG
SOPAN

SUGAR
CANE

PAPAYA
AND
BANANAS

JUNGLE

BLUSOI RIVER

RICE
PADIS

We climbed onto the bamboo platform of the first stilted *pondok*. There were about ten young men inside besides our friends and this was a particularly happy reunion, since most of them were Da'an and some had been away from their families for over a year. Bayung delivered the 'migratory' bantam to his cousin and the other boys had each brought messages from home.

Word spread through the *kampong* that some visitors had arrived and more people climbed into the *pondok* to welcome us. There had never been an *orang barat* in Kampong Sopan and, without sounding flippant, it was difficult to explain why we had wanted to come across from the north. They shook their heads grimly, remembering the harshness of their own trips.

There were twenty or so inhabitants in the *kampong*. The average age was about twenty-two and the population was wholly transient, although one old-timer had been there for four years. Kampong Sopan was no more than a work camp, a place to live whilst the men collected *gaharu*.

We had walked straight into the fruit season and while the Da'an chattered Paul and I were happy to loll lazily against the bamboo walls, chain-munching the most delicious bananas that we had ever eaten. They were only three inches long, about an inch thick and were called *pisang emas* (golden bananas). They were the heavenly nuggets of the fruit world. Even the strong, healthy hunting dogs were addicted to the sweet *pisang emas*. We laughed as we watched them delicately peeling off the soft skins, nibbling daintily with their incisors.

There are numerous stories throughout Borneo of how disaster befalls people who laugh at animals, but my favourite was reported by Spenser St John, in 1862: Many years ago a great *kepala* gave a feast and lots of people came to his longhouse. In the middle of the feast his beautiful daughter arrived. She was very spoilt and was only interested in annoying the guests. In their efforts to get rid of her they put dirt in her food. But this did no good. So (as is the way in the best Dayak tales) they put poison in it.

The *kepala* was very angry and he decided he would have his revenge on the whole congregation. So he went to get his dog. He shaved off all its fur and painted it with vertical black and white stripes. Then he got it drunk and carried it back into the *ramai* where he placed it in the middle of the room. The dog started to stagger around and looked so ridiculous that everybody roared with laughter – even the host couldn't keep a straight face. They were all turned to stone.

By nightfall our attention had been diverted from *pisang emas* to papayas and then, via sugarcane, to durians. We had both tried this legendary fruit in Singapore, several years earlier, but they had been simmering in the tropical sun on a market stall for hours and we'd never had the urge to repeat the experience.

When they are not fresh or after they have been opened a few minutes durians start to send up a penetrating stench like blocked drains. For this reason alone, they are illegal on the public transport system in Singapore and we'd had to smuggle our purchase across the city hidden under the back seat of a bus - whilst we sat in the front one.

These Sopan durians were something very different. Rushed inside as soon as they fell from the tallest trees, where the wind had chilled them, they could not have been fresher and their thick creamy flesh was delicious. After only ten minutes the empty skins, like spiky green leather, and the shiny mahogany stones begin to smell. Similarly, by that time they have penetrated your whole system and have been converted almost entirely to gas - with spectacular results. For two days all your bodily waste, your burps (and there are lots of them) and your breath are strongly perfumed with old durian.

When Paul and I hobbled down to a nearby stream to *mandi* that evening, we were already thoroughly converted to the durian appreciation association (not a large, but certainly a dedicated sect). We were doubled over by the sheer weight of fruit and the fascinating gaseous convulsions in our stomachs. I had to sit still for half an hour, unable to move until five monstrous durian belches had burst forth, effectively lessening my body weight by about eight kilos.

That first night in Kampong Sopan I paid the price of my gluttony. I was woken by some ominous internal rumblings and, with somebody's muffled giggling behind me (probably Paul's), I went skating through the darkness along the slimy path to the river. After half an hour spent groaning in shallows I was not sleepy any more so I sat for a while on the platform and considered the successes and the failures of our expedition.

I was convinced beyond doubt that we were the only westerners ever to travel along the valley of the Iban 'River of Death,' across the Central Müllers and down the Djuloi River. We had been congratulating ourselves on this success between mouthfuls of fruit ever since we arrived in Kampong Sopan:

"Dive in! You deserve every bit of that."

"Oh no, please. Couldn't have done it without you . . Have another?"

On the other hand a guilty feeling had haunted me ever since we had started across the mountains and, in need of every fraction of my resources, I had driven it from my mind. Now I was forced to face the fact that we had not fully accomplished our mission. I had hoped that once we entered the Müllers I would be able to offer the bonus that would persuade our guides either to detour off the trail or to set up a base-camp from where to spend some time looking for signs of the Punan.

I had radically underestimated the speed - to the Punan alien and unfriendly - at which we would have to travel. If the nomads *had* shown themselves, I for one, head down and dreaming of chocolate, would never have seen them. I was already thinking of returning to explore the *sarang burung* caves of the Ot Danum, and perhaps use them as a re-supplied base-camp from which to make short explorations (of up to three or four days) into the surrounding area.

For the moment however, we were looking forward to some R and R in Banjarmasin, at the mouth of the Barito River. BJ (as it's known amongst expats in Kalimantan) is famous for R and R. Ours would consist, I hasten to add, only of some fairly lightweight debauchery involving steak, chips, lots of chocolate and several bottles of *arak*.

We did not feel free to talk openly about the pleasures that awaited us downriver because our Da'an friends, after restocking their provisions in Taj'ak Bangkan, would turn back to the Müllers to make the crossing all over again. It was a humbling thought.

They planned to spend two more months camping on the Mandai Hulu side of the mountains, collecting *gaharu*. I hoped that from our wages and the sale of their *gaharu* they would make enough money to enjoy some of the easy-living and partying that they would undoubtedly have earned.

The voracious mosquitoes, the keepers of the curfew, drove me back inside and, after tentatively shoving a snarling dog away from my sleeping-mat, I curled up and closed my eyes. The *kampong* cockerels had begun to herald the day an hour ago - regardless of the fact that it would still be pitch black for another three hours. I concentrated to ignore them and for a while I was successful.

Waking up in a village in Borneo was rarely as I had hoped or had imagined it would be: the sunlight cutting cheerfully through the slatted bamboo walls, the crackling wood as somebody gently coaxes the early fire and far away across the valleys gibbons calling to break the silence.

This is all romantic nonsense. In Sopan, as in most *kampongs*, every living thing wakes simultaneously with only one ambition: to make more noise than all the other things that have just woken. There seems to be some unwritten law that the long hours of the night's silence must be balanced by forty minutes of chaos.

Two dogs started a vicious, snarling fight on my feet. A cockerel roosting on a perch three feet below my head crowed. (I could see its scraggy neck through the boards - but I couldn't reach it.) Someone in the next room decided that it was absolutely vital that the rice pot be cleaned immediately . . and that the most effective way to do it would be to belt it on the base with a sturdy log. The man on the bunk at my head slammed his radio on and Indonesian pop music wailed into the room, terrifying even the fighting dogs.

Kolop's friend, Hutuk, and another man (they didn't have

radios) started to clear their throats as only South East Asians can do. They hawked and coughed and slapped their necks and Hutuk held his nose to get more leverage.

As I pulled my sheet over my head I heard Paul's voice rise above it all: "Oh for fuck's sake! He'll blow a bloody lung like that!"

Kampong Sopan consisted of four sturdy *pondoks* and a *ladang* that was well stocked and cared for. The river was full of fish, the jungle was full of wildlife and the inhabitants, in addition to their fruit and rice, were full of *babi* and deer. Decency Village was a good place to live.

Because of the rainfall that was still descending up on the Müllers we waited for three days in Sopan for the Djuloi River to drop back to more or less its usual level. We passed our time strolling around the village, bathing and visiting each of the four shacks in turn. In a *pondok* high up the bank on the opposite side of the stream lived the man who had already been four years in Sopan. He was also a Da'an and would be a rich man when he eventually made the trip back to his family in Nanga Raun. In addition to *gaharu* collecting he carved handles and sheaths for the Kampong Sopan's parangs.

Unfortunately he had acquired several pots of paint from somewhere and now all his sheaths with their intricate rattan bindings were painted bright blue.

It was no secret if somebody in the village was going hunting because the moment he stepped out of the hut with a pig-spear he would be surrounded by dogs, with their heads thrown back howling like foxhounds.

The dogs of the *kampong*, fiercely maintaining their own positions in the strict hierarchy, were obviously from the same stock. Bred through generations into the instantly recognisable Sopan breed, they were short but sturdy, sandy coloured with dark muzzles and they were quick and willing fighters. They outnumbered their masters by two-to-one and slept their nights curled between the bodies of the men, sharing warmth, or in the backs of the large fireplaces amongst the heated stones.

Boss was unquestionably top dog. He was identical in markings to the others but unlike them - liable to receive only a kick if they wandered unwanted through a hut - everyone had a word for Boss.

"What news, Boss?"

"Wanna hunt *babi*, Boss?"

It seemed the polite thing to do, when Boss wandered past, for someone to interrupt their conversation to casually reach out and cup his testicles, as if weighing them. Perhaps they were considering the next generation of hunting dogs, but either way it never seemed to make Boss the slightest bit nervous.

"You can do that if you want to." I told Paul. "Boss won't mind."

"That's the dog's bollocks, that's what that is," Paul said, nodding towards the ambling Boss.

We were faced with a further one-day hike downriver to the *palangkan* (literally a jetty) where we could wait for a boat to Taj'ak Bangkan. There was no regular service, everything depended on the condition of the river: we might have to wait, one, two, three days or maybe a whole week. This *palangkan* was Sopan's only link with the outside world.

We were disappointed to learn that Narok and Bujang would not be coming with us to Taj'ak Bangkan. Our goodbyes were going to have to be said in Sopan and the beery farewell that had been planned was destined to be far less hearty with only two-thirds of the old posse.

The boat trip was much more expensive than we had expected - due partly to the dangerous, rocky nature of the river and partly to the high price of fuel in the *hulu*. We were going to pay Kolop and Bayungs' return fares to Taj'ak Bangkan as an extra bonus and we simply couldn't afford to pay for the others. Kolop was going to collect their provisions and I promised that we would send some beers back for them - along with Narok's shoes.

Hutuk, from Nanga Sarai, had been four months in Sopan and was ready to sell his stash of *gaharu*, so he decided to join our little procession.

We were both very unhappy about saying goodbye to the two young *Gaharu* hunters and did so as quickly as possible. Each of us was well aware of how much we had been through together and also painfully certain that we were unlikely ever to travel together again.

It was twenty-five kilometres to the *palangkan*. The green twisting valley and the rocky chasms of the Djuloi were beautiful but Hutuk's continuous hacking throat-clearing made us realise how lucky we had been with our companions.

"He must have tonsils like a bricky's thumb," grumbled Paul.

We both had some stalks of sugarcane from the *ladang*

strapped to our backs and they were a great energy boost. Another lesson to remember for our return was that travelling through the rainforest would be much easier during the fruit season.

The *palangkan* was no more than a *pondok* frame with a fireplace and we quickly threw our plastic sheet across and tied up our bunks for the night. We had rice enough to last if we had to wait for two days and Bayung immediately swam across the river to scavenge around the base of a towering durian tree and returned with two fresh durians.

At mid-afternoon we were excited to hear the steady hum of a *speed* and figured happily that we would be in town by dark. But the boatman dropped his passengers and explained that he had to go back downriver to a camp where someone was ill and that he would return for us early the next morning.

There were two lads on the boat. They were travelling to the caves to collect birds' nests. One was a young, thin Ot Danum. He was the only young Dayak that we met in Kalimantan who could not speak Bahasa. Whilst his friend *pondok*-ed with us, he made his own camp on the riverbank. He disappeared into the jungle with his *parang* and reappeared after ten minutes dragging four nearly perfect six-by-two scaffold boards. With these he quickly knocked up a bunk.

Paul was flabbergasted: "There must be a bloody Jewson's in there!"

I awoke before dawn and went to sit alone in the darkness to enjoy the sensations of my last night in the jungle. I was sitting comfortably on a fallen log near the river when the most amazing dawn display of the gibbons began. They were in the branches right on the ridge across the river so for once we not only heard them but we were able to watch their lanky loops through the treetops whilst we breakfasted on *nasi inggris* and more fallen durian.

Then something wonderful happened. Something that provoked us, for the first time, to openly discuss our return. Two hornbills chugged along the river in front of us (flying left to right) and swooped upwards, gliding on a swan-like wingspan for the last second to roost high on a naked branch. One of them threw back its head so that its massive bill jerked upward and *ca-ca-cack-cackled*.

If it were not for the fact that we had to change money (and eat chocolate) it is doubtful whether we would have got on the boat that morning.

We saw more wildlife in the five hours that it took to travel down to Taj'ak Bangkan than we did either in the Mandai Hulu or in the mountains. This surprised us all the more because instead of travelling in relative silence as we had with our canoes - disregarding of course the accompanying sobs and Anglo-Saxon oaths - we were now zipping down the river in front of an Evenrude outboard.

We saw so much wildlife that I began to keep a list. And there was so much wildlife that, because I was writing my list, Paul saw more than me. He saw: hornbills, Brahminy kites, two species of kingfisher, iguana, red and grey leaf monkeys, *babis*, *kijang*, mouse-deer, marten and an Argus pheasant.

We stopped briefly at another *gaharu* hunter's camp where the Posong River joined the Djuloi. We ate wonderful mouse-deer *satay* with the boatman's friends and gazed wistfully at some unripe bunches of fluffy rambutan hanging from a tall tree. This fruit - literally meaning 'hairy' in Indonesian - is a particularly delicious member of the lychee family.

One of the *gaharu* hunters was in a lot of discomfort with

what seemed to be dysentery and I gave him some re-hydration sachets and the last of our antibiotics.

Clutching a mouse-deer *satay* for the road (and mouse-deer *satays* are a lot more nourishing than you might imagine) we buzzed back into the current.

Despite our enjoyment of the boat ride we were glad when, after five hours, we glided towards a pontoon on the edge of Taj'ak Bangkan.

"Look," said Paul, pointing towards a figure at the edge of the pontoon, "It's a woman."

"Calm down Mowgli." I laughed.

Our first responsibility was, of course, to settle our more basic needs. There were three general stores in TB. We went to the closest one and within half an hour we were such valued customers that Eros, the Muslim lady who owned it, offered us sleeping-mats on her floor for the night. We would also eat our evening meal in the shop - tinned beef with rice (no escape) and fried eggs.

The boys had already moved into a large weatherboard bungalow that served as the 'guess-how.' I was happy that we were not going to stay there with them because I had paid their wages the evening before and was glad that they need feel no further responsibility towards us.

We walked up to the 'guess-how' to find a large gathering of Dayak wanderers. It was not long before we were back to old habits, sharing out Gudang Garam, drinking *kopi susu* and trailing fingers over our map, this time with an air of achievement as the only *orang barat* ever to arrive in town from the Djuloi Hulu.

Taj'ak Bangkan struck us as a very sad village. It aspired to be developed and yet was too much of a backwater to live up to its own hopes. The poorer downriver end of this *kampong melayu* was particularly sad. Women sat on filthy verandas wearing tattered sarongs and grubby bras, devoid of the inherent dignity of the Dayaks. They were Muslims and in their own opinions had sunk as low as they could go. So they were guiltily drunk on illicit alcohol.

The land all around the *kampong*, like the people, had been degraded by 'progress.' Not here had centuries of circulated *ladangs* drained the land of its nutrients. Bulldozers had done the job in less than a decade. The land was almost dead and the *orang melayu* of Taj'ak Bangkan lived in a kind of limbo. They wanted Sky Television, Coca Cola and Guns'n'Roses yet in that direction lay even greater cravings and more heart-rending dissatisfaction.

Kolop more than any of us was obviously upset and saddened by TB. The atmosphere of small-town blues in the single-table poolroom (the village's only entertainment) soon drove us back into the darkness. We ended up drifting up and down the dusty street amongst gangs of zombie-lads who were trying, in their best shirts, to make it Friday night.

We lamely said our goodbyes outside the 'guess-how' and gave Kolop several bottles of *arak* (procured by Eros) to share with our friends back in Kampong Sopan. As a parting gift Paul presented him with the Californian sunglasses that he had kept a covetous eye on throughout the trip. By now the Da'an's most talked-about jungle dandy will be blundering myopically around in the forest's perpetual twilight.

The *orang barat gila* have their revenge.

Post Script
Back to the World

There is never enough time – or paper – to say everything you want to say and I feel that there are many other things that I would have liked to include in this book. 'There were a few practical things to be said,' as Hemingway once wrote, 'if I could have made this enough of a book it would have had everything in it':

The journey back out of the interior, sleeping in the bow of a motorised *sampan*. The reverse culture shock that so rarely comes because 'civilisation' has a way of seeping up the rivers of the world – like osmosis. But in the Barito Hulu it hit us with a power that made it seem almost alien. "We just popped in to borrow a couple of English paperbacks," I told the manager at Indomoro Gold Mine . . . and we were served with cold roast beef with horseradish sauce, fresh-baked bread, apple pie and ice cream and, best of all, chilled Mars bars that had been flown in from Singapore in a refrigerated plane.

The gang at Indomoro seemed to us to be veritable angels: in their hospitality they surpassed the wildest culinary fantasies of our weeks in the fever trees. We toasted Heineken Export in appropriate style in the bar but our shrunken stomachs prohibited us from keeping pace with our host's generosity.

If this could have been more of a book it would have had a chapter dedicated to Rupert Ridgeway (*An Englishman Abroad*). Barbour-jacketed and brief-cased, commuting once again from his Barito Hulu forestry project to his house in Jakarta – just another day at the office for Rupert.

With two hours to spare, before our expired visas landed us with a fine and a possible position on the immigration blacklists, we left Kalimantan for the marble shopping malls of Brunei and a few nights sleeping on a veranda in the world's biggest stilted water village. We watched Whitney Houston performing at the pristine Jerudong amusement park and tried to remind ourselves that somewhere nearby, back in the rainforest, a band of hunters dressed only in torn Y-fronts would be eating *babi* and passing the *tuak*.

If it could have been possible our hitchhiking trip out of Brunei and down the spine of Sarawak would have found a place on these pages. Longhouses, caves, markets and fishing boats were our sleeping places during that journey and we got more rides than I could count during those memorable five hundred miles. We celebrated Paul's birthday in Bintulu and I bought him a T-shirt that said 'Creep.' Paul, being Paul, wore it with pride.

There's nothing here either about Judi, the tattooed headman of an Iban longhouse, who invited us to be his guests and spent a total of eight hours (and several jugs of *tuak*) in tattooing the biceps of two *orang barat gila* with needles dipped in rice soot and sugar-cane juice. Needless to say, we both think about Judi often.

If this were more of a book Kuching, too, would be here. Four o'clock in the morning when the market comes to life. Rats running around the legs of the Iban fishermen on the wharf. A score of Chinese dressed in white, like spectres, silently practising Tai Chi on the riverbank by the old courthouse. Muslims heading for the first prayer call of the day. Laughter, shouting and dawn mist from the Sarawak River mixing with the smell of the curry sauce that's served with *roti* pancakes for breakfast. On the far bank of the river, the white walls of the Rajah's Palace reflecting the first light. The ghost of Joseph Conrad everywhere.

If it could have had everything this book would have had our last meal at the hawker centre opposite the Kuching Hilton, and our last view of Borneo as the plane banked out over the South China Sea. It would have had to tell of our happy arrival in England and perhaps even the curry and RICE! with which my mother welcomed us back home.

Six months later the fever trees of Borneo were still playing a powerful part in my life and finally I went into hospital to quell the malaria attacks that had been wracking me every few weeks.

I'm certain that nothing will ever diminish my memories of, and affection for, the people of Borneo – and the Da'an in particular. If this could have been more of a book, it would have been more of a tribute to them.

Glossary

Apa Kabar?	hello (literally 'what news?')	*Ladang*	clearing
Arak	rice spirit	*Mandau*	headhunting sword
Babi	pig	*Mandi*	wash,. shower
Bagus	good! (exclamation)	*Naik*	ascend / mount
Baik	good (adjective)	*Nasi*	cooked rice
B*arang*	baggage	*Omong kosong*	gossip - literally 'empty chatter'
Belanda	Dutch	*Orang*	person
Belum	not yet	*Orang barat gila*	crazy westerner
Beram	drink made from fermented rice	*Orang hutan*	jungle person (orang-utan)
Bilik	apartment with longhouse	*Padi*	rice crop / field
Damar	resin	*Pak*	Sir/Mr
Enak	delicious	*Parang*	knife
Gaharu	aloeswood	*Pondok*	hut
Gila	crazy	*Ramai*	party
Hati	careful	*Rumah makan*	dining room
Hulu	upriver, The Interior	*Rumah panjang*	longhouse
Ikan	fish	*Sakit*	sick
Inggris	English	*Selamat datang*	welcome
Kabar baik	very well - response to greeting	*Selamat jalan*	goodbye (literally bon voyage')
Kamar kecil	toilet literally 'little room'	*Selamat pagi*	good morning
		Selamat minim	cheers!
Kampong	village	*Sudah*	already
Kepala	village headman	*Tidak ada masalah*	no problem
Kijang	barking deer	*Tuak*	wine made from the fermented sap of a palm tree
Kopi	coffee (*susi*-white, *panas* - hot)	*Turun*	climb down / descend
		Ular	snake (*Ular hitam* King Cobra)

Maverick in Madagascar
(The next offering from Mark Eveleigh)

Mark's next expedition leads him into the wilderness of another of the world's great islands. Madagascar, the mystic 'Isle of the Moon', is renowned for its unique wildlife, its fascinating tribes and its astounding and varied landscapes. It is an island where sorcery and magic still thrive and it is the home of the fabled white pygmies.

The adventurer sets off alone in search of these famed and feared pygmies and soon realises that 'The Great Red Island' offers more mysteries than he bargained for. His search leads him first across the island's steamy north in the company of a formidable hump-backed zebu bull. He then turns westwards towards the remote Bungolava Mountains and, following a chain of clues, sets out along the very trail that the pygmy kings once used in their exodus out of the high plateau. Disregarding local warnings about bandits (whose magic makes them immune to bullets), blood-guzzling spirit-animals and ghosts that take the form of beautiful girls to trap their victims, he sets out on foot across the lawless expanses of the 'Zone Rouge'.

With dauntless guide Eloi (a karate expert, clad in a homemade bulletproof vest) he narrowly side steps the bandit's ambush attempts and visits a chain of isolated villages where no westerner has ever been. Villages where the days are governed by superstition and the nights by the fear of sudden massacre at the hands of the Dahalo, the deadly bandit tribe who rule the vast savannahs of the Zone Rouge.

At a tiny village – with the catchy name of Ankazamandiladong – he meets a descendent of the 'white pygmies' and the old man tells him the true story of his people's extinction.

Publication date: October 2000

(The author would like to thank Lowe Alpine, Polartec and Air Madagascar for their sponsorship of 'The Isle of the Moon Expedition – Madagascar 1999')

Other titles from TravellersEye

Discoveries

The Jungle Beat – fighting terrorists in Malaya

Author		Roy Follows
Editor		Dan Hiscocks
ISBN:	0 953 0575 77	R.R.P £7.99

This book describes, in his own words, the experiences of a British officer in the Malayan Police during the extended Emergency of the 1950's. It is the story of a ruthless battle for survival against an environment and an enemy which were equally deadly, and it ranks with the toughest and grimmest of the latter-day SAS adventures.

"The Jungle Beat is tough book on the Malayan Emergency Campaign. It tells the story with no holds barred: war as war is. A compelling reminder of deep jungle operations."

General Sir Peter de la Billière

Touching Tibet

Author		Niema Ash
Editor		Dan Hiscocks
ISBN:	0 953 0575 50	R.R.P £7.99

After the Chinese invasion of 1950, Tibet remained closed to travellers until 1984. When the borders were briefly re-opened, Niema Ash was one of the few people fortunate enough to visit the country before the Chinese re-imposed their restrictions in 1987. *Touching Tibet* is a vivid, compassionate, poignant but often amusing account of a little known ancient civilisation and a unique and threatened culture.

"Excellent - Niema Ash really understands the situation facing Tibet and conveys it with remarkable perception."

Tenzin Choegyal (brother of The Dalai Lama)

Dreams

Discovery Road

Authors		Tim Garratt & Andy Brown
Editor		Dan Hiscocks
ISBN:	0953 0575 34	R.R.P £7.99

Their mission and dream was to cycle around the southern hemisphere of the planet, with just two conditions. Firstly the journey must be completed within 12 months, and secondly, the cycling duo would have no support team or backup vehicle, just their determination, friendship and pedal power.

"We are taken on a voyage of self discovery and are confronted with some of the crucial issues facing everyone living in the world today. Readers will surely find themselves reassessing their lives and be inspired to reach out and follow their own dreams."

Sir Ranulph Fiennes, Explorer

Frigid Women

Authors		Sue & Victoria Riches
Editor		Gordon Medcalf
ISBN	0953 0575 26	R.R.P £7.99

In 1997 a group of twenty women set out to become the world's first all female expedition to the North Pole. Mother and daughter, Sue and Victoria Riches were amongst them. Follow the expedition's adventures in this true life epic of their struggle to reach one of Earth's most inhospitable places, suffering both physical and mental hardships in order to reach their goal, to make their dream come true.

"This story is a fantastic celebration of adventure, friendship, courage and love. Enjoy it all you would be adventurers and dream on."

Dawn French

A Trail of Visions

Guide books tell you where to go, what to do and how to do it. A Trail of Visions shows and tells you how it feels.

Route 1: India, Sri Lanka, Thailand, Sumatra

Photographer & Author	Vicki Couchman
Editor	Dan Hiscocks
ISBN: 1 871349 338	R.R.P £14.99

"A Trail of Visions tells with clarity what it is like to follow a trail, both the places you see and the people you meet."   Independent on Sunday

Route 2: Peru, Bolivia, Ecuador, Columbia

Photographer & Author	Vicki Couchman
Editor	Dan Hiscocks
ISBN 0 935 0575 0X	R.R.P £16.99

"The illustrated guide."   The Times

Heaven & Hell

An eclectic collection of anecdotal travel stories – the best from thousands of competition entries.

"...an inspirational experience. I couldn't wait to leave the country and encounter the next inevitable disaster."   The Independent

Traveller's Tales from Heaven & Hell

Author	Various
Editor	Dan Hiscocks
ISBN: 0 953 0575 18	R.R.P £6.99

More Traveller's Tales from Heaven & Hell

Author	Various
Editor	Dan Hiscocks
ISBN: 1 903070 023	R.R.P £6.99

TravellersEye Club Membership

Each month we receive hundreds of enquiries from people who've read our books or entered our competitions. All of these people have one thing in common: an aching to achieve something extraordinary, outside the bounds of our everyday lives. Not everyone can undertake the more extreme challenges, but we all value learning about other people's experiences.

Membership is free because we want to unite people of similar interests. Via our website, members will be able to liase with each other about everything from the kit they've taken, to the places they've been to and the things they've done. Our authors will also be available to answer any of your questions if you're planning a trip or if you simply have a question about their books.

As well as regularly up-dating members with news about our forthcoming titles, we will also offer you the following benefits:

Free entry to author talks / signings
Direct author correspondence
Discounts off new & past titles
Free entry to TravellersEye events
Discounts on a variety of travel products & services

To register your membership, simply send in your name and address via post or email.

TravellersEye Ltd
30 St Marys Street
Bridgnorth
Shropshire
WV16 4DW
Tel: (01746) 766447
Fax: (01746) 766665
email: books@travellerseye.com
website: www.travellerseye.com